GIS Tutorial

WORKBOOK FOR ArcView 9

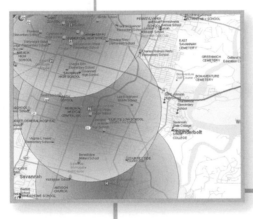

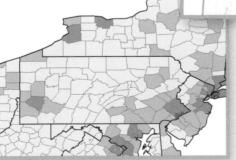

Wilpen L. Gorr

Kristen S. Kurland

ESRI Press
REDLANDS, CALIFORNIA

ESRI Press, 380 New York Street, Redlands, California 92373-8100

Copyright © 2005 ESRI

All rights reserved. First edition 2005
10 09 08 07 06   2 3 4 5 6 7 8 9 10

Printed in the United States of America

Library of Congress Cataloging-in-Publication Data
Gorr, Wilpen L.
    GIS tutorial : workbook for ArcView 9 / Wilpen Lewis Gorr, Kristen Seamens Kurland.—1st ed.
       p.   cm.
    ISBN 1-58948-127-5 (pbk. : alk. paper)
    1. ArcView. 2. Geographic information systems. I. Kurland, Kristen Seamens, 1966– II. Title.
  G70.212G74   2005
    910'.285—dc22   2005014578

ISBN-13: 978-1-58948-127-5
ISBN-10: 1-58948-127-5

Ask for ESRI Press titles at your local bookstore or order by calling 1-800-447-9778. You can also shop online at www.esri.com/esripress. Outside the United States, contact your local ESRI distributor.

ESRI Press titles are distributed to the trade by the following:

In North America, South America, Asia, and Australia:
Independent Publishers Group (IPG)
Telephone (United States): 1-800-888-4741
Telephone (international): 312-337-0747
E-mail: frontdesk@ipgbook.com

In the United Kingdom, Europe, and the Middle East:
Transatlantic Publishers Group Ltd.
Telephone: 44 20 8849 8013
Fax: 44 20 8849 5556
E-mail: transatlantic.publishers@regusnet.com

Cover design by Suzanne Davis

Copyediting by Tiffany Wilkerson

Print production by Cliff Crabbe

Testing and review by Miriam Schmidts

Contents

Acknowledgments   xv
Preface   xvii

GIS Tutorial 1   Introduction

Launch ArcMap   2
Open an existing map   3
Map layers   4
   Turn a layer on   4
   Turn a layer off   4
   Add a layer   5
   Change a layer's display order   6
   Change a layer's color   7
   Change a layer's outline color   8
Zoom and pan   9
   Zoom In   9
   Fixed Zoom In   9
   Zoom Out   10
   Fixed Zoom Out   10
   Pan   10
   Zoom to Full Extent   10
   Zoom to the Previous Extent   11
   Zoom to the Next Extent   11
Magnifier window   12
   Opening the magnifier   12
   Magnifier properties   13
Overview window   14
   Opening the Overview window   14
Spatial boookmarks   16
Measure distances   17
   Measure the horizontal distance of Colorado   17
   Change distance measurements   18
Identify features   19
   Identify various U.S. states   19
   Identify various U.S. cities   20
   Restricting Identify Results   21
Selecting features   22
   Select button   22
   Selecting multiple features   22

Clearing selected features   23
Selection Color   23
Changing selection symbol   24
Selectable layers   25

Find features   26

Work with feature attribute tables   28
Open the table of the US Cities layer   28
Show the connection between layers and tables   29
Show only selected records   29
Clear selections   30
Select more than one record from the table   30
Zoom to selected feature   31
Switch selections   31
Clear selections   32
Sort a field   32
Move a field   33

Label features on the map   34
Set label properties   34
Label features   34
Remove labels   35
Convert labels for selected features to annotation   35

Relative paths and saving maps   37
Absolute path names   37
Relative path names   37
Saving layers as relative path names   37
Save the project and exit ArcMap   38

Exercise Assignment 1-1   **Statistics on U.S. housing**   39
Exercise Assignment 1-2   **Erin Street crime watch**   40

GIS Tutorial 2   Map Design   43

Launch ArcMap   44

Create choropleth maps   45

    Add a layer to the view   45

    Change a layer's name   46

    Select a census attribute to display state population   47

Create group layers   48

    Add a group layer to the map   48

    Add a layer to the group   49

    Change the symbology for states   50

    Select a census attribute to display county population   51

    Saving layer files   53

    Adding group layers   53

    Removing group layers   53

Create threshold scales for dynamic display   54

    Set a visible scale based on the current scale   54

    Set a maximum scale based on the current scale   55

    Clear a layer's visible scale   56

    Set a minimum visible scale for a specific layer   57

    Set a maximum visible scale for a specific layer   58

Create choropleth maps using custom attribute scales   59

    Create custom classes in a legend   59

    Manually change class values   60

    Manually change class colors and hues   62

Pin (point) maps   63

    Create a pin map of U.S. cities by population   63

Create a pin map based on feature query   65

    Create a new map   65

    Add data to the map   66

    Create ground polygons   66

    Display a queried subset of Pennsylvania cities   67

    Change the layer's name and symbol   68

    Add Pennsylvania's state capital city   69

    Change the layer's name and symbol   70

Create hyperlinks   71

    Create a dynamic hyperlink   71

    Launch the hyperlink   72

    Create MapTips   73

Exercise Assignment 2-1   **Map showing schools in the city of Pittsburgh by enrollment**   74

Exercise Assignment 2-2   **Map showing K–12 population versus school enrollment**   75

GIS Tutorial 3 GIS Outputs 77

Launch ArcMap 78
Open an existing map 79
Use interactive GIS 80
Produce print layouts 81
  Choose a built-in layout template 81
  Set up and customize the template page 82
Create a custom map template and map series 84
  Start a new map 84
  Complete the new map project 85
  Set up the layout view 86
  Add elements 87
  Use the custom template for a new map 88
Create a custom map template for multiple maps 90
  Create a new map 90
  Add elements 91
Add reports to a layout 92
  Open an existing map 92
  Make a selection of records 92
  Start the report 93
  Finish the report 94
  Add the report to a layout 95
  Add final touches to the layout 96
Add graphs to a layout 97
  Open an existing map 97
  Select records for graphing 97
  Create a graph in ArcMap 98
  Export data 99
  Import data into Microsoft Excel 99
  Create a graph in Microsoft Excel 100
  Add the Microsoft Excel graph to the layout 101
Export layouts as files 102
Other outputs 103
Exercise Assignment 3-1 *Layout comparing males, females, and young population in Orange County, California* 104
Exercise Assignment 3-2 *Walking map of historic districts in downtown Pittsburgh* 105

GIS Tutorial 4   *Geodatabases*   107

Launch ArcMap   108
Launch ArcCatalog   109
Create a new personal geodatabase   110
  Create a new geodatabase   110
  Import shapefiles   111
  Import a data table   112
  Add layers to ArcMap   113
  Change layer properties   113
Modify a geodatabase   114
  Examine and modify Layer Attribute Tables   114
  Modify a primary key   115
  Calculate a new column   116
Join tables   118
  Join a table to a map   118
  Symbolize a map   120
Aggregate data   122
  Examine tables to join   122
  Join tables   123
  Extract a subset of points   124
  Spatially join point and polygon layers   126
  Count points by polygon ID   127
  Join a count table to a polygon map   128
  Symbolize the choropleth map   129
  Symbolize the point map for drill down   130
Export data from a geodatabase   132
  Export a table from a personal geodatabase   132
  Export a layer from a personal geodatabase   133
Use ArcCatalog utilities   134
  Copy and paste geodatabase layers   134
  Rename and delete geodatabase layers   135
  Compact a geodatabase   135
Exercise Assignment 4-1   **Compare county financial information in a map**   136
Exercise Assignment 4-2   **Map by census tract a count of schools and the number of K–12 students enrolled in schools**   138

GIS Tutorial 5 Importing Spatial and Attribute Data 141

Sources of maps and data 142
 ESRI Web site 142
 Navigate to free ESRI data 143
 Download ESRI basemaps 144
 Add the data in ArcMap 147
 Geography Network 148
 Download Census TIGER/Line Data 149
 Download census tracts and data for a county 150
 Extract files 151
 U.S. Census Bureau 152
 American FactFinder 153
 Create and download American FactFinder data tables 154
Vector spatial data formats 156
 Coverages 156
 Add a coverage in ArcMap 157
Convert a coverage to a shapefile 158
 Shapefiles 159
 Add a shapefile in ArcMap 160
 Interchange (.e00) files 161
 Start ArcCatalog 161
 Annotation layers 162
 CAD files 165
 Add a CAD file as a layer for display 166
 Add a CAD file as a layer for edit and analysis 167
 Export shapefiles to CAD 169
 Copy the shapefile to the root directory 169
 XY event files 170
World and U.S. projections 172
 World projections 172
 Change the map's projection to Mercator 173
 Change the map's projection to Hammer-Aitoff and then to Robinson 174
 Projections of the USA 175
 Albers equal area conic projection 175
State Plane coordinate system 176
 Add a map without State Plane coordinates 176
 Set the coordinate projection for the map 177
 Convert 2000 census tracts to a State Plane shapefile 179
 Add a map with State Plane coordinates 180
Stored metadata 181
 Start ArcCatalog and view metadata 181
Attribute data 183
 Adding and opening .dbf (dBASE) files 183
 Adding and opening comma delimited .csv files 184
 Microsoft Access tables 185
Exercise Assignment 5-1 *Maps showing population changes for Florida counties* 186
Exercise Assignment 5-2 *Create a voting district map for a local election* 188

GIS Tutorial 6   *Digitizing* 191

Create a new polygon shapefile   192
Create a new polygon shapefile   192
Start ArcMap: Open a map document   193
Add the shapefile to a map   194

Digitize and edit the polygon layer   195
Open the Editor toolbar   195
Practice digitizing a polygon   196
Practice editing a polygon   197

Vertices   199
Move vertex points   199
Add vertex points   200
Delete vertex points   200

Drawing and editing tips   201
Advanced Edit tools   201
Precision snapping   201
Specify a segment length   201
Edit tasks   202
Adding other graphics   202

Digitize the commercial zone polygons   203
Add feature attribute data   204
Label the commercial zones   205

Digitize a point layer   206
Create a point layer for evacuation shelters   206
Add evacuation shelter points   207
Add a name field to the EvacShelter attribute table   208
Add name attributes to the EvacShelter records   209

Digitize a line layer   210
Create a line shapefile for an evacuation route   210
Change the line symbol for the evacuation route   210
Prepare area for digitizing   211
Start editing   211
Digitize by snapping to features   212
Save your edits and the map   213

Spatial adjustment   215
Add aerial photos to a map   215
Adjust the transparency values of the aerial photos   216
Add a building outline   217
Move the building   218
Rotate the building   219

Transform the building to the aerial photo   220
Add displacement links   220
Edit displacement links   222
Adjust the building   223

Exercise Assignment 6-1   **Digitizing police beats**   224
Exercise Assignment 6-2   **Using GIS to track campus information**   226

GIS Tutorial 7 **Geocoding** 229

Geocode data by zip code 230
    Open the Pennsylvania zip code map 230
    Add the FLUX Attendee data file 231
    Build address locators for zip codes 232
    Specifying a reference table (zip codes) 233
    Add address locator to map 235
    Batch match 236
    Prepare table for geocoding 236
    Review unmatched zip codes 238
    Fix and rematch zip codes 239
    Rematch zip codes 240
Geocode to streets 241
Prepare data and street maps 242
    Create an address locator for streets 243
    Specify a reference table (streets) 244
    Create address locator 245
    Add address locator to a map 246
Interactively locate addresses 247
    Show address on map 248
Perform batch geocoding 250
    Prepare table for geocoding 250
    Correct addresses using interactive rematch 252
    Match interactively 252
Correct street layer addresses 254
    Open a new map 254
    Create a new address locator 255
    Geocode clients' addresses to CBD streets 256
    Identify and isolate streets for unmatched address 257
    Identify and isolate unmatched streets 258
    Modify the attributes of CBDStreets 259
Use alias tables 262
    Add an alias table and rematch addresses 262
Exercise Assignment 7-1 **Geocode household hazardous wastes participants to zip codes** 264
Exercise Assignment 7-2 **Geocode ethnic businesses to Pittsburgh streets** 266

GIS Tutorial 8 **Spatial Data Processing** 269

Launch ArcMap   270
Open an existing map   271
Use data queries to extract features   272
   Use the ArcMap Select By Attributes dialog   272
   Show selected features and convert to shapefile   273
   Use the ArcMap Select Features tool   274
Clip features   275
   Use the ArcMap Select By Location tool   275
   Show selected features and convert to shapefile   276
   Clip the Manhattan streets   277
Dissolve features   279
   Open an existing map   279
   Dissolve zip codes using the ArcMap command line   280
Append layers   283
   Open an existing map   283
   Create an empty polygon layer for appending   284
   Append several shapefiles into one shapefile   284
Union layers   286
   Open an existing map   286
   Union shapefiles   287
ModelBuilder   289
   Open an existing map   289
   Create a new model   290
   Add a Clip operation to the model   291
   Connect PATractStatePlane layer to Clip tool   292
   Connect Union function to layers   293
   Run the model   295
   Display the new shapefile   296
Exercise Assignment 8-1   **Build a study region for Colorado counties**   298
Exercise Assignment 8-2   **Dissolve property parcels to create a zoning map**   300

GIS Tutorial 9 *Spatial Analysis* *303*

Buffer points for proximity analysis   304
   Open map   304
   Buffer bars   305
   Extract assault offenses in bar buffers   306
Conduct a site suitability analysis   308
   Open a map   308
   Add X and Y columns to car beats   308
   Compute car beat centroids   308
   Map car beat centroids   310
   Buffer car beat centroids   311
   Buffer retail businesses   312
   Select major streets   313
   Buffer major streets   314
   Intersect buffers   315
Apportion data for noncoterminous polygons   316
   Approach to apportionment   317
   The math of apportionment   318
   Preview of apportionment steps   319
   Create Tract ID and AGE22Plus fields in the attributes of block centroids   320
   Sum Age22Plus by tracts   322
   Intersect car beats and tracts   323
   Overlay the intersection of car beats and tracts with block centroids   324
   Join the summary attributes to the spatial join output   325
   Compute apportionment weights   326
   Compute apportionment values   327
   Sum weights by tract   328
   Sum undereducated by car beats   329
   Join Sum_UnderEducated to the car beat layer   330
   Map undereducated population by car beat   331
   Wrap up   332
Exercise Assignment 9-1   *Analyze population in California cities at risk for earthquakes*   333
Exercise Assignment 9-2   *Neighborhood walking distances and urban grocery store site selection*   335

Appendix A   Data License Agreement   339
Appendix B   Installing the Data and Software   343

Acknowledgments

We would like to thank all who made this book possible.

GIS Tutorial was used for several years in GIS courses at Carnegie Mellon University before it went to ESRI Press for publication. During this time, the students and teaching assistants who used the book in their classes provided us with significant feedback. Their thoughtful comments guided our revisions and helped improve the content and overall quality of this book.

Faculty at other universities who have taught GIS using drafts of *GIS Tutorial* have also provided valuable feedback. They include Don Dixon of California State University at Sacramento, Mike Rock of Columbus State Community College, Piyusha Singh of State University of New York at Albany, An Lewis of the University of Pittsburgh, and George Tita at the University of California at Irvine.

We are very grateful to the many public servants and vendors who have generously supplied us with interesting GIS applications and data, including Kevin Ford of Facilities Management Services, Carnegie Mellon University; Barb Kviz of the Green Practices Program, Carnegie Mellon University; Susan Golomb and Mike Homa of the City Planning Department, City of Pittsburgh; Richard Chapin of infoUSA, Inc.; Pat Clark and Traci Jackson of Jackson Clark Partners, Pennsylvania Resources Council; Commander Kathleen McNeely, Sgt. Mona Wallace, and John Shultie of the Pittsburgh Bureau of Police; Chief Robert Duffy, Lt. Todd Baxter, Lt. Michael Wood; and Jeff Cheal of the Rochester, New York Police Department; Kirk Brethauer of Southwestern Pennsylvania Commission *(www.spcregion.org)*; and Tele Atlas for use of their USA datasets contained within the ESRI Data & Maps 2004 Media Kit.

Finally, thanks to the entire team at ESRI, especially Christian Harder, Judy Hawkins, and Brian Parr. Special thanks to Jennifer Galloway for the book's design and production, Tiffany Wilkerson and Colleen Langley for copyediting, and Miriam Schmidts for testing the exercises.

Preface

GIS Tutorial is the direct result of the authors' experiences teaching GIS to students at high schools and university, as well as working professionals. *GIS Tutorial* is a hands-on workbook that takes the reader from the basics of using ArcGIS Desktop interfaces to performing advanced spatial analysis. Instructors can use this book in the classroom, or the individual can use it for self-study.

If you are new to ArcGIS Desktop and are using this book as a self-study guide, we recommend you work through the exercises in order. However, the tutorials are independent of each other, and you can use them in the order that best fits you or your class's needs.

In tutorial 1, readers will learn the basics of working with existing GIS data and maps. In tutorials 2 and 3, readers will learn how to build maps from GIS data and how to create, then add, graphs and reports to their maps. The exercises in tutorial 4 teach the reader how to create geodatabases and import data into them. Tutorial 5 has the reader explore the basic GIS data types and use the Internet to gather GIS data. Editing spatial data is a large part of GIS work, and in tutorial 6 readers learn how to manage an edit session, digitize vector data, and transform data to match real-world coordinates. In tutorial 7, the reader will learn how to map address data as points through a process called address geocoding. In tutorials 8 and 9, the reader performs spatial analysis using geoprocessing tools and analysis workflow models.

To reinforce the skills learned in the step-based content and to provoke critical problem-solving skills, there are *Your Turn* tasks and advanced exercise assignments within each tutorial. The quickest way to increase your GIS skills is to follow step-based content with independent work. The *Your Turn* tasks and exercise assignments provide this important follow-up by having the reader perform tasks and solve problems without the aid of step-by-step direction.

This book comes with two CDs. One contains the data, the other contains a 180-day trial CD of ArcView 9.1. You will need to install the software and the data in order to perform the exercises in this book. (If you already have ArcView 9.x, ArcEditor 9.x, or ArcInfo 9.x installed, you only need to install the data.) Instructions for installing the two CDs that come with this book are included in the appendix.

We sincerely hope you enjoy *GIS Tutorial*. For teacher resources and updates related to this book, go to *www.esri.com/esripress/GISTutorial*.

Work with map layers
Zoom and pan
Magnifier and Overview windows
Spatial bookmarks
Measure distances
Identify features
Select features on a map
Find features
Work with feature attribute tables
Label features

GIS Tutorial 1

Introduction

This first tutorial will make you familiar with some of the basic functionality of ArcMap and illustrate the fundamentals of GIS. You will work with map layers and underlying feature attribute data tables for U.S. states, cities, counties, and streets. All layers you will use are made up of geographic features consisting of points, lines, and polygons. Each geographic feature has a corresponding data record, and you will work with both features and their data records.

Launch ArcMap

ArcMap is the primary mapping component of ArcGIS Desktop software from ESRI. ESRI offers three licensing levels of ArcGIS Desktop, each with increasing capabilities, namely ArcView, ArcEditor, and ArcInfo. Together, ArcMap and two other components that you will use later in this workbook (ArcCatalog and ArcToolbox) make up ArcView, the world's most popular GIS software.

1   From the Windows taskbar, click Start, All Programs, ArcGIS, ArcMap.

Depending on how ArcGIS and ArcMap have been installed or which Windows operating system you're using, there may be a slightly different navigation menu from which to open ArcMap.

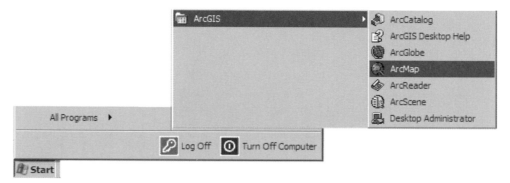

2   In the resulting ArcMap window, click the An existing map radio button and click OK.

Open an existing map

1   Browse to the drive on which the Gistutorial folder has been installed (e.g., C:\Gistutorial), click
    the **Tutorial1-1.mxd** (or Tutorial1-1) icon and click Open.

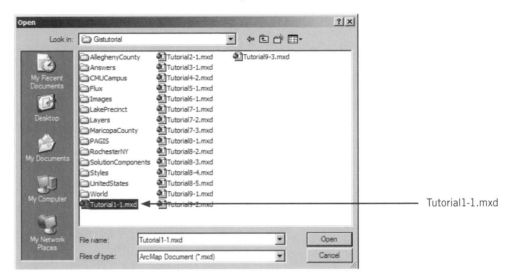

Tutorial1-1.mxd

The Tutorial1-1.mxd project opens in ArcMap showing a map consisting of the US States layer
(boundaries of the lower forty-eight contiguous states). The US Cities layer (not yet turned on)
is the subset of cities with populations greater than 300,000. Note that your Tools menu, which
is anchored on the right side of the screen below, may be free-floating on your screen or docked
somewhere else on the interface. If you wish, you can anchor it by clicking in its top area, dragging
it to a side of the map display window and releasing when you see a thin rectangle materialize. If
you do not see the Tools menu at all, click View, Toolbars, Tools to make it visible.

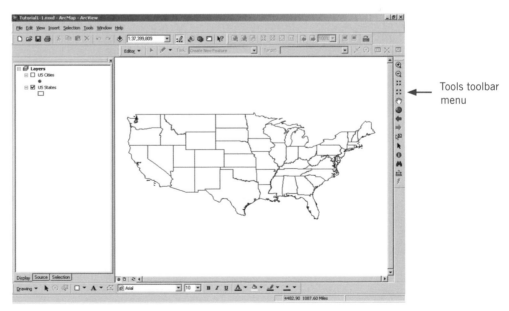

Tools toolbar
menu

Map layers

Map layers are references to data sources such as point, line, and polygon shapefiles; geodatabase feature classes; raster images; and so forth, representing spatial features that can be displayed on a map.

Turn a layer on

1   Click the small check box to the left of the US Cities layer in the table of contents to turn that layer on.

The table of contents is the panel on the left side of the view window. If the table of contents accidentally closes, click Window, Table of Contents to reopen it. A check mark appears if the layer is turned on. Nothing appears if it is turned off.

Check box turns a layer on and off in the table of contents

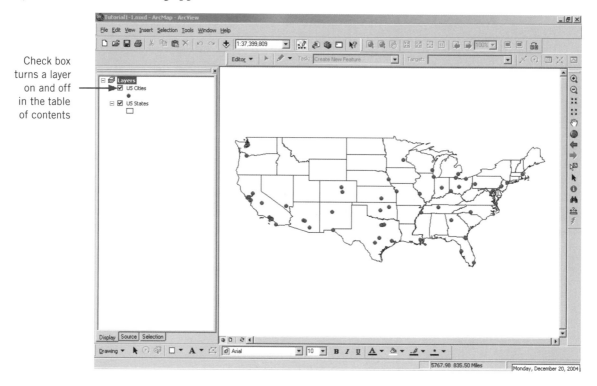

Turn a layer off

1   Click the small check box to the left of the US Cities layer in the table of contents again to turn the layer off.

2   Click the check box again to turn the layer on.

Add a layer

1   **Click the Add Data button.**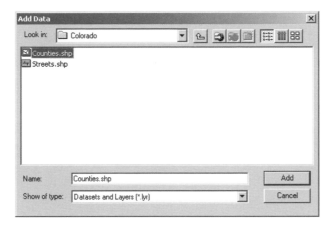

2   **In the Add Data browser, browse to \Gistutorial\UnitedStates\Colorado.**

3   **Click Counties.shp.**

4   **Click Add.**

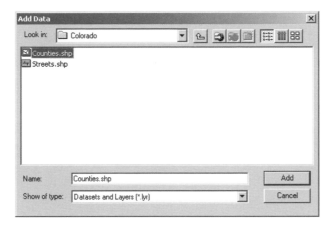

ArcMap randomly picks a color for the Colorado counties layer. The color can be changed later.

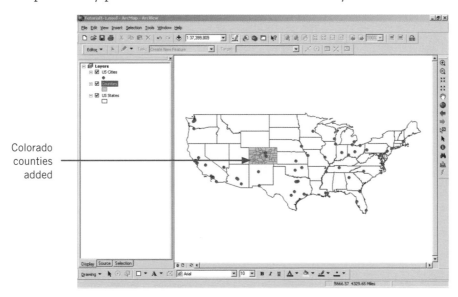

Colorado
counties
added

YOUR TURN

Use the Add Data button to add Streets.shp, also found in the \Gistutorial\UnitedStates\Colorado folder. These are street centerlines for Jefferson County, Colorado.

Note: Click OK if you see a message relating to projections.

Change a layer's display order

1   In the table of contents, click and hold down the left mouse button on the name of the
US Cities layer.

2   Drag the US Cities layer down to the bottom of the table of contents.

ArcMap draws layers from the bottom up. Because the US Cities layer is now drawn first, its
points are covered by the US States and Counties layers and cannot be seen.

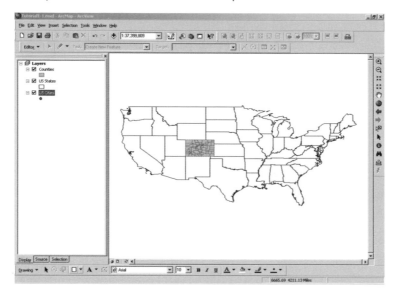

3   Click and hold down the left mouse button on the US Cities layer.

4   Drag the US Cities layer back to the top of the table of contents.

Because US Cities is now drawn last, its points can be seen again.

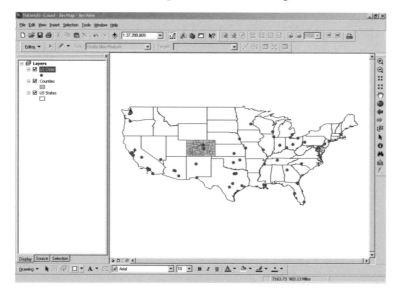

Change a layer's color

1   Click the Counties layer's legend symbol.

The legend symbol is the rectangle below the layer name in the table of contents.

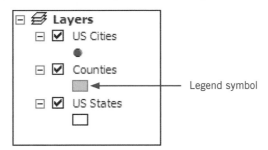

2   In the resulting Symbol Selector window, click the Fill Color button in the Options section.

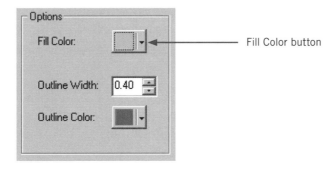

3   Click the Tarragon Green tile in the Color Palette.

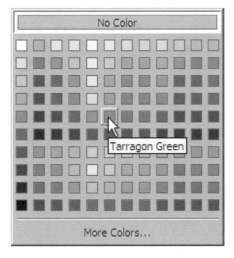

4   Click OK.

The layer's color will change to Tarragon Green on the map.

Change a layer's outline color

1 Click the Counties layer's legend symbol.

2 Click the Outline Color button in the Options section of the Symbol Selector dialog box.

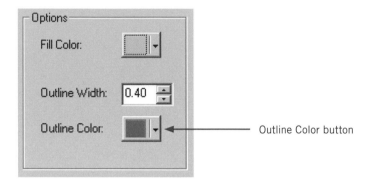

Outline Color button

3 Click the Apple Dust tile in the Color Palette.

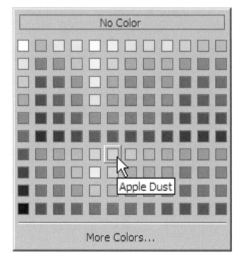

4 Click OK.

The effect of colors on maps will be explored more in chapter 2 of the tutorial.

YOUR TURN

Repeat the steps outlined above, this time changing the colors of the other layers to your liking.

Zoom and pan

Zooming and panning enlarges or reduces the display and shifts the display to reveal different areas of the map. The zoom and pan buttons are found on the Tools toolbar.

Zoom In

1   **Click the Zoom In button.**

2   **Click and hold down the mouse button on a point above and to the left of the state of Florida.**

3   **Drag the mouse below and to the right of the state of Florida and release the mouse button.**

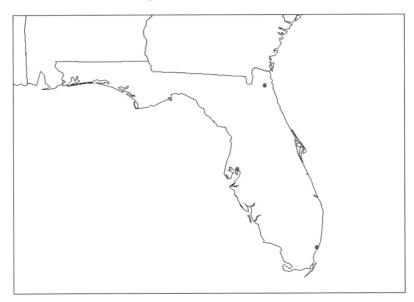

4   **Click once on the screen to zoom in. The display recenters on the point you click.**

This is an alternative to dragging a rectangle for zooming in.

Fixed Zoom In

1   **Click the Fixed Zoom In button.**

This zooms in a fixed distance on the center of the current zoomed display.

Zoom Out

1   Click the Zoom Out button.

2   Click once on the map to zoom out from the point you pick.

Fixed Zoom Out

1   Click the Fixed Zoom Out button.

This zooms out a fixed distance from the center of the current zoomed display.

Pan

Panning shifts the current display to the left, right, up, or down without changing the current scale.

1   Click the Pan button.

2   Move the cursor anywhere onto the map display.

3   Hold down the left mouse button and drag the mouse in any direction.

4   Release the mouse button.

Zoom to Full Extent

1   Click the Zoom to Full Extent button.

This zooms to a full display of all layers, regardless of whether they are turned on or turned off.

Zoom to the Previous Extent

1 **Click the Zoom to Previous Extent button.**

This returns the map display to its previous extent. Continue to click this button to step back through the views.

Zoom to the Next Extent

1 **Click the Zoom to Next Extent button.**

This moves forward through the sequence of zoomed extents you have viewed. You can continue to click this button until you reach the most recently viewed extent.

YOUR TURN

Zoom to the county polygons in Colorado and the streets in Jefferson County, Colorado.

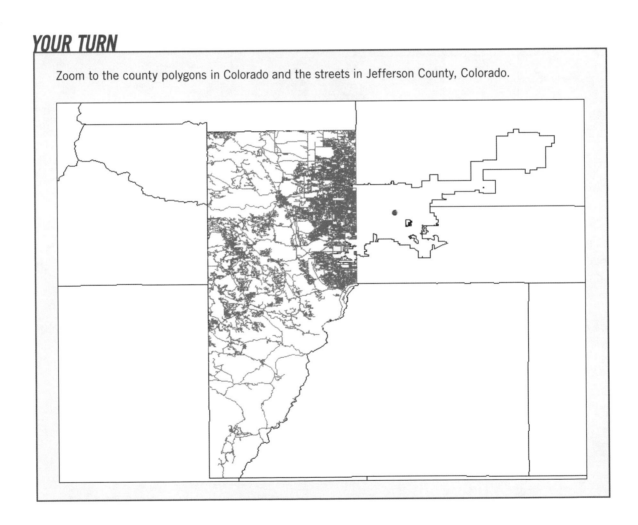

Magnifier window

The magnifier window adjusts the map display to see more detail or get an overview of an area. This window works like a magnifying glass: as you pass the window over the map display, you see a magnified view of the location under the window. Moving the window does not affect the current map display.

Opening the magnifier

1   Click Window, Magnifier.

2   Drag the magnifier over an area of the map to see crosshairs for area selection and then release to see the zoomed details.

Magnifier window

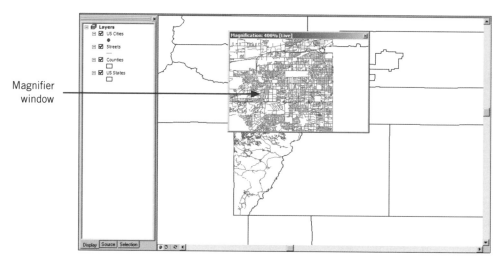

3   Drag the magnifier to a new area to see another detail on the map.

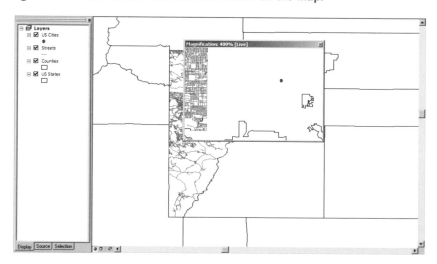

Magnifier properties

1 Right-click the title bar of the magnifier window.

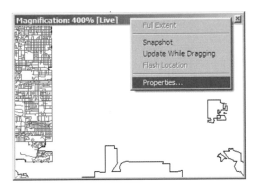

2 Click Properties.

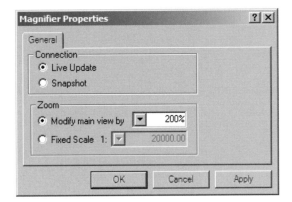

3 Change the Zoom percentage to 200%.

4 Click OK.

5 Drag the magnifier to a different location and see the resulting view.

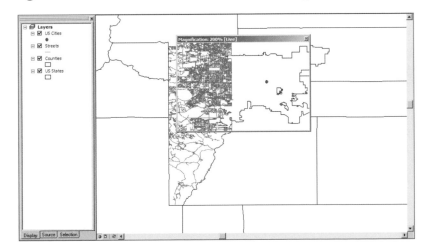

6 Close the magnifier window.

Overview window

The Overview window shows the full extent of the layers in a map. A red box shows the area currently zoomed to. You can move the red box to pan the map display. You can also make the red box smaller or larger to zoom the map display in or out.

Opening the Overview window

1   **Click View, Zoom Data, Full Extent.**

2   **Zoom to a small area of the map (one or two states).**

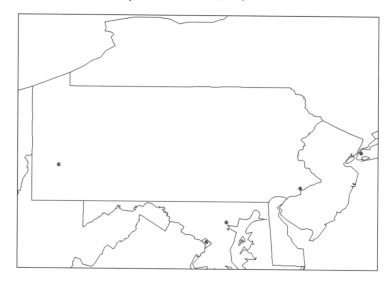

3   **Click Window, Overview.**

The current extent of the map display will be highlighted with a red hatch pattern.

4   **Move the cursor to the center of the hatch pattern and click and drag to move it to a new location.**

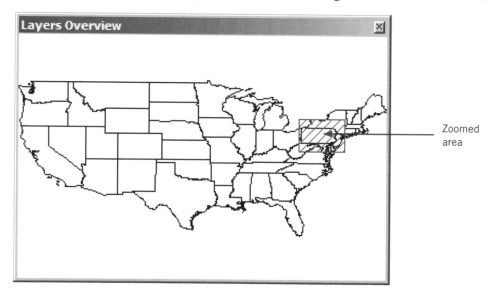

Zoomed area

The extent of the map display updates to reflect the changes made in the Layers Overview window.

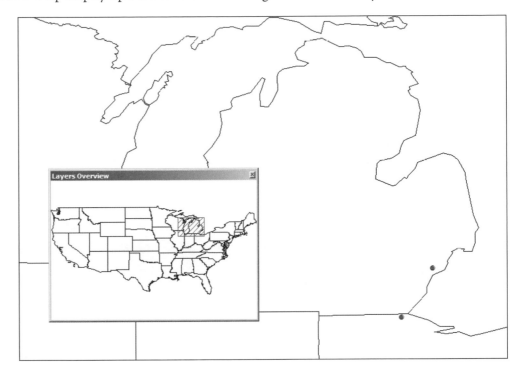

Spatial bookmarks

Spatial bookmarks save the extent of a map display or geographic location so you can return to it later without having to use the Pan and Zoom tools.

1 **Close the Layers Overview window.**

2 **Click View, Zoom Data, Full Extent.**

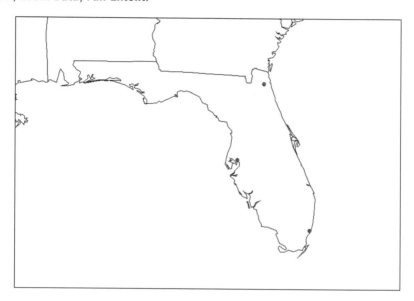

3 **Zoom to the state of Florida.**

4 **Click View, Bookmarks, Create.**

5 **Type Florida in the Bookmark Name field.**

6 **Click OK.**

7 **Click View, Zoom Data, Full Extent.**

8 **Click View, Bookmarks, Florida.**

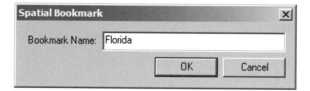

ArcMap will automatically zoom to the saved bookmark of Florida.

YOUR TURN

Create spatial boookmarks for the states of California, New York, and Colorado. Try out your bookmarks. Use View, Bookmarks, Manage to remove the California bookmark.

Measure distances

Measure the horizontal distance of Colorado

1   Use your bookmark (or use the Full Extent and Zoom In tools) to zoom to Colorado.

2   From the Tools toolbar, click the Measure button.

3   Click once on the left boundary of the state of Colorado.

4   Drag the mouse to the right boundary of Colorado and double-click.

The resulting distance is shown on the status bar found on the lower left corner of the screen. The distances for this layer are shown in miles. The distance should be about 375 miles.

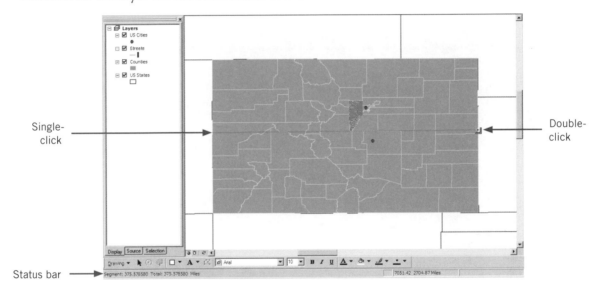

Change distance measurements

1   Click View, Data Frame Properties, and the General tab.

2   In the Units frame, change the Display units to Kilometers.

3   Click OK.

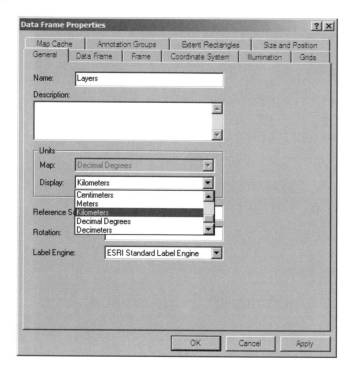

YOUR TURN

Measure the vertical distance (top to bottom) of Colorado. The distance should be about 275 miles or 445 kilometers.

Change the display units back to miles and measure the length and height of the United States. The length is approximately 2,700 miles and the height 1,600 miles, but these measurements are difficult to make precisely.

Identify features

To display the data attributes of a map feature, click the feature with the Identify tool. This tool is the easiest way to learn something about a location in a map.

Identify various U.S. states

1   **Turn off all layers except US States.**

2   **From the Tools toolbar, click the Identify button.**

3   **Click inside the state of Texas.**

The state will temporarily flash and its attributes appear in the Identify Results dialog box.

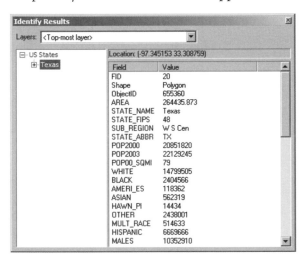

4   **Right-click the name of the feature in the left window (in this case Texas) and click Set Bookmark.**

ArcMap will create a zoomed bookmark of that feature.

5   **Close the Identify Results window.**

Identify various U.S. cities

1   Turn the US Cities layer on.

2   Click the Identify button.

3   Click any of the points for the cities.

Make sure the point of the arrow is inside the circle when you click the mouse button. Notice which feature flashes—that is the feature on which you will get information. If the entire state flashes, you have missed the city, and the Identify Results dialog will give you information about the state and not the city.

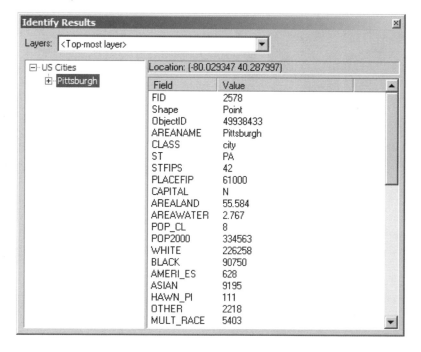

4   Continue clicking other states to see the identify results.

ArcMap will identify the features in the layer at the top of the Table of Contents first (Top-most layer). Since US Cities is above US States, it will be identified first. Hold down the Shift key to pick multiple cities.

Restricting Identify Results

1   Click the Layers drop-down list in the Identify Results dialog.

2   Click US States.

This will restrict the Identify selection
to features in this layer only and will
ignore features in the other layers.

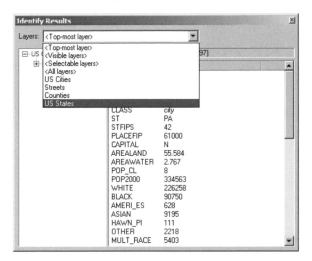

3   Click any city point feature.

ArcMap will identify the US States only because its layer is set in the dialog box.

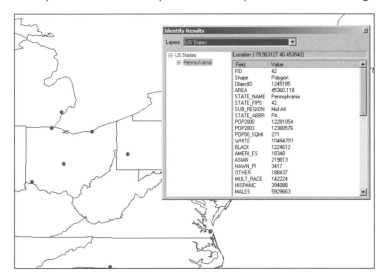

4   Close the Identify Results window.

YOUR TURN

Restrict the Identify Results to the US Cities layer and identify cities. Practice making bookmarks for
various cities. Also see if you can remember how to go to the bookmarks once they have been created.

Selecting features

Selecting features identifies the features on which you want to perform certain operations. For example, before you move, delete, or copy a feature, you must select it. Selected features also appear highlighted in the layer's attribute table and in the map.

Select button

1 **From the Tools toolbar, click the Select Features button.**

2 **Click inside any of the US States polygons.**

The state will be highlighted with a thick, bright blue line.

Selecting multiple features

1 **Hold down the Shift key and click inside multiple states.**

All of the selected states will be highlighted with a thick, bright blue line.

Clearing selected features

1   Click Selection, Clear Selected Features, or click once anywhere outside the features on the map.

Selection Color

1   Click Selection, Options.

2   Click the color box in the Selection Color frame.

Selection
Color box →
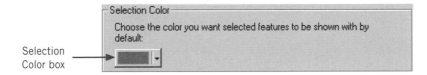

3   Pick a new color.

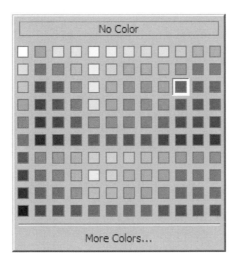

4   Click OK.

Changing selection symbol

1   Right-click the layer US Cities in the table of contents.

2   Click Properties.

Note that the resulting Layer Properties window is one that you will use often. It allows you to modify many properties of a map layer.

3   Click the Selection tab.

4   Pick a new symbol and/or color for the point features.

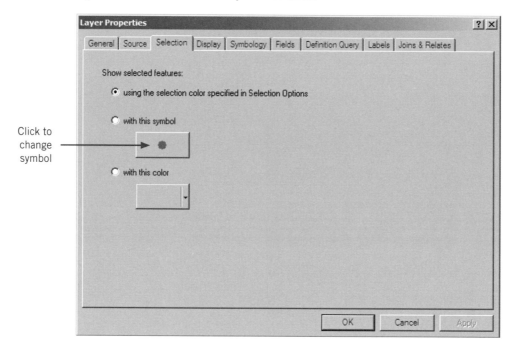

5   Click OK.

Selectable layers

Making a layer selectable allows features to be selected via the Select Features tool, Select by Graphics, Find tool, and so forth.

1 Click Selection, Set Selectable Layers.

2 Click off the check boxes for Streets, Counties, and US States to make only US Cities selectable.

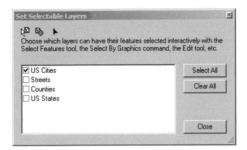

3 Click Close.

4 Click the Select Features button **and pick a city.**

That city gets the selection symbol and color that you chose on the previous page.

5 Clear the selected features.

YOUR TURN

Create a new layer from selected features by selecting multiple cities in one state. After the cities are selected, right-click the US Cities layer, click Selection, and click Create Layer from Selected Features.

Find features

The Find tool is used to locate features in a layer or layers based on their attribute values. You can also use this tool to select, flash, zoom, bookmark, identify, or unselect the feature in question.

1   **From the Tools toolbar, click the Find button.**

2   **Type Dallas as a city name to find.**

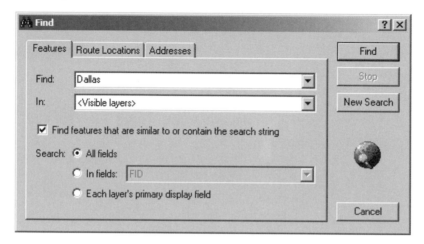

3   **Click Find.**

The results will appear in the following section of the Find dialog box.

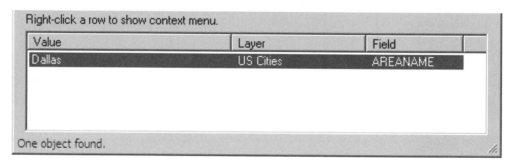

4 Right-click the city name and click Zoom to feature(s).

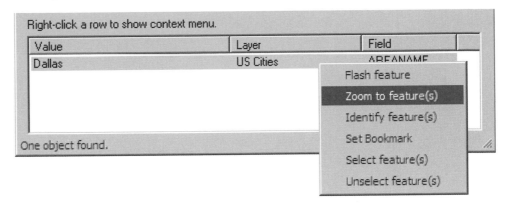

5 If necessary, clear the selected features.

YOUR TURN

Find other cities and practice showing the features using other find options such as Flash Features, Identify Feature(s), and Set Bookmark.

Work with feature attribute tables

Tabular attribute data associated with map features can be viewed via the layer's attribute table. To explore the attributes of a layer on a map, open its attribute table to select features and find features with particular attributes.

Open the table of the US Cities layer

1   **Right-click the US Cities layer in the table of contents.**

2   **Click Open Attribute Table.**

The table opens, containing one record for each US City point feature. Every layer has an attribute table with one record per feature.

3   **Scroll down in the table until you find Chicago (the order of records may be different on your computer) and click the record selector for Chicago to select that record.**

If a feature is selected on the map, it will also be selected in the attribute table. You will see this on the next page.

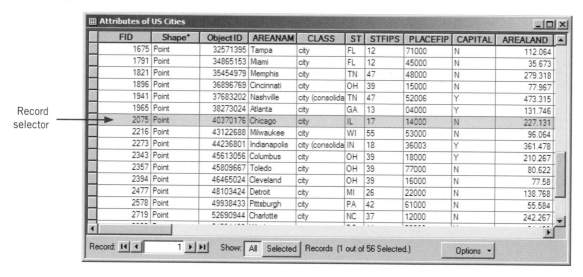

Record selector

Show the connection between layers and tables

1   Resize the Attributes of US Cities table to see both the map and table on the screen.

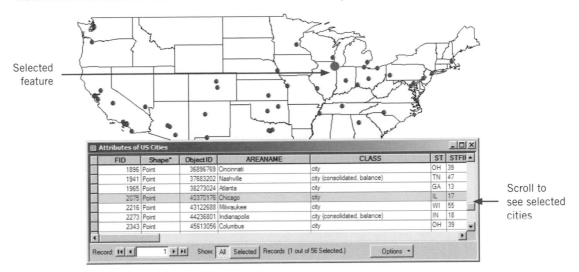

Selected feature

Scroll to see selected cities

2   Click the Select Features button 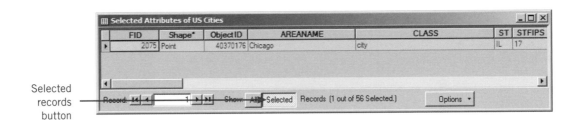 and click various cities on the map.

3   Scroll through the Attributes of US Cities to see the selected cities.

Show only selected records

1   In the Attributes of US Cities table, click the Selected Records button.

Selected records button

This will show only the records for the features selected in the map.

2   Click the All Records button to show all records again.

Clear selections

1   In the Attributes of US Cities table, click the Options button. (If you cannot see the Options button, widen the table to the right until it appears.)

2   Click Clear Selection.

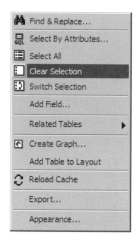

Select more than one record from the table

1   In the Attributes of US Cities table, click once on the record selector for Atlanta.

2   Hold down the Ctrl key and select the following records: Jacksonville, Miami, and Tampa.

This will highlight these selected features both in the Table and Map windows. Scroll up or down to find these records.

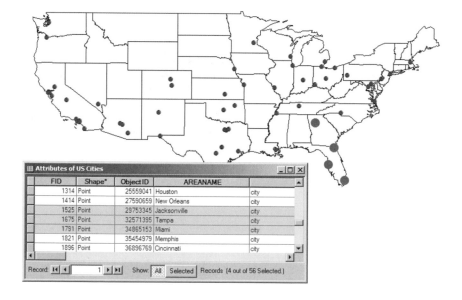

3   Hold down the Ctrl key and click the Atlanta record again to deselect it.

Zoom to selected feature

1 Click View, Zoom Data, Zoom to Selected Features.

This will zoom to the three selected cities in Florida.

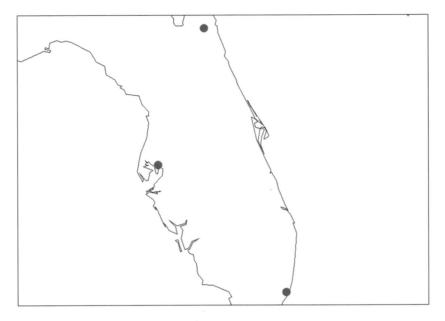

Switch selections

1 In the Attributes of US Cities table, click the Options button.

2 Click Switch Selection.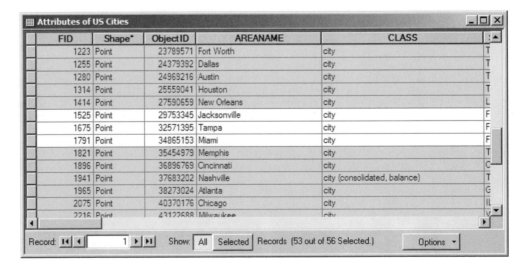

This reverses the selection. In other words, it selects all of those that were not selected and deselects those that were selected.

FID	Shape*	ObjectID	AREANAME	CLASS	
1223	Point	23789571	Fort Worth	city	T
1255	Point	24379392	Dallas	city	T
1280	Point	24969216	Austin	city	T
1314	Point	25559041	Houston	city	T
1414	Point	27590659	New Orleans	city	L
1525	Point	29753345	Jacksonville	city	F
1675	Point	32571395	Tampa	city	F
1791	Point	34865153	Miami	city	F
1821	Point	35454979	Memphis	city	T
1896	Point	36896769	Cincinnati	city	C
1941	Point	37683202	Nashville	city (consolidated, balance)	T
1965	Point	38273024	Atlanta	city	G
2075	Point	40370176	Chicago	city	IL
2216	Point	43122688	Milwaukee	city	W

Record: 1   Show: All Selected   Records (53 out of 56 Selected.)   Options ▾

Clear selections

1   In the Attributes of US Cities table, click Options and Clear Selection.   [▣] Clear Selection

Sort a field

1   In the Attributes of US Cities table, right-click the **AREANAME** field name.

2   Click Sort Ascending.   [▣] Sort Ascending

This will sort the table from A to Z by the name of each U.S. city.

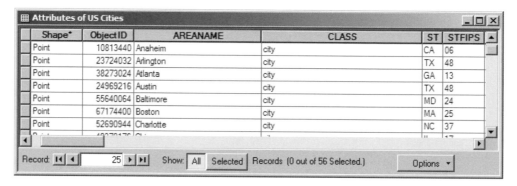

3   Scroll to the right in the table and right-click the POP2000 field name.

4   Click Sort Descending.   [▣] Sort Descending

This will sort the field from the highest populated city to the lowest populated city.

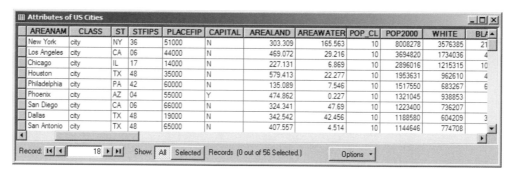

Move a field

1 Click the gray title of the POP2000 field in the Attributes of US Cities table.

2 Click, drag, and release the POP2000 field to the left of another field.

The field moves to the left of the other field(s).

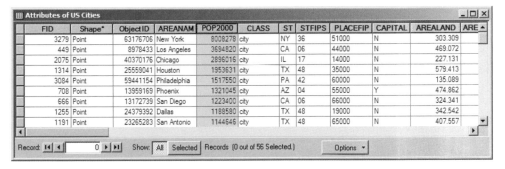

3 Close the Attributes of US Cities.

YOUR TURN

Move and sort by other field names. Try sorting by multiple fields. For example, you could sort US Cities alphabetically or by whether or not they are state capitals.

To sort by multiple fields, rearrange the table's fields so the field whose values will be sorted first appears directly to the left of the field whose values will be sorted second. While holding down the Ctrl key, click the heading of the two fields you want to use to sort the records. Right-click the name of one of the selected fields and choose a sort order. When you sort, the selected fields will be in the sort order you chose.

Label features on the map

Labels are text items on the map that are dynamically placed and whose text value is derived from one or more feature attributes.

Set label properties

1 Zoom to Florida if the map is not already zoomed to that state.

2 Right-click the US Cities layer in the table of contents.

3 Click Properties.

4 Click the Labels tab.

5 Click the Label Field drop-down arrow and click **AREANAME** if not already selected.

6 Click OK.

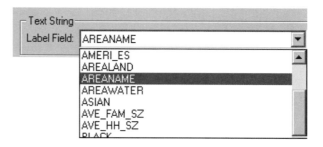

Label features

1 Right-click the US Cities layer in the table of contents.

2 Click Label Features.

All of the features in the map will be labeled.

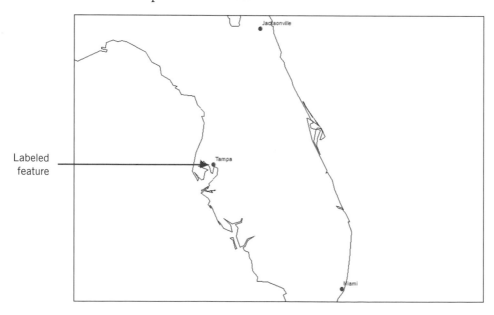

Remove labels

1   Right-click the US Cities layer in the table of contents.

2   Click Label Features.

Labels in the map will be turned off.

3   Click Label Features again to turn them back on.

Convert labels for selected features to annotation

1   Use the Select Features button to select the Florida cities if they are not already selected.

2   Right-click the US Cities layer in the table of contents.

3   Click Convert Labels to Annotation.

4   In the Store Annotation section, choose In the map. In the Create Annotation For section, choose Selected features.

5   Click Convert.

YOUR TURN

Explore other label commands, including Label tools from the Draw toolbar and advanced label tools from the Labeling toolbar. Explore online help for more information on labeling.

Relative paths and saving maps

When a layer is added to a map, the path name to the data is stored in the map, but the layer is not copied from its original location. When a map is opened, ArcMap locates the layer data it needs using these stored path names. If ArcMap cannot find the data for a layer, the layer will appear in the ArcMap table of contents but it won't be drawn. Instead, a red exclamation mark (!) will appear next to the layer to indicate that it needs to be repaired.

Absolute path names

An example of an absolute full path is C:\Gistutorial\Tutorial1.mxd. To share maps saved with absolute paths, everyone who uses the map must either do so on the same computer or have the data on their computer in exactly the same folder structure (e.g., C:\Gistutorial). This is not conducive for a computer lab environment since instructors, teaching assistants, and students all work on different machines. Instead, the relative path option is favored.

You can view information about the data source for a layer by clicking the Source tab in the Layers Properties box.

Relative path names

An example of a relative path is \Gistutorial\Tutorial1.mxd. Relative paths in a map specify the location of the layers relative to the current location on disk of the map document (.mxd file). Because relative paths do not contain drive letter names, they enable the map and its associated data to point to the same directory structure regardless of the drive that the map resides on. If a project is moved to a new drive, ArcMap will still be able to find the maps and their data by traversing the relative paths.

This option, for example, allows you to share maps that you made with data on your local F:\ drive with people who only have a C:\ drive. This also allows you to easily move the map and its data to a different hard drive on your computer, or give the map and its data to another person to copy to their computer.

Saving layers as relative path names

1   **Click File, Map Properties.**

2   **Click Data Source Options.**

3   **Click the Store relative path names radio button.**

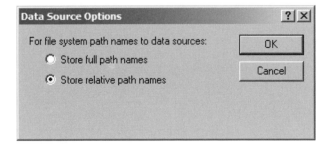

4   **Click OK and OK again to close the Map Properties dialog box.**

Save the project and exit ArcMap

1 Click File, Save As.

2 Navigate to the **\Gistutorial** folder and save the map as **Tutorial1-2.mxd**.

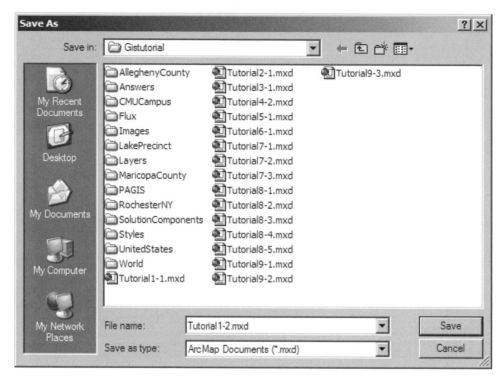

Saving your work session in ArcMap is referred to as saving your map. When you save a map, you save it to a map document file, which has an .mxd file extension. When working with ArcMap you usually spend time setting properties that affect the look, feel, and functionality of your map and its layers. For example, in this map you added layers, changed their symbology, and created bookmarks. By saving this map, all of this work is preserved in the Tutorial 1-2.mxd file, which you can reopen anytime or share with others.

3 Click File, Exit.

Exercise Assignment 1-1

Statistics on U.S. housing

Public housing policies of the 1960s and 1970s have had many negative impacts. Many cities have public housing developments that are ghettos—often geographically isolated and characterized by extreme poverty, low family status, and lack of amenities. GIS can be used to compare demographic information on housing characteristics for public housing or housing in general. In this exercise, you will compare statistics for U.S. states with the number of housing units, number of renter- and owner-occupied units, and highest number of vacant units.

Start with the following:

- **\Gistutorial\UnitedStates\States**—polygon layer of U.S. states with census 2000 information.

    Attributes of States table—attribute table for U.S. states that includes the following fields needed for the assignment:

HSE_UNITS	number of housing units per state
RENTER_OCC	number of renter-occupied units per state
OWNER_OCC	number of owner-occupied units per state
VACANT	number of vacant units

Change the map and get statistics

Create a new map called C:\Gistutorial\Answers\Assignment1\Assignment1-1.mxd with the above layer of the US States added and modified as a hollow-filled color with a medium gray outline. Using the US States attribute table and a bright red selection color, select the five states having the highest number of vacant units. Label these selected states only with the state name and number of vacant units for each state.

Create data document
- **Create a Microsoft Word document called C:\Gistutorial\Answers\Assignment1\Assignment1.doc.**
- **In the Word file, create a table with statistics as follows for the five states with the highest number of vacant units only: mean, minimum, and maximum number of housing units, renter occupied, owner occupied, and vacant.**

Field	Mean	Minimum	Maximum
HSE_Units			
Renter_Occ			
Owner_Occ			
Vacant			

Hint: Getting statistics
- Use the Attributes of States table and right-click each field to get the appropriate statistics for the five records selected (those with the highest number of vacant units).

EXERCISES

Exercise Assignment 1-2

Erin Street crime watch

Crime prevention depends very much on what the criminology literature calls "informal guardianship": residents and their neighbors keep an eye on suspicious behavior and intervene in some fashion. Police departments therefore actively promote and support crime watch or block watch citizen groups and keep them informed on crime trends. Suppose that the police commander of a precinct has a notebook computer, ArcMap, and a portable color projector for use at crime watch meetings. Your job is to get the commander ready for a meeting with the 100 block Erin Street crime watch group.

Start with the following:

- **C:\Gistutorial\PAGIS\Midhill\Street**—arc layer for street centerlines in the Middle Hill neighborhood of Pittsburgh. Note: This is a TIGER street centerline map from the U.S. Census Bureau. You will study and use TIGER maps extensively in GIS.
  - **Attributes of Street table**—attribute table for streets in the Middle Hill neighborhood that includes the following fields needed for the assignment:
    - **Fname** = street name
    - **Address Ranges**
    - **LeftAdd1** = beginning house number on the left side of the street
    - **LeftAdd2** = ending house number on the left side of the street
    - **RgtAdd1** = beginning house number on the right side of the street
    - **RgtAdd2** = ending house number on the right side of the street
- **C:\Gistutorial\PAGIS\Midhill\Curbs**—arc layer for curbs in the Middle Hill neighborhood of Pittsburgh.
- **C:\Gistutorial\PAGIS\Midhill\Building**—polygon layer for buildings in the Middle Hill neighborhood of Pittsburgh.
- **C:\Gistutorial\PAGIS\Midhill\Mid911**—point layer for 911 calls in the Middle Hill neighborhood of Pittsburgh.
  - **Attributes of Mid911 table**—attribute table for mid911 points that includes the following fields needed for the assignment:
    - **Nature_Code** = call type
    - **Date** = date of crime
    - **Address** = addresses of crime locations

Change the map and get statistics

Create a new map with the above layers called C:\Gistutorial\Anwers\Assignment1\Assignment1-2.mxd that includes a zoomed view of the Erin Street block selected and labeled with street names. Display streets, curbs, and buildings as medium-light gray lines, and 911 calls as bright red circles. Create a spatial bookmark of the zoomed area called Erin Street.

Create data document

- Create a list of addresses, dates of calls, and call types for crimes in the 100 block of Erin Street (see hints). Some of these will have address names of Davenport, Erin, Trent in the table. Use your word processing package to add a table of addresses in **C:\Gistutorial\Answers\ Assignment1\Assignment1.doc.**

Address	Date	Call Type

Hints

- The 100 block of Erin Street is the segment of Erin Street whose address range is from 100 to 199 and perpendicular to streets Webster and Wylie. The crime reports are prepared for the area between Erin Davenport and Erin/Trent. Use both the attribute table and Identify tool to find and label these streets.
- Although it appears that there are only six points, there are actually thirteen total because some calls are at the same location. Use the Select Features button (perhaps with a window) and information in the attribute table to get the data on all relevant calls.
- Fields can be exported from the attribute table. In the table, choose "Options" and "Export." Save the selected records to a .dbf file. Open in Microsoft Excel and paste from there into Microsoft Word.

What to turn in

If you are working in a classroom setting with an instructor, you may be required to submit the exercises you created in tutorial 1. Below are the files you are required to turn in. Be sure to use a compression program such as PKZIP or WinZip to include all three files as one .zip document for review and grading. Include your name and assignment number in the .zip document (YourNameAssn1.zip).

ArcMap projects

C:\Gistutorial\Assignments\Assignment1\Assignment1-1.mxd

C:\Gistutorial\Assignments\Assignment1\Assignment1-2.mxd

Word document

C:\Gistutorial\Assignments\Assignment1\Assignment1.doc

Create choropleth maps
Create group layers
Create threshold scales for dynamic display
Create choropleth maps using custom attribute scales
Create pin (point) maps
Create hyperlinks
Create Tool Tips

GIS Tutorial 2

Map Design

In this tutorial you will learn all steps necessary to compose common maps from available map layers. One type of map that you will create is a choropleth map that color codes polygons to convey information about areas. The second is a "pin map" that uses point markers to display spatial patterns in point data. You will continue to use U.S. states and counties, plus census tracts and detailed census data for the Commonwealth of Pennsylvania. All maps that you will produce are of interest to demographers and policy makers.

Launch ArcMap

1   From the Windows taskbar, click Start, All Programs, ArcGIS, ArcMap.

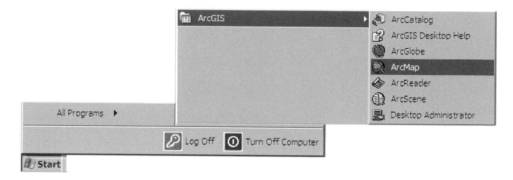

2   Click the An existing map radio button in the ArcMap dialog box.

3   Click OK.

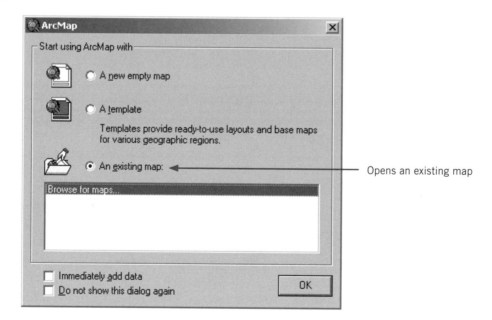

4   Browse to the drive on which the Gistutorial folder has been installed (e.g., C:\Gistutorial), select the **Tutorial2-1.mxd** project, and click the Open button.

ArcMap opens a map with no layers added. You will add the layers needed for the tutorial next.

Create choropleth maps

A choropleth map is a map in which polygon areas are colored or shaded to represent attribute values. You will use population to create choropleth maps for states, counties, and census tracts.

Add a layer to the view

1   **Click the Add Data button.**

2   **Navigate to the folder where you have the Gistutorial data installed and click \Gistutorial\ UnitedStates\.**

3   **Click States.shp and click Add.**

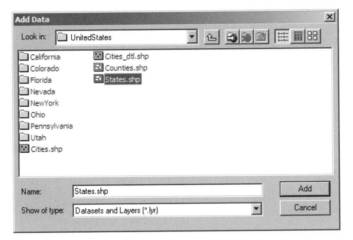

The forty-eight states of the continental United States are drawn in the map display in a color randomly picked by ArcMap. You will change the color of the states later in the tutorial.

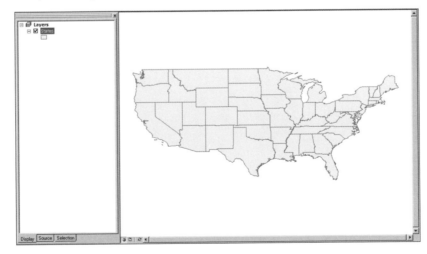

Change a layer's name

1   Right-click the States layer in the table of contents.

2   Click Properties.

3   Click the General tab.

Notice that the current layer name is "States."

4   Type **Population by State** as the new layer name.

5   Click OK.

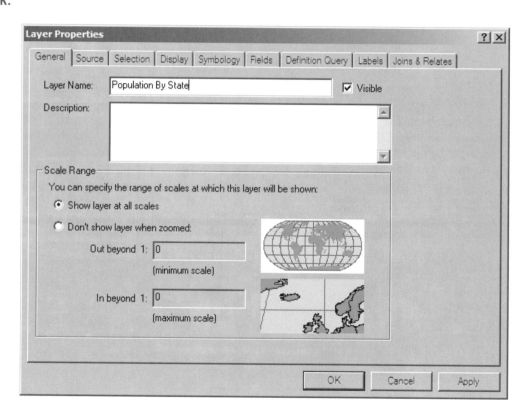

Select a census attribute to display state population

1   Right-click the Population by State layer in the table of contents.

2   Click Properties.

3   Click the Symbology tab.

4   In the Show box, click Quantities and click Graduated colors.

5   In the Fields box, click the Value drop-down list and click POP2003.

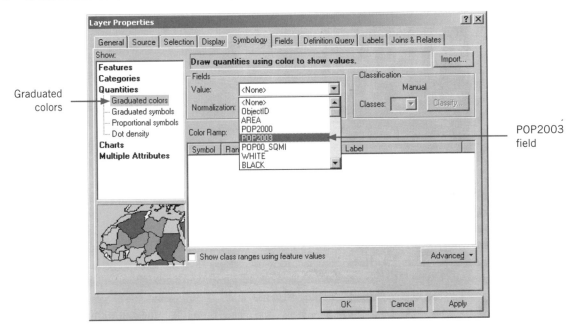

6   Click OK.

The result is a classification consisting of five value ranges of 2005 population ranging from lowest to highest population with darker colors for higher population. ArcMap picks an arbitrary color fill for the polygons. You will learn how to change the colors and classifications later.

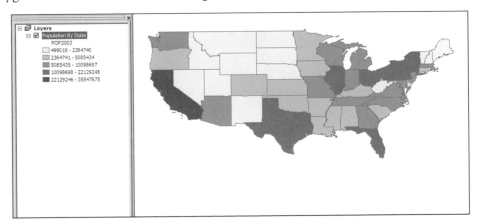

Create group layers

Group layers are layers that contain other layers, allowing for better organization of the layers in your map. Group layers have behavior similar to other layers in the table of contents. Turning off the visibility of a group layer turns off the visibility of all its component layers.

Add a group layer to the map

1   Right-click Layers in the table of contents.

2   Click New Group Layer.

3   Right-click the resulting New Group Layer and click Properties.

4   Click the General tab.

5   Type **Population By County** as the group layer name.

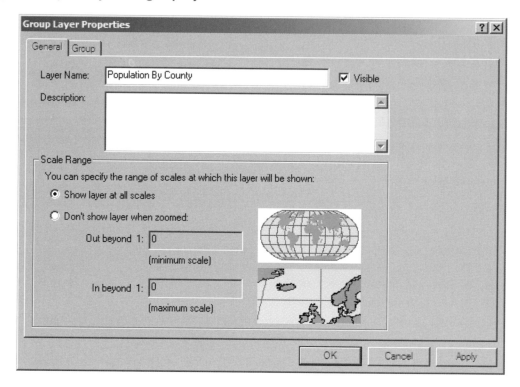

Add a layer to the group

1   Click the Group tab in the Group Layer Properties window.

2   Click the Add button.

3   Navigate to your **\Gistutorial\UnitedStates** folder.

4   Click **States.shp** and the Add button again.

5   Double-click the **Counties.shp** file.

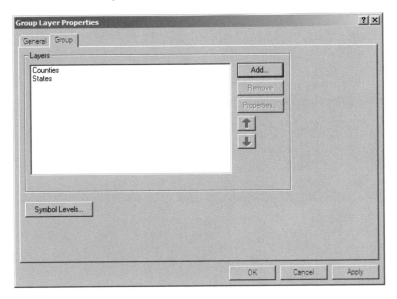

6   Click OK.

The U.S. counties are displayed in the map with a color randomly selected by ArcMap.

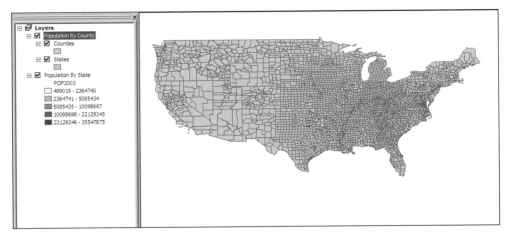

Change the symbology for states

1 **Click once on the legend symbol below the States layer name.**

You are changing the symbology for the States layer that you just added, not the one you added at the beginning of the tutorial.

2 **In the Symbol Selector's Options panel, change the Fill Color to No Color, key in an Outline Width of 1.5, and change Outline Color to Black.**

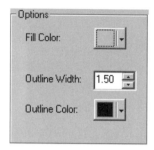

3 **Click OK.**

4 **Within the Population By County group layer, click the States layer and drag it above the Counties layer.**

If by mistake you drag the States layer outside of the Population By County group, just drag it back inside the group. This is another way to add layers to a group—simply add them to your map then drag them inside a group.

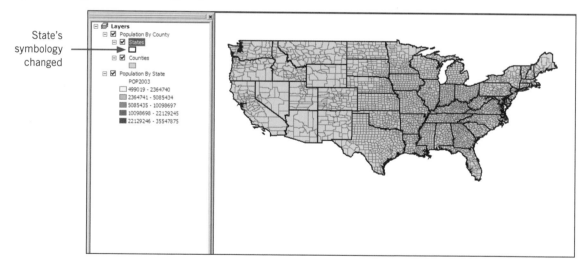

State's symbology changed

Select a census attribute to display county population

1   Right-click the Counties layer in the table of contents.

2   Click Properties.

3   Click the Symbology tab.

The current symbol for the counties layer is Single symbol.

4   In the Show box, click Quantities and click Graduated colors.

5   In the Fields panel, click the Value drop-down list and click POP2003.

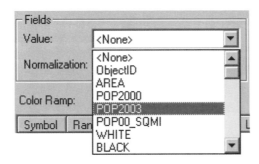

6   Click OK.

The result is a classification of the U.S. counties into five value ranges of 2003 population that are listed lowest to highest.

7   Collapse the tree structures in the table of contents by clicking the boxes that have minus signs (−) for Population By County and Population By State.

You can reverse this process by clicking the boxes again, which now have plus signs (+) indicating that they can be expanded.

YOUR TURN

Note: You must complete this Your Turn *exercise before continuing. You will use this group layer later in the tutorial.*

Turn off the Population By County group layer and the Population By State layer.

Create a new group layer called Population By Census Tract.

Add the census tract layers for Utah and Nevada and the States layer to the Population By Census Tract group layer. (The census tract layers are located at \Gistutorial\UnitedStates\Utah\UtahTracts.shp and \Gistutorial\UnitedStates\Nevada\NevadaTracts.shp.)

Classify the census tracts using graduated colors based on the POP2003 field.

You can continue this for the other states with data downloaded from sites reviewed in tutorial 5.

Saving layer files

1 Turn on all of the layer groups.

2 Right-click the layer group name Population By County.

3 Click Save As Layer File.

4 Navigate to the **\Gistutorial\Layers** folder.

5 Type **PopulationByCounty.lyr** in the Name field.

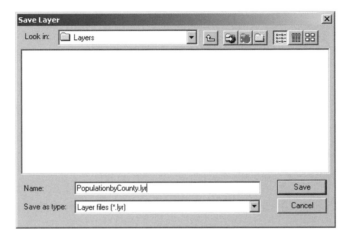

6 Click Save.

The layer file is now stored in the Layers folder. It can be added to any map that you create.

Adding group layers

1 Click the Add Data button.

2 Navigate to **\Gistutorial\Layers**.

3 Click **PopulationByCounty.lyr**.

4 Click the Add button.

Removing group layers

1 Right-click the duplicate Population By County layer group that was just added.

2 Click Remove.

Create threshold scales for dynamic display

If a layer is turned on in the table of contents, ArcMap will draw it, regardless of the map scale. To help you automatically display layers at an appropriate scale, you can set a layer's visible scale range and define the range of scales at which ArcMap draws the layer.

Set a visible scale based on the current scale

1 Turn off the Population By Census Tract group layer and turn on Population By County and Population By State.

2 Zoom to a few states in the northeast part of the country.

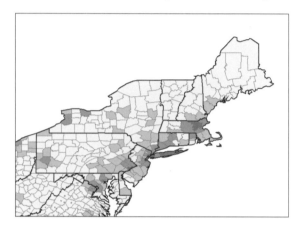

3 If necessary, expand the Population By County group layer, then right-click the Counties layer in the Population By County group layer.

4 Click Visible Scale Range, Set Minimum Scale.

ArcMap sets the scale to display this layer when zoomed in this close or closer. Zooming out any further will turn off the polygons for this layer.

5 Click the Zoom to Full Extent button.

Now the county polygons will not display.

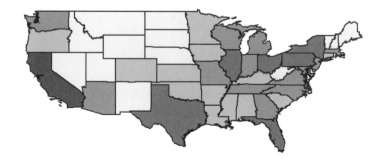

Set a maximum scale based on the current scale

1   Zoom in until the county polygons are displayed again.

2   Right-click the States layer in the Population By County group layer.

3   Click Visible Scale Range, Set Maximum Scale.

4   Zoom in a little closer.

The black outline polygons for the states are not displayed when zoomed in beyond the maximum scale just set. Zooming out enough will turn on the state polygons again.

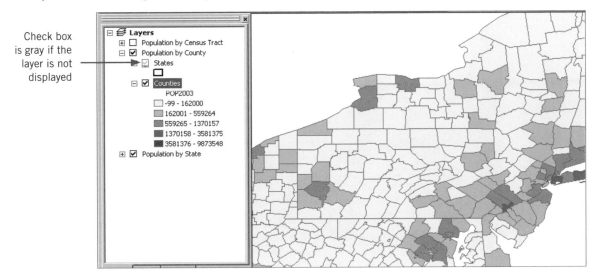

Check box is gray if the layer is not displayed

Clear a layer's visible scale

1   Right-click the States layer in the Population By County layer group.

2   Click Visible Scale Range, Clear Scale Range.

The outline polygons for the states are displayed again when zoomed at this scale.

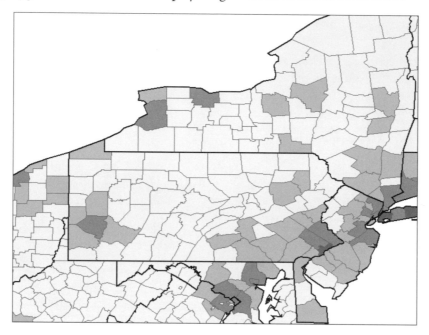

Set a minimum visible scale for a specific layer

1   Zoom to the full extent of the map.

2   Turn the Population By Census Tract group layer back on.

3   In the table of contents, right-click the NevadaTracts layer and click Properties.

4   Click the General tab.

5   Click the Don't show layer when zoomed radio button.

6   Type **8,000,000** in the Out beyond field.

If you zoom out beyond this scale, the layer will not be visible.

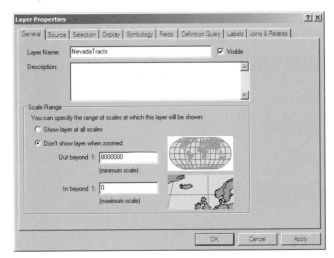

7   Click OK.

ArcMap will not show the Nevada census tract polygons when zoomed out past a scale of 1:8,000,000.

Scale is
1:31,000,000

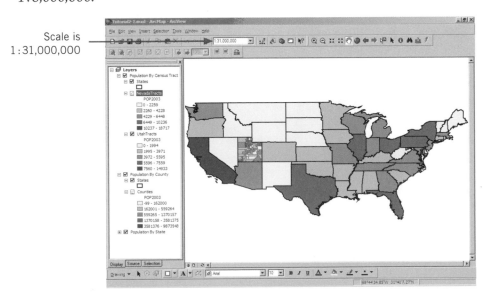

Set a maximum visible scale for a specific layer

1   Right-click the Population By State layer and click Properties.

2   Click the General tab.

3   Click the Don't show layer when zoomed radio button.

4   Type **10,000,000** in the In beyond field.

5   Click OK.

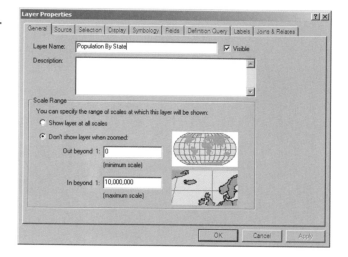

If you zoom in below this scale (1 : 10,000,000) the layer will not be visible.

Scale is
1 : 9,500,000

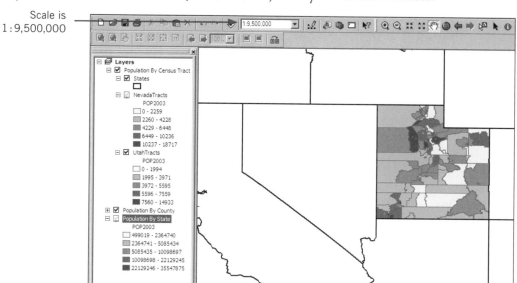

YOUR TURN

Set the minimum scale for the Counties layer to 9,000,000 and its maximum scale to 8,000,000.

After changing scales, zoom in and out to make sure you understand what changing those values accomplished.

Create choropleth maps using custom attribute scales

Earlier in this tutorial, you created a choropleth map out of the Population By States layer by classifying it with graduated colors based on the POP2003 attribute field. When you chose to symbolize the layer with graduated colors, ArcMap automatically applied a classification method called Natural Breaks to divide the features in the map into five separate value classes. Although Natural Breaks is the default method, ArcMap allows you to choose other methods for classifying your data.

Create custom classes in a legend

1   **Zoom to the full extent.**

2   **Turn off all layers except Population By State, and expand that layer in the table of contents so that you can see its classes.**

3   **Right-click the Population By State layer and click Properties.**

4   **In the Layer Properties dialog box, click the Symbology tab.**

5   **In the Classification panel, click the Classes drop-down list and select 6.**

6   **In the Classification panel, click Classify.**

The Classification dialog box shows the current classifications, statistics, and break values.

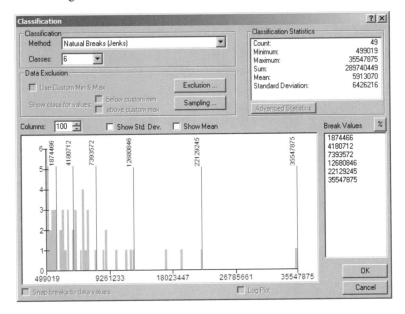

Manually change class values

1 Click the drop-down list for the Classification Method and click Manual.

2 In the Break Values panel, click the first value, 1874466, to highlight it.

Notice the blue graph line corresponding to that value turns red.

3 Type **2000000** and press Enter to move to the next break value.

4 Continue by entering the following break values: **4000000, 8000000, 12000000, 18000000, 9999999999**.

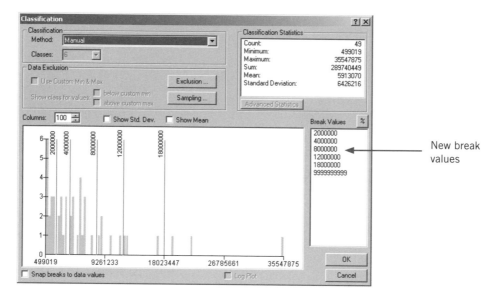

5 Click OK.

6 In the Label field of the Symbology tab, change the first value to **0–2,000,000** and the last label to **18,000,001 and greater,** then add commas to the remaining range labels.

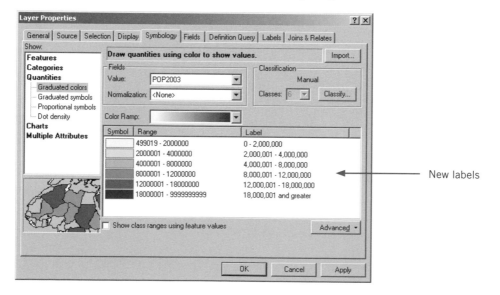

7   Click OK.

The Population By State layer will change to reflect the new break values and labels. This is much easier to read than the Natural Breaks classification.

8   Right-click the Population By State layer in the table of contents and click Save As Layer File.

9   Browse to the \Gistutorial\Layers folder, key in PopulationByState in the name field, and click Save.

YOUR TURN

Change the classification break values for the Counties, Nevada Census Tracts, and Utah Census Tracts layers based on the population (POP2003) field. Use the same method as above to manually change the values. Be sure to change the labels in the legend.

Right-click a layer name and Zoom to Layer to see how your classification scheme looks on the choropleth map.

Manually change class colors and hues

Colors for classes can be changed manually. Generally, it is best to have more classes with light colors and a few with dark colors (the human eye can differentiate light colors more easily).

1 Right-click the Population By State layer and click Properties.

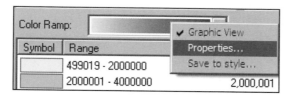

2 In the Layer Properties dialog box, click the Symbology tab.

3 Right-click the Color Ramp and click Properties.

4 Click the color box beside Color 1 and select Arctic White.

5 Click the color box beside Color 2 and select Ultra Blue then click OK twice.

The Population By State map will change to reflect the colors.

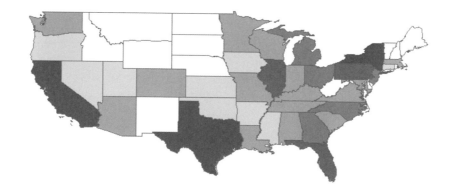

You can also double-click each color symbol to change the classification colors individually.

Double-click
color symbol →

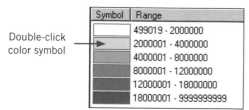

Pin (point) maps

Pin maps, otherwise known as point maps, show exact locations of data or events using individual point markers for each record. In this example, you will create a pin map showing the range of populations in U.S. cities using graduated symbols.

Create a pin map of U.S. cities by population

1   Turn off all the layers in your map and create a new group layer called Population By City.

2   Add the data layers **\Gistutorial\UnitedStates\States.shp** and **\Gistutorial\UnitedStates\Cities.shp**.

3   Double-click States in the Population By City group layer to open its Layer Properties window.

4   Click the Symbology tab, change the symbol to a hollow fill with a black outline of 1.5, and click OK, then click OK again.

5   Double-click Cities in the Population By City group layer to open its Layer Properties window.

6   Click the Symbology tab and change the layer's symbology from Single Symbol to Quantities, Graduated Symbols.

7   In the Fields panel, change the Value to POP2000, the template symbol to a red circle, symbol size to 2–18, and assign the break points and legend labels as shown below.

8   Click OK.

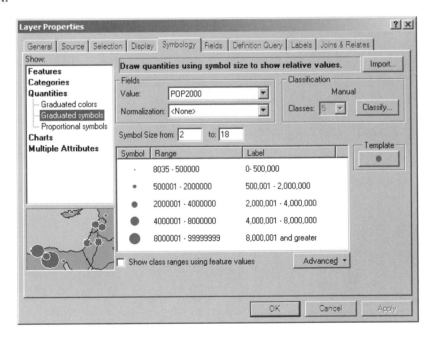

The resultant pin map shows U.S. cities classified by population.

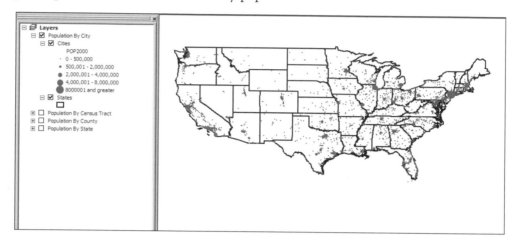

9 Click File, Save.

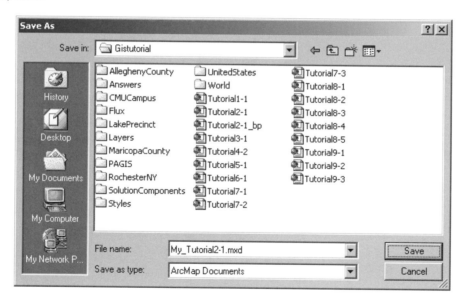

Create a pin map based on feature query

Pin maps can be created by selecting a subset of features from an existing layer. For example, suppose you have a layer containing all the cities in Pennsylvania, but you only want to display the cities with populations between 10,000 and 49,000. To display the correct cities, you can create a definition query to filter out all the cities with population values outside the desired range.

Create a new map

1 **Click File, New.**

2 **Click the My Templates tab and Blank Document from the New dialog box.**

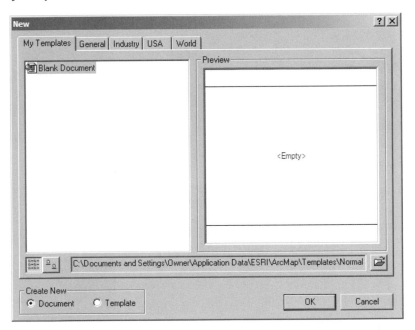

3 **Click OK.**

Add data to the map

1   Click the Add Data button.

2   Navigate to the folder where you have the Gistutorial data installed, click **\Gistutorial\ Unitedstates\Pennsylvania**, and add the following layers: **PACounties.shp** and **PACities.shp**.

This displays a map showing county polygon features for Pennsylvania and detailed cities. ArcMap picks an arbitrary color fill and point marker for the polygons and points.

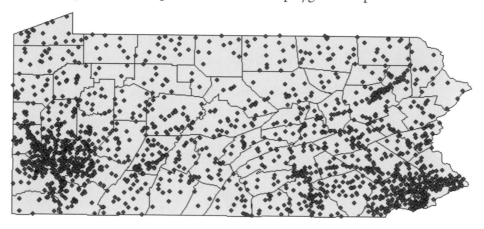

Create ground polygons

To draw attention away from a feature, colors should be very light or, in the case of these polygons, have no color at all.

1   Right-click the PACounties layer and click Properties.

2   Click the General tab and change the name of the layer to Pennsylvania Counties.

3   Click the Symbology tab, click the symbol, and click the Hollow fill style from the Symbol Selector.

4   Click OK and OK again.

Display a queried subset of Pennsylvania cities

1   **Right-click the PACities layer and click Properties.**

2   **Click the Definition Query tab.**

3   **Click the Query Builder button.**

4   **In the Query Builder window double-click "FEATURE".**

5   **Click the Get Unique Values button.**

6   **Click "=" as the logical operator.**

7   **In the Unique Values List, double-click '10,000 to 49,999'.**

The completed query ("FEATURE" = '10,000 to 49,999') will yield a layer with only the cities in Pennsylvania that are between 10,000 and 49,999. If the query has an error, just edit it in the lower panel of the Query Builder, or delete it by clicking Clear and then repeat steps 4 through 6.

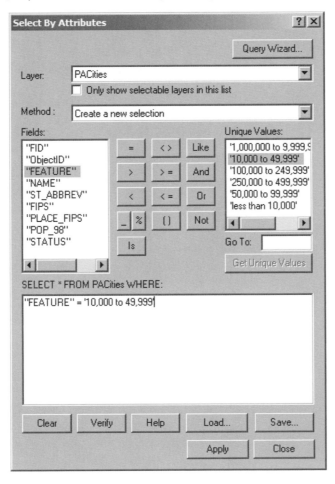

8   **Click OK twice to execute your query and close the Layer Properties dialog box.**

Change the layer's name and symbol

1   Right-click the PACities layer and click Properties.

2   Click the General tab and change the name of the layer to **Population 10,000 to 49,999**.

3   Click the Symbology tab.

4   Click the Symbol button.

5   Click the Circle 2 symbol icon.

6   Change the color to Ultra Blue and the size to 8.

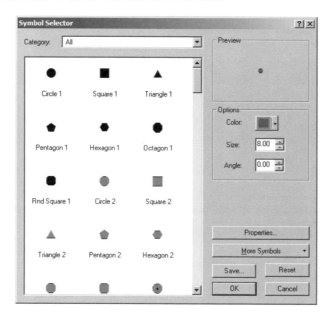

7   Click OK, then click OK again.

The resulting map uses blue circles to show the cities in Pennsylvania with a population between 10,000 and 49,999.

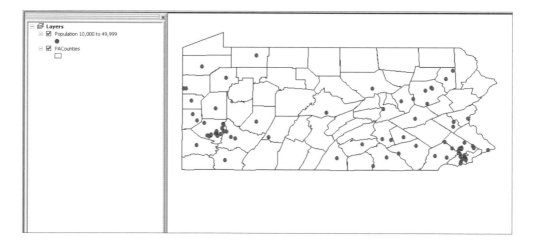

Add Pennsylvania's state capital city

1 Click the Add Data button.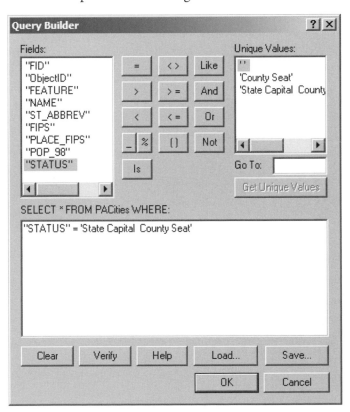

2 Navigate to the folder where you have the Gistutorial data installed, click **\Gistutorial\ Unitedstates\Pennsylvania,** and add the **PACities.shp** again.

3 Right-click the PACities layer and click Properties.

4 Click the Definition Query tab.

5 Click the Query Builder button.

6 In the Fields list of the Query Builder window double-click "STATUS".

7 Click the Get Unique Values button.

8 Click "=" as the logical operator.

9 Double click 'State Capital County Seat'.

The completed query ("STATUS" = 'State Capital County Seat') will yield a layer with only this city, Pennsylvania's state capital of Harrisburg.

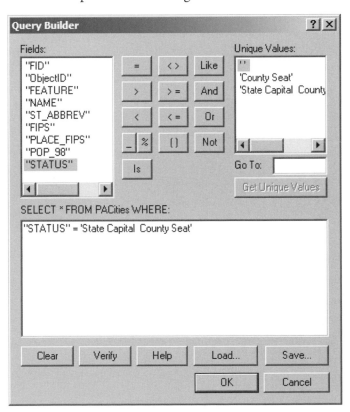

10 Click OK and OK again.

Change the layer's name and symbol

1 Right-click the PACities layer and click Properties.

2 Click the General tab and change the name of the layer to State Capital.

3 Click the Symbology tab.

4 Click the Symbol button.

5 Scroll down and click the Star 3 symbol icon.

6 Change the color to Solar Yellow and the size to 25.

7 Click OK and OK again.

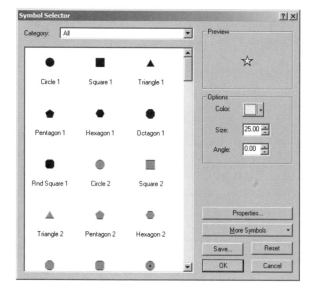

The resultant map shows the state capital of Harrisburg.

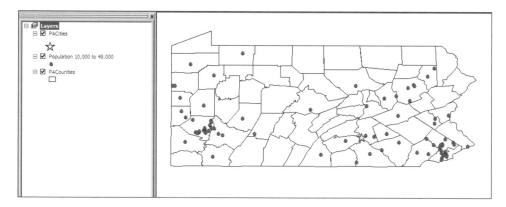

YOUR TURN

Add the PACities layer once more and create a definition query that displays Pennsylvania's two largest cities, Philadelphia and Pittsburgh, and show the two cities with a symbol that makes them stand out on the map. *Hint: The query should be "NAME" = 'Pittsburgh' OR "NAME" = 'Philadelphia.'*

Create hyperlinks

The Hyperlink tool allows access to documents or Web pages by clicking features. There are three types of hyperlinks: documents, URLs, and macros.

Create a dynamic hyperlink

1   **Click the Identify button.**

2   **Click the city feature for Harrisburg. (Harrisburg is the state capital and should be displayed with a star.)**

3   **In the Identify Results window, right-click Harrisburg in the left panel and select Add Hyperlink from the context menu.**

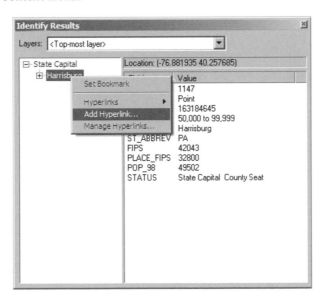

4   **Click the Link to a URL radio button and type *http://www.harrisburg.com.***

5   **Click OK, then close the Identify Results window.**

Launch the hyperlink

1   **From the Tools toolbar, click the Hyperlink button.**

Make sure the layer containing the feature with the hyperlink you want to access is checked (visible) in the table of contents.

2   **Move the cursor to the city of Harrisburg feature.**

When you are over a feature for which a hyperlink exists, the cursor turns into a pointing hand and you see a pop-up tip with the name of the target. This takes some practice. Keep hovering the cursor over the feature and you will eventually get it. Try placing the tip of the "lightning bolt" on the feature.

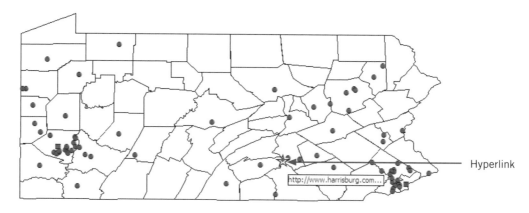

3   **Click the feature to go to the Harrisburg Web site.**

YOUR TURN

Add another hyperlink for Harrisburg *for www.senatorsbaseball.com.* Visit the ArcGIS Desktop Help topic for creating field-based hyperlinks. *Hint: In the help system's Contents tab, navigate to ArcMap>Querying Maps>Displaying a Web Page or Document about a feature.*

Create MapTips

When you hover your pointer over a feature on a map, it is possible to have an attribute of that feature automatically displayed as a MapTip.

1   Right-click the Population 10,000 to 49,999 layer in the table of contents.

2   Right-click Properties and click the Fields tab.

3   Select Name to be the Primary Display Field.

4   Click the Display tab and check Show MapTips.

5   Click OK.

6   From the Tools toolbar, click the Select Elements button.

7   Hover over any city in the Population 10,000 to 49,999 layer to see its name.

8   Click File, Save as, browse to **\Gistutorial**, type **Tutorial2-2.mxd** as the name, and click Save.

Exercise Assignment 2-1

Map showing schools in the city of Pittsburgh by enrollment

The City of Pittsburgh School Board wants to do an extensive evaluation of local schools. They have collected data about all schools, public and private. The data about these schools is entered in a GIS program. The initial project identifies schools as either public or private and shows their enrollment. Your task is to make a GIS map for the school board comparing the enrollment of public and private schools. You will use point features of different sizes to show this. *Note: Data for this exercise was obtained from the City of Pittsburgh City Planning Department and enrollment numbers may not reflect the actual count.*

Start with the following:

- **C:\Gistutorial\PAGIS\Neighborhoods.shp**—polygon layer of Pittsburgh neighborhoods.
- **C:\Gistutorial\PAGIS\Schools.shp**—point layer of all schools.
- **Attributes of Schools table** for Pittsburgh Schools using the following fields:
    DISTRICT = school type (public, private, or Pittsburgh diocese)
    Enroll 95 = number of students enrolled
    STATUS = OPEN or CLOSED

Create pin map with hyperlink

Create a new map called C:\Gistutorial\Answers\Assignment2\Assignment2-1.mxd showing the enrollment of students in both public and private schools that are currently open. Include Pittsburgh neighborhood polygons but have the main focus of the map be on the public schools. Hyperlink the Web site *http://schenleyhs.pghboe. net* to the point record for Schenley High School (home of Andy Warhol). If you cannot find this Web site, hyperlink a similar site.

Hints
- Private schools are those labeled private and diocese (Catholic).
- Be sure to rename the data frame and layers. Think carefully about your color and classification schemes.

Exercise Assignment 2-2

Map showing K–12 population versus school enrollment

Knowing the population of school-age children in Pittsburgh might lead to some interesting conclusions as to which schools have a higher enrollment or which schools need additional attention. Perhaps some schools will close or others will import students from surrounding areas. In this exercise, you will create a choropleth map showing the population by census tract for the entire state of Pennsylvania, then a map zoomed into the city of Pittsburgh for the K–12 school-age population. Layers will turn on or off depending on the zoom level. You will also show schools by enrollment to pick ones that might possibly close.

Start with the following:

Note: You must add each layer one a a time in the order listed below. Otherwise map layers will not overlay properly.

- **C:\Gistutorial\UnitedStates\Pennsylvania\PATracts.shp**—polygon layer of Pennsylvania census tracts, 2000.
- **C:\Gistutorial\UnitedStates\Pennsylvania\PACounties.shp**—polygon layer of Pennsylvania counties.
- **C:\Gistutorial\PAGIS\BlockGroups.shp**—polygon layer of Pittsburgh census block groups, 2000 that will be shown when zoomed into the Pittsburgh area.
- **C:\Gistutorial\PAGIS\Neighg**—polygon layer of neighborhoods. Be sure to use this instead of the "Neighborhoods" layer. It matches the geographic projection of census block groups, which you will learn about later.
- **C:\Gistutorial\PAGIS\Schools.shp**—point layer of Pittsburgh schools.

Create choropleth maps with scale thresholds

Create a new map called C:\Gistutorial\Answers\Assignment2\Assignment2-2.mxd that shows the Pennsylvania census tracts for K–12 school-age population (ages 5–17) for the entire state as well as additional details about the city of Pittsburgh. Create a bookmark to help you easily zoom into the Pittsburgh details.

When zoomed to the entire state, do not show the city of Pittsburgh details, but turn on these layers when zoomed into that area. Have the Pennsylvania details turned off when zoomed into the Pittsburgh details.

When zoomed into Pittsburgh, also show the K–12 population as census block groups and neighborhood outlines. This will give more details than census tracts do and also show the neighborhood boundaries which the school board is more familiar with. At the zoomed level, include the point layer for Pittsburgh public schools that are still open but with low enrollment (over 0 and under 200 students).

Hints
- Create two layer groups: one for the state of Pennsylvania and one for Pittsburgh details so you can turn them on or off as necessary. You decide what layers should be included in each layer group.

Questions

Create a Microsoft Word file called C:\Gistutorial\Answers\Assignment2\Assignment2.doc with answers to the following questions:

1   The seven public schools meeting the criteria (over 0 and under 200 enrollment) are in what neighborhoods?
2   Name a school that may close. Explain why you picked this school.

What to turn in

If you are working in a classroom setting with an instructor, you may be required to submit the exercises you created in tutorial 2. Below are the files you are required to turn in. Be sure to use a compression program such as PKZIP or WinZip to include all three files as one .zip document for review and grading. Include your name and assignment number in the .zip document (YourNameAssn2.zip).

ArcMap projects

C:\Gistutorial\Assignments\Assignment2\Assignment2-1.mxd
C:\Gistutorial\Assignments\Assignment2\Assignment2-2.mxd

Word document

C:\Gistutorial\Answers\Assignment2\Assignment2.doc with answers to the above questions.

OBJECTIVES

Use interactive GIS
Produce print layouts
Create a custom map template and map series
Create a custom map template for multiple maps
Add reports to layouts
Export layouts as files
Generate other outputs

GIS Tutorial 3

GIS Outputs

A GIS can produce many forms of output, from interactive desktop projects similar to maps in tutorials 1 and 2, to printed maps for distribution, to image files for placement in presentations or on Web sites. Final map compositions created in ArcMap are constructed in Layout mode. While in this mode, users see their current map on a virtual page (the layout) and can add map elements to it such as a title, map legend, north arrow, or scale bar. In addition, it is possible to add graphs or tabular reports to layouts. Layouts can be designed in various sizes, from regular letter-sized paper to very large sheets used in plotters. Finally, while not covered in this tutorial workbook, it is possible to produce interactive maps for Web sites using packages such as ArcIMS software from ESRI.

Launch ArcMap

1   From the Windows taskbar, click Start, All Programs, ArcGIS, ArcMap.

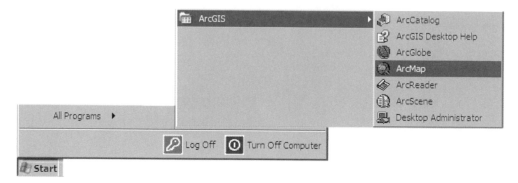

2   Click the An existing map radio button in the ArcMap dialog box.

3   Click OK.

Open an existing map

1   Browse to the drive on which the Gistutorial folder has been installed (e.g., C:\Gistutorial), select **Tutorial3-1.mxd**, and click the Open button.

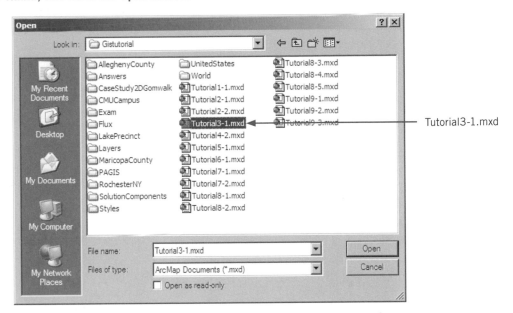

Tutorial3-1.mxd opens in ArcMap showing a map of the United States with state capitals displayed.

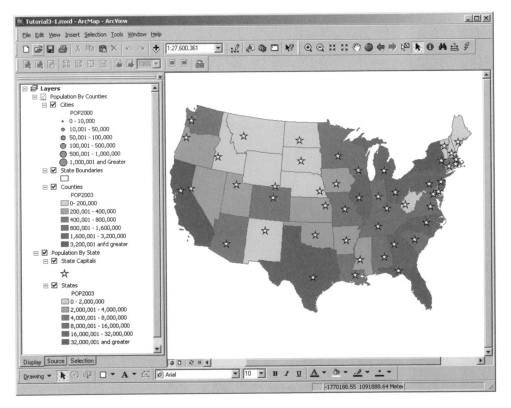

Use interactive GIS

The map document you just opened builds on work that you did in tutorials 1 and 2. It provides the ability to scan the entire area of interest, the continental United States; to get information on state e-government Web sites; and to pick an area to zoom into for more detailed information. Feature labels and MapTips provide additional information. Applying GIS in this way is quite powerful and popular. A good example is crime mapping by municipal police departments. The area-wide scan uses choropleth maps of crime counts by area to provide general information on neighborhoods where crimes are increasing or decreasing. The analyst can then drill down to small areas to see detailed information on individual crime points. See the sample crime maps at *www.icpsr.umich.edu/NACJD/cmtutorial.html*. You can link to the maps from the "About the CrimeMap Tutorial" section of that page.

YOUR TURN

Start by using the Hyperlink tool (the lightning bolt on the Tools toolbar) to access some state e-government Web sites by clicking state capitals. Try any state along the west or south coast of the United States (after clicking the Hyperlink button, dots will appear in the center of stars that have hyperlinks).

Zoom into an area about the size of a state to see the threshold scales at work. Try the MapTips over any city or county. Bookmarks are available to help you move around and get back to the continental United States.

Produce print layouts

Often, it is desirable to produce a paper copy or file copy of a map for distribution. ArcMap has a Layout View for this purpose and several built-in templates for producing layouts.

Choose a built-in layout template

1   **Click View, Bookmarks, Continental U.S.**

2   **Click View, Layout View.**

3   **Outside the rectangle containing the map, right-click any portion of the Layout View border.**

4   **Click Change Layout, then click the General tab. Select the LandscapeClassic.mxt and Finish.**

The .mxt extension is for map layout templates.

Set up and customize the template page

1 Right-click the top border of the layout, outside any rectangles containing map elements, and click Page and Print Setup.

2 In the Map Page Size frame, click the Standard Sizes drop-down list and select Letter. Click the Landscape Orientation option in the Map Page size frame and again in the Paper frame, and click OK.

3 Double-click the title place holder (< Double-click to enter map title >) on the left side of the map.

4 In the Properties window, type **U.S. Population and Cities**, click the Change Symbol button, change the color from white to black, click OK, then click OK again.

5 Double-click inside the brown left panel of the layout, outside the rectangles containing the legend and map title placeholder.

6 In the Properties window, change the Fill Color from brown to white and click OK.

7 Right-click the data frame name (Layers) in the table of contents and click Properties. Click the Frame tab, change the Background Color from light blue to white, and click OK.

8 Double-click the small text placeholder in the lower left corner of the map, type something like **Map Designed by "Your Name"**, and click OK.

Small text placeholder

9 Click File, Save As, browse to the **\Gistutorial** folder, name the map **Tutorial3-2.mxd**, and click Save.

The resulting layout has a new title, colors, and your name.

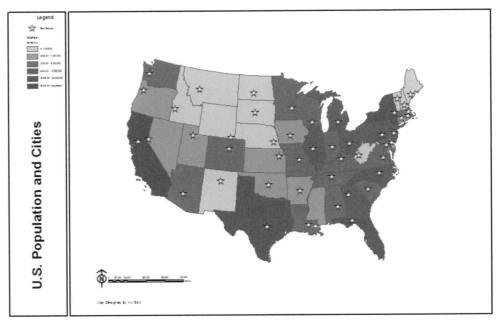

YOUR TURN

Return to Data View and turn off the Population By States group (but leave the Population By County group on). Do not worry about your map appearing blank.

Use a Bookmark to zoom to one of the available cities (Los Angeles, for example).

Change back to Layout View and change the layout template to LetterLandscape.mxt (right-click the layout outside the data frame).

Make modifications and additions as necessary.

If you have a printer, you can preview the effect of your print settings by clicking File, Print Preview. To make changes to your print settings click File, Print, Setup. When you're ready to print, click File, Print, OK.

Save the results as Tutorial3-3.mxd.

Create a custom map template and map series

Sometimes it is desirable to produce a number of maps, each with the same design and layers but with some features changed or different attributes displayed.

Start a new map

1 **Click File, New, then click the My Templates tab. Select the Blank Document template and click OK. If you wish to save changes to your current map click Yes, otherwise click No.**

Starting from a blank document is the only way to create a custom template.

2 **Click View, Data View.**

3 **Click the Add Data button.** **Browse to the \Gistutorial\UnitedStates\ folder and double-click States.shp.**

4 **Right-click the States layer in the table of contents, click Properties. Click the General tab, and change the Layer Name to Population.**

5 **Click the Symbology tab and in the show box, click Quantities, Graduated Colors and in the Fields frame change the value to AMERI_ES (you may have to scroll down to see this field in the list).**

It is a good idea to use the same break values or scale for all maps in a map series to facilitate comparisons. Start with the attribute that has the minimum value by state (population, in this case), which is Native Americans (AMERI-ES). Others that will be in the map series are ASIAN, WHITE, BLACK, and HISP.

6 **Click Classify, change the number of Classes to 7, change the Method to Manual, and key the following Break Values starting at the bottom of the list: 9999999999, 10000000, 5000000, 1000000, 500000, 100000, 50000.**

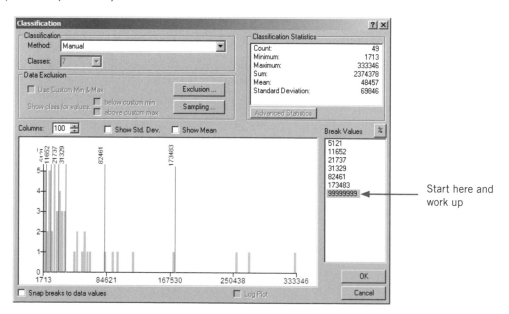

Complete the new map project

1   Click **OK** to return to the Layer Properties window.

2   In the Layer Properties window, change the first symbol label from 1713–50000 to 0–50,000.

3   Key in comma separators for the remaining labels, change the last label from
     10000001–999999999 to 10,000,001 and greater, and click **OK**.

4   Right-click the Population layer in the table of contents, click Save As Layer File, browse to the
     \Gistutorial\Layers folder, key in **PopulationStatesNativeAmericans.lyr**, and click Save.

Set up the layout view

1   **Click View, Layout View.**

In the next steps, you will use the vertical and horizontal rulers to set guides for positioning map elements on the layout page. If these rulers do not currently appear along the top and left margins of your layout display, from the Tools menu, click Option, then, in the Options dialog box, click the Layout View tab and check the Show box in the Rulers frame.

2   **Click at 8.5 inches on the top horizontal ruler to create a vertical blue guide line at that location.**

If you place your guide at the wrong place, right-click its arrow, click Clear Guide, and start again.

3   **Do the same at 7 inches on the left vertical ruler.**

4   **Right-click the boundary of the layout, click Guides, and make sure that Snap to Guides is checked.**

5   **Click anywhere on the map to activate its frame and grab handles if they are not already visible.**

6   **Click, hold, and drag the upper right grab handle of the layout to the intersection of the two guides, then release.**

The grab handle will snap precisely to the intersection of the guides when you release.

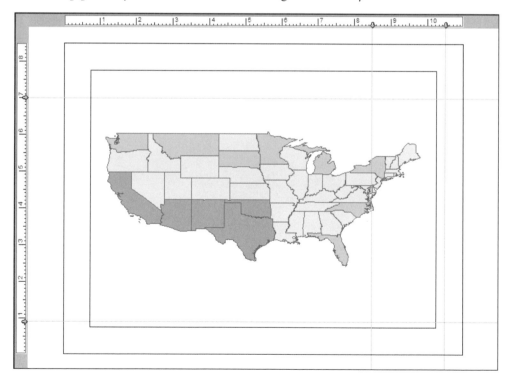

Add elements

1   Click Insert, Title.

2   Click outside the resulting title, then double-click the title, type **Native American Population (2001)** in the text box, click OK, and center the title above your map.

3   Click the horizontal ruler at 10.5 inches to create a new vertical guide.

4   Click Insert Legend, click Next four times, and click Finish.

5   Click the right edge of the blue frame of the legend and drag it to the right so that it snaps to the 10.5 inch guide.

6   Click the horizontal ruler at 9 inches to create a new vertical ruler.

7   Click the top left grab handle of the legend and drag to the right and down to make it smaller and so that it snaps to the 9 inch guide.

8   Click Insert, Text, then click outside the resulting small text box, click it again, and drag it away from the map to the lower-right corner of the layout.

9   Double-click the text box and type **Map designed by "Your Name"**.

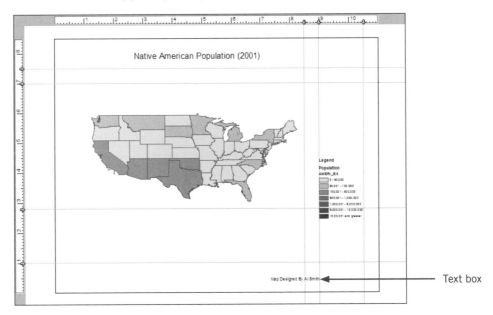

Native American Population (2001)

Text box

10   Click File, Save As, change the file type to ArcMap Documents (.mxd), name the map **Tutorial3-NativeAmericans.mxd**, and click Save.

11   Click File, Save As, browse to the **\Gistutorial** folder, change the Save As Type to ArcMap Templates (*.mxt), name the template **Tutorial3-Template**, and click Save.

Note: Once you save the layout as a template, your selection for ArcMap Document will no longer be available in the Save As dialog.

Use the custom template for a new map

1   Click File, New.

2   In the New window, click the Browse button, browse to the **\Gistutorial** folder, and double-click **Tutorial3-Template.mxt**.

3   Click View, Data View.

4   Right-click the Population layer in the table of contents, click Properties, the Symbology tab, and the Import button.

5   In the Import Symbology dialog, click the Browse button, browse to the **\Gistutorial\Layers** folder, double-click **PopulationStatesNativeAmericans.lyr**, and click OK.

6   In the Import Symbology Matching Dialog, click the Value Field drop-down arrow, click ASIAN, and click OK.

7   In the Layer Properties window, change the color ramp to another monochromatic scheme (shadings of the same color) and click OK.

8   Right-click the Population layer in the table of contents, click Save As Layer File, browse to the **\Gistutorial\Layer** folder, key in **PopulationStatesAsians.lyr**, and click Save.

9   Click View, Layout View.

10 Double-click the map title, change Native American to Asian, and click OK.

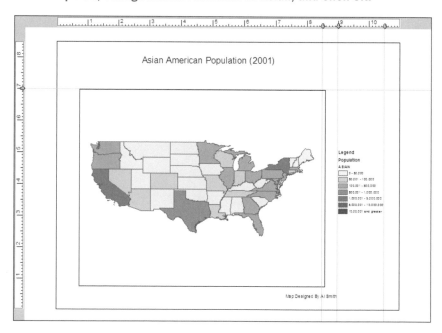

11 Click File, Save As, browse to the **\Gistutorial** folder, name the file **Tutorial3-Asians.mxd**, and click Save.

YOUR TURN

Complete the map series by making maps for at least one of the following: Blacks, Whites, or Hispanics.

Name the maps Tutorial3-Blacks.mxd, Tutorial3-Whites.mxd, and Tutorial3-Hispanics.mxd.

Save layer files for each Population layer.

Create a custom map template for multiple maps

To facilitate comparisons, it is a good idea to place two or more maps on the same layout. Our population maps by racial/ethnic groups are ideal for this because they all share the same break points, making comparisons easy.

Create a new map

1   Click File, New, then, in the My Templates tab, click Blank Document, and click OK.

2   If necessary, click View, Layout View.

3   Right-click the border of the layout, click Page and Print Setup, change the standard page size to Letter, click both Portrait radio buttons in the Page and Paper frames, and click OK.

4   Right-click the vertical ruler and click Clear All Guides. Do the same to the horizontal ruler.

5   Click the horizontal ruler at the 0.5-, 6.5-, and 8.0-inch marks.

6   Click the vertical ruler at the 0.5-, 5.4-, 5.6-, and 10.5-inch marks.

7   Click and drag the layers frame so that its upper left corner snaps to the intersection of 10.5-inch horizontal guide and 0.5-inch vertical guide.

8   Click and drag the lower right grab handle of the data frame to snap it at the 5.6-inch horizontal guide and 6.5-inch vertical guide.

9   Click Insert, Data Frame and drag/modify the new data frame to fit in the guides below the original frame.

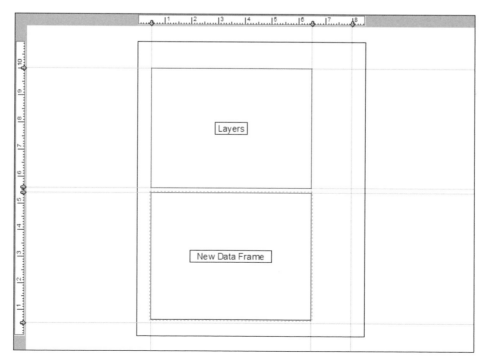

Add elements

1   In the table of contents, right-click the Layers data frame, click Add Data, browse to the \Gistutorial\Layers folder, and double-click **PopulationStatesNativeAmericans.lyr**.

2   In the table of contents, right-click the New Data Frame, click Add Data, and double-click **PopulationStatesAsians.lyr**.

3   Click Insert, Legend.

4   Click Next four times, and then Finish.

5   Drag the legend so that it snaps on the right to the 8-inch vertical guide in the middle of the page, then resize it to fit the available space.

6   Click Insert, Title, click outside the Title frame, and then double-click the Title frame.

7   In the Properties window, type **Population of Native Americans**, press the Enter key, type **And Asians**, change the angle to 90, click the Change Symbol button, change the Size to 20, and click OK twice.

8   Position the Title frame on the top right of the layout.

9   Change the color ramp of one of the layers in the table of contents to match the color ramp of the other layer.

10 Click File, Save As, name the map **Tutorial3-NativeAmericansAndAsians**, and click Save.

Add reports to a layout

ArcMap has a built-in capability to make tabular reports. These can be added to layouts to provide detailed information.

Open an existing map

1   Click File, Open, browse to the **\Gistutorial** folder, and double-click **Tutorial3-NativeAmericans.mxd**.

If you do not have this file in the \Gistutorial folder, browse to \Gistutorial\SolutionComponents\ Tutorial3\ and you will find a copy there.

2   Click File, Save As, and type **Tutorial3-NativeAmericansReport.mxd** for the File Name, then click Save.

3   Click View, Data View.

Make a selection of records

1   Right-click the Population layer in the table of contents and click Open Attribute Table.

2   Scroll to the right in the Attributes of Population to find the AMERI_ES column, right-click the AMERI_ES column heading, and click Sort Descending.

3   Scroll left in the table until you see the State column.

4   If necessary, make the table large enough so you can see the first twelve state records. Click the row selector for the top row, then hold and drag down to select the top twelve rows in the table (California through Minnesota).

You will generate a report for the selected records only.

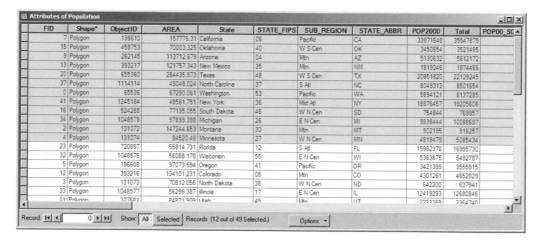

5   Close the Attributes of Population window.

Start the report

1   Click View, Layout View.

2   Click Tools, Reports, Create Report, and wait until the Report Properties window opens.

3   In the Available Fields box, double-click STATE_NAME, AMERI_ES, and POP2003.

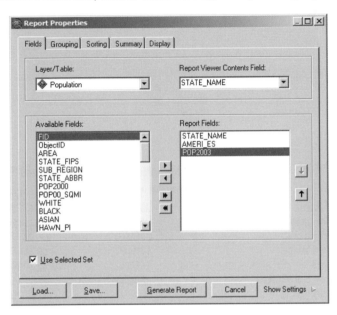

4   Click the Sorting tab and change None in the AMERI_ES row to Descending.

5   Click the Display tab, check the box to the left of the Title item, change the Text property from Report Title to Native American Population in the Top 12 States, change the Font to Arial by clicking the [...] box and selecting the font from the resulting pop-up window, and then click OK.

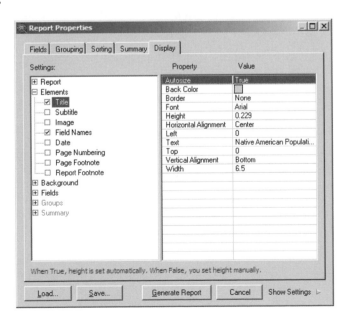

Finish the report

1   In the Settings box, click the plus sign (+) to the left of the Fields item to expand it.

2   Click the STATE_NAME field and change its text to **State**; click the AMERI_ES field and change its text to **Native Americans**; and click the POP2003 field and change its text to **Total**.

3   Change the fonts of these fields to Arial.

4   Click the Generate Report button.

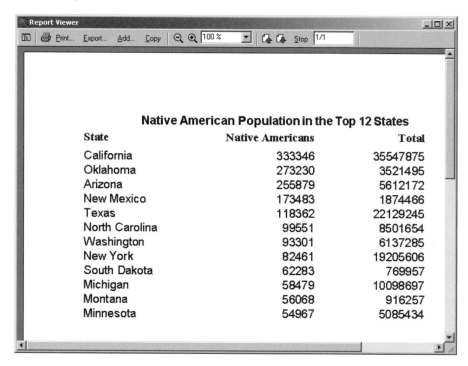

5   In the Report Viewer window, click Export, select Rich Text Format (*.rtf) from the Save as type drop-down list, name the report **NativeAmericans**, click Save, and close the Report Viewer.

This saves the report output for later use.

6   In the Report Properties window, click Save, type **NativeAmericans** as the File Name, and click Save, Close.

This saves the report specification as an RDF (report), which allows you to modify it and generate a new report output. It can be loaded in the Report Properties window.

Add the report to a layout

1 In the Layout View, click Insert Object.

2 In the Insert Object window, click the Create from File radio button, browse to the **\Gistutorial** folder, and double-click **NativeAmericans.rtf** (the rich text format report output).

3 Click OK in the Insert Object window.

The report is now on the layout but needs to be resized and moved.

4 Click anywhere on the map to activate its frame, right-click the frame, click Properties, click the Frame tab, change the border color to no color, and click OK.

5 Click the vertical ruler on the left at 8.5 inches to create a horizontal guide, and click and drag the map frame up to this guide.

6 Click the vertical ruler at 1 inch to create a horizontal guide and click and drag the report frame down so that its lower right corner is at the 1-inch horizontal, 8.5-inch vertical guide intersection.

7 Click the vertical ruler on the left at 2.8 inches, click the upper left grab handle of the report, and drag it down until the top of the report snaps to the new guide.

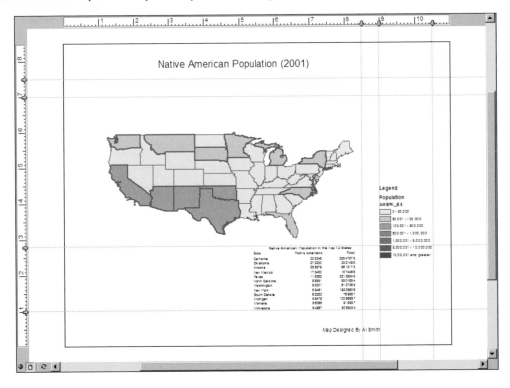

Add final touches to the layout

1 Click View, Data View.

2 Right-click the Population layer in the table of contents and click Properties.

3 Click the Labels tab, check the Label Features in This Layer box, and click OK.

4 Click View, Layout View.

5 Click File, Save.

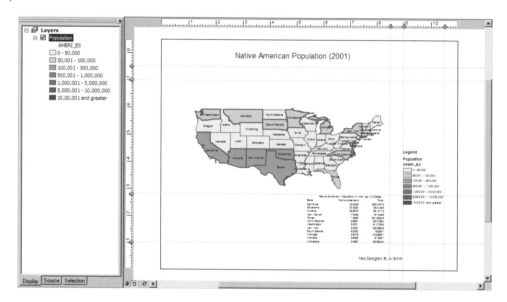

YOUR TURN

Create a report for another racial or ethnic group corresponding to a layout that you created earlier, and add it to the layout.

Save your layout using Save As and adding "Report" to the end of the .mxd file name.

Add graphs to a layout

The graphs available from ArcMap are easy to use, but have limitations. In this section you will build an ArcMap graph and then build the same graph in Microsoft Excel, both for use on an ArcMap layout. The Excel graph gives you more control over the graph design, but it takes several more steps than the ArcMap graph.

Open an existing map

1   Click File, Open, browse to the **\Gistutorial** folder, and double-click **Tutorial3-NativeAmericans.mxd**.

2   Click View, Data View.

Select records for graphing

1   Right-click the Population layer in the table of contents and click Open Attribute Table.

2   In the Attributes of Population window, scroll to the right until you can see the AMERI_ES column.

3   Right-click the AMERI_ES column heading and click Sort Descending.

4   Scroll back to the left, to the beginning of the table, click the first row's record selector, hold and drag down to include Minnesota, then release to select the first twelve rows.

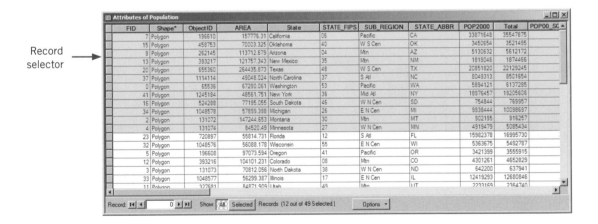

Record selector

5   Close the table and click View, Layout View.

The graph that you will create next will use only the records that you selected.

Create a graph in ArcMap

1 Click Tools, Graphs, Create.

2 In the Graph Wizard, Step 1, click Next.

3 In Step 2, make sure that Use selected set of features or records is checked, uncheck the ObjectID field, scroll down and check AMERI_ES, and click Next.

4 In Step 3, change the Title to **Population of Native Americans**, check Label X Axis With, check Show Graph on Layout, and click Finish.

5 Click anywhere on the map to activate its frame, right-click the frame, click Properties, change the Border Color to No Color, and click OK.

6 Click the vertical ruler at 7.8 inches to create a new guide, and drag the map frame up so that its top snaps to the new guide.

7 Click anywhere on the graph to activate its frame.

8 Click the vertical ruler at 0.8 inches to create a new guide, and drag the graph frame down so that its bottom right side snaps to the new guide and the intersection of the 8.5-inch vertical guide.

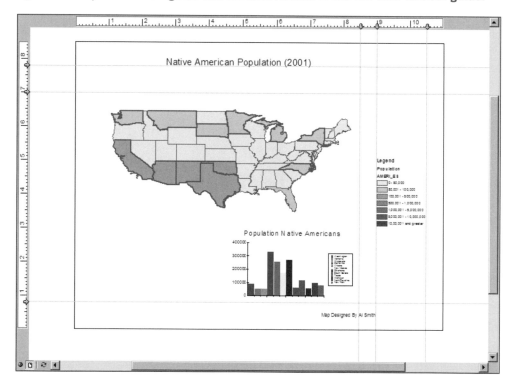

The result is an attractive graph, but it would be better if you could control the sorting of the bars, for example in descending order.

Export data

1   Click View, Data View.

2   Right-click the Population layer in the table of contents and click Open Attribute Table.

The top twelve states should still be selected, although they will not appear as a contiguous group of records.

3   In the lower right corner of the Attributes of Population window, click the Options button, then click Export, browse to the **\Gistutorial** folder, change the name of the output file from Export_Output.dbf to **NativeAmericanPopulation.dbf**, click Save, click OK, and click No when asked to add it to your map.

4   Close the Attributes of Population table.

Import data into Microsoft Excel

1   Launch Microsoft Excel (you may minimize ArcMap, but do not close your project), click File, Open, browse to your **\Gistutorial** folder, change the Files of Type to dBase Files (*.dbf), and double-click NativeAmericanPopulation.dbf.

2   Click column headings and use Edit, Delete to delete all but STATE_NAME and AMERI_ES columns.

3   Change the column headings from STATE_NAME to State and AMERI_ES to Population.

4   Select all cells with data and click Data, Sort, click the Descending radio button for Population, and click OK.

	A	B
1	State	Population
2	California	333346
3	Oklahoma	273230
4	Arizona	255879
5	New Mexico	173483
6	Texas	118362
7	North Carolina	99551
8	Washington	93301
9	New York	82461
10	South Dakota	62283
11	Michigan	58479
12	Montana	56068
13	Minnesota	54967

Create a graph in Microsoft Excel

1 Click the Chart Wizard button in Excel.

2 In the Chart Wizard, click Next until finished.

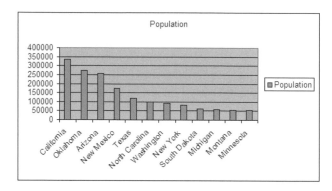

3 Click the frame of the Population legend to the right of the graph and press Delete on your keyboard.

4 Resize the graph so that it is about 3 inches wide and 2 inches tall.

5 Double-click the horizontal axis.

6 In the resulting Format Axis window, click the Alignment tab. Then click and hold the red dot at the end of the Text line and rotate up to vertical.

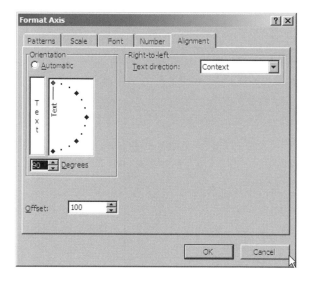

7 Click the Scale tab, enter values of 1 for the first three text boxes, and click OK.

8 Double-click the vertical axis of the graph, click the Scale tab, change the Major Unit to 100000, and click OK.

9 Double-click any of the bars on the graph, change the color to a bright green, and click OK.

Add the Microsoft Excel graph to the layout

1   In Excel, click the boundary of the graph to activate its frame.

2   Click Edit, Copy.

3   Close Excel (save as an Excel workbook if you like).

4   Switch to ArcMap, which should still be open, and click View, Layout View.

5   Click the Population graph to activate its frame and press **Delete** on your keyboard.

6   Click Edit, Paste and relocate/resize your Excel graph.

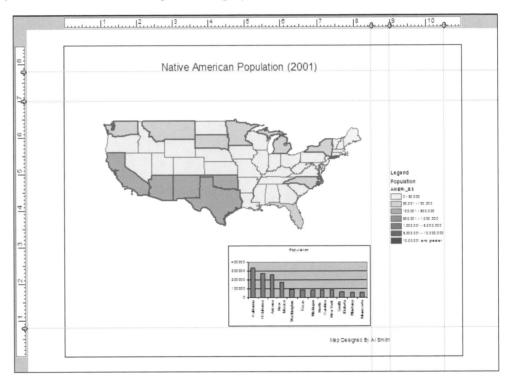

7   Click File, Save As, key in **Tutorial3-Graph.mxd** as the File Name, and click Save.

Export layouts as files

It is often desirable to include maps in Microsoft Word documents or Microsoft PowerPoint presentations, or on Web sites. ArcMap allows you to export layouts in a variety of file formats.

1 In Layout View of **Tutorial3-Graph.mxd**, click File, Export Map.

2 In the Export Map dialog box, click the Save as type drop-down arrow and click JPEG (*.jpg).

3 Browse to the **\Gistutorial** folder and click Save.

You now have a very nice JPEG file, displayed below, that you can import as a picture into a variety of software packages or upload to a Web site.

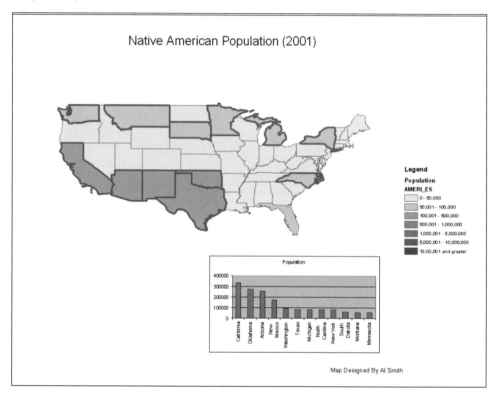

4 Save and close ArcMap.

Other outputs

We have covered several outputs of GIS in this tutorial, including interactive GIS, print layouts, and file exports of layouts. There are many more GIS outputs, and while not covered in this chapter, we will list a few more here for your information.

1. Spatial data processing—GIS provides unique outputs that no other kind of software can produce because it incorporates world coordinate systems and related algorithms. A major GIS output is a point on a map that represents a street address. Points are generated from street addresses (like 4800 Forbes Ave., Pittsburgh, PA 15213) through a unique GIS process called address matching. It is then possible to use another spatial data processing step, spatial overlay, to assign area identifiers (like county, census tract, and so on) to such points. We will cover geocoding, address matching, and spatial overlay in later tutorials.

2. Web-based, interactive GIS—the ArcIMS package from ESRI—is an easy way to provide most of the functionality of tutorials 1 and 2 on the Web. You can try out sample Web sites at *www.esri.com/software/ internetmaps/index.html.* This is not a difficult package to learn, given your current GIS knowledge, but ArcIMS is limited to organizations that can afford the package and have staff who can implement and maintain it.

3. Free GIS package for map display and querying—ArcExplorer—is a simple, free GIS package that includes functionality similar to tutorials 1 and 2. Its designer's interface is similar to that of ArcIMS in many respects. See *www.esri.com/software/arcexplorer/index.html.*

Exercise Assignment 3-1

Layout comparing males, females, and young population in Orange County, California

It is often necessary to compare U.S. census variables side by side on a map layout. In addition to creating layer groups, map layouts with multiple maps can help to visualize information about multiple attributes and aid analysis of those attributes. In this problem, you will create a map layout with three census variables by population percentages for the number of males, females, and total young people (ages 22–29) in Orange County, California. An alternative set of maps could be made to show population density.

Start with the following:

- **C:\Gistutorial\UnitedStates\California\OrangeCountyTracts.shp**—census tract polygon boundaries for Orange County, California, Census 2000.

Create a comparison map of census data

Create a new map called C:\Gistutorial\Answers\Assignment3\Assignment3-1.mxd that includes an 11×8.5-inch landscape layout with a total of three data frames. Be sure to acknowledge the data sources.

Hints
- In two data frames, show the percentage of males and the percentage of females in Orange County, California, using the same cutpoints in the classifications.
- In the third data frame, show the percentage population ages 22–29.
- Use the Layer Properties, Symbology tab to show the population as a percentage of the total population for the year 2000 (use POP2000 field to normalize the data).
- Use your judgment as to the color, sizes, titles, and other map elements to add or modify.

Export the map as a JPEG file called C:\Gistutorial\Answers\Assignment3\Assignment3-1.jpg.

Exercise Assignment 3-2

Walking map of historic districts in downtown Pittsburgh

Many city planning departments are using GIS as a tool to create maps for their cities. These maps can be used in planning documents, tourist attraction documents, or Web sites for visitors in a city. Visit Pittsburgh's Department of City Planning Web site to see examples of maps *(www.city.pittsburgh.pa.us/cp)*. Click "Walking Tours" to see maps and photos of Pittsburgh's historic sites. In this exercise, you will create maps that the planning department can use to promote historic areas. In the layout, you will create an overall view of the historic sites in the Central Business District as well as a zoomed map for one area. Later, these maps can be added to a Web site using ArcIMS for "live" access.

Start with the following:

- **C:\Gistutorial\PAGIS\CentralBusinessDistrict\CBDOutline.shp**—polygon feature of Pittsburgh's Central Business District neighborhood outline.
- **C:\Gistutorial\PAGIS\CentralBusinessDistrict\CBDBLDG.shp**—polygon features of Pittsburgh's Central Business District buildings.
- **C:\Gistutorial\PAGIS\CentralBusinessDistrict\CBDStreets.shp**—line features of Central Business District streets.
- **C:\Gistutorial\PAGIS\Histsite.shp**—polygon features of historic areas in Pittsburgh's Central Business District. This layer shows historic district polygons for the entire city of Pittsburgh. You will focus only on those historic areas within the Central Business District neighborhood.
- **C:\Gistutorial\PAGIS\Histpnts.shp**—point features of historic sites in Pittsburgh's Central Business District. This layer shows points for the entire city of Pittsburgh. You will focus only on those historic points within the Central Business District neighborhood.

Create a large-scale map

Create a new map called C:\Gistutorial\Answers\Assignment3\Assignment3-2.mxd with an 8.5×14-inch layout containing two data frame maps—one scaled at 1:14,000 showing all of the historic districts in the Central Business District, and one scaled at 1:2,400 showing one of the historic districts (you choose the focus) in detail. See hints for how to set a fixed scale in a layout.

Keep in mind basic mapping principles such as colors, ground features, and so forth, covered in previous chapters. Choose labels and other map elements that you think are appropriate for each map as well as the overall layout. Include a photograph of a building that you download from the City of Pittsburgh Web page and save to the C:\Gistutorial\Answers\Assignment3 folder.

Draw the Historic Sites polygons as a transparent layer (see hints) so you can see the buildings under the sites and the Central Business District as a thick outline.

Export your map as a PDF file called C:\Gistutorial\Assignment3\Assignments\Assignment3-2.pdf.

EXERCISES

Hints

Drawing a layer transparently

- Click the View menu, point to Toolbars, and click Effects. The Effects toolbar appears.
- Click the Layer drop-down arrow and click the layer you want to adjust.
- Click Adjust Transparency.
- Drag the slider bar to adjust the transparency.

Setting a Fixed Scale in a Layout Data Frame

- Click the black pointer tool and select a data frame in a layout.
- Right-click the data frame and click Properties.
- Check (and change as necessary) the map and distance units for the data frame.
- Click the Data Frame tab.
- Click the Fixed Scale radio tab and enter your new scale here.

What to turn in

If you are working in a classroom setting with an instructor, you may be required to submit the exercises you created in tutorial 3. Below are the files you are required to turn in. Be sure to use a compression program such as PKZIP or WinZip to include all three files as one .zip document for review and grading. Include your name and assignment number in the .zip document (YourNameAssn3.zip).

ArcMap projects

C:\Gistutorial\Answers\Assignment3\Assignment3-1.mxd
C:\Gistutorial\Answers\Assignment3\Assignment3-2.mxd

Exported maps

C:\Gistutorial\Answers\Assignment3\Assignment3-1.jpg
C:\Gistutorial\Answers\Assignment3\Assignment3-2.pdf

Downloaded image of a building

C:\Gistutorial\Assignments\Assignment3\XX.XX

OBJECTIVES

Create a new personal geodatabase
Modify a personal geodatabase
Join tables
Aggregate data
Export data from a personal geodatabase
Use ArcCatalog utilities

GIS Tutorial 4

Geodatabases

Spatial data, such as you have seen in shapefiles, can have many formats. Tutorial 5 will examine several such formats, but in this tutorial we first provide an introduction to the powerful and modern relational database format. A geodatabase is a collection of maps and database tables stored in a relational database management system. The best way to explore GIS data is with ArcCatalog—the ArcGIS Desktop tool for exploring and managing your GIS data.

Launch ArcMap

1   **From the Windows taskbar, click Start, Programs, ArcGIS, ArcMap.**

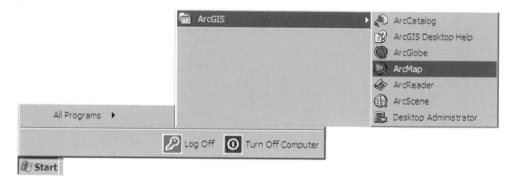

Depending on how ArcGIS and ArcMap have been installed, there may be a different navigation menu.

2   **Click the A new empty map radio button in the ArcMap dialog box and click OK.**

3   **Click File, Save As, browse to the Gistutorial folder, key in Tutorial4-1 in the File name field, and click Save.**

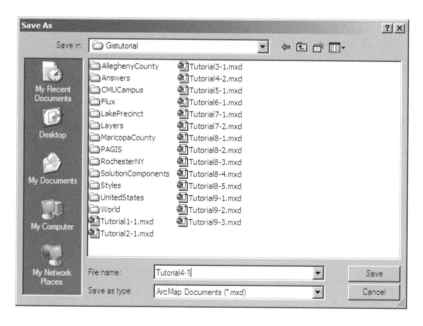

Launch ArcCatalog

1   **Click the ArcCatalog button.**

ArcCatalog opens.

2   **In the catalog tree, navigate to your Gistutorial folder, then expand it by clicking the small box with the plus sign (+) to its left. Do the same for the MaricopaCounty folder, and then click the MaricopaCounty folder to expose that folder's contents in the Contents tab of the preview pane to the right.**

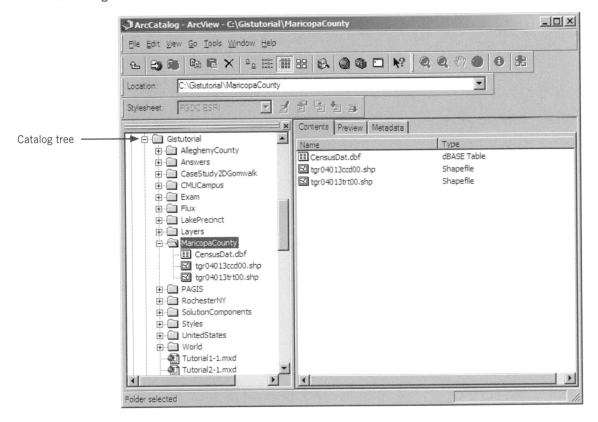

Create a new personal geodatabase

ArcCatalog shows that there are two shapefiles in the Maricopa County folder (Maricopa County, Arizona, includes the city of Phoenix and other cities). Both shapefiles were downloaded for free from the ESRI Geography Network (see tutorial 5). One is year 2000 census tract boundaries (tgr04013trt00.shp) and the other is county civil divisions (tgr04013ccd00.shp), which include city boundaries. The "tgr" stands for TIGER file, 04 is the FIPS code for Arizona, and 013 is the FIPS code for Maricopa County.

Create a new geodatabase

1   In the catalog tree of the ArcCatalog window, right-click the MaricopaCounty folder, click New, Personal Geodatabase.

ArcCatalog creates an empty geodatabase that you can now populate with feature classes and stand-alone tables. (Feature classes are the thematic layers stored in a geodatabase and are typically referred to as layers once loaded into ArcMap.)

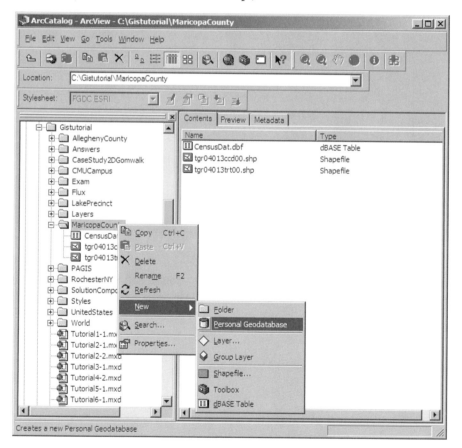

2   In the catalog tree, right-click New Personal Geodatabase, click Rename, type MaricopaCountyIncome, and press Enter on your keyboard.

Import shapefiles

1   Right-click the MaricopaCountyIncome geodatabase, then click Import, Feature Class (Single).

2   In the Feature Class to Feature Class dialog box, click the browse button next to the Input Features field, browse to **Gistutorial\MaricopaCounty**, double-click to open the folder, double-click **tgr04013ccd00.shp**, type **tgr04013ccd00** as the Output Feature Class name, and click OK. Close after ArcCatalog finishes importing.

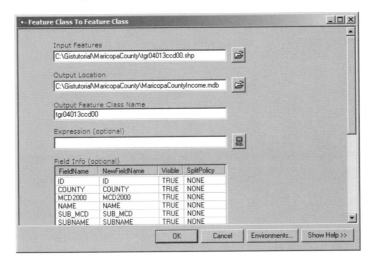

ArcCatalog imports the shapefile into the geodatabase with the same name.

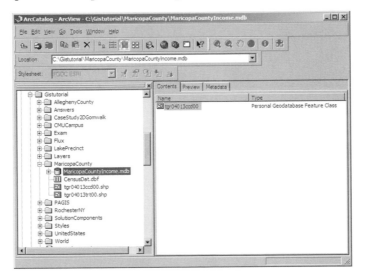

YOUR TURN

Import tgr04013trt00.shp into the MaricopaCountyIncome personal geodatabase.
Important note: You must complete this task in order to perform later steps of this tutorial.

Import a data table

Next you will import a 2000 census data table at the tract level that was downloaded from the *www.census. gov* Web site. See tutorial 5 for details on how to download data from this Web site. Eventually you will join this table to the tract map you just imported, tgr04013trt00, and use it to map income disparities between Native Americans and Hispanics and Whites at both the city and tract levels.

1   In the ArcCatalog window, click the ArcToolbox button.

2   In the ArcToolbox window, expand the Conversion Tools toolbox by clicking the plus sign (+) to its left.

3   Expand the To Geodatabase toolset by clicking the box with a plus sign (+) to its left.

4   Double-click Table to Geodatabase (multiple).

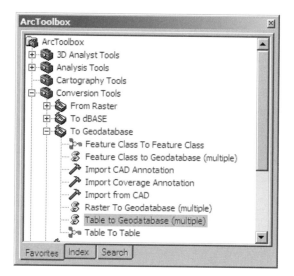

5   In the Table to Geodatabase window, browse to **Gistutorial\MaricopaCounty** for the Input table, click **CensusDat.dbf**, and click Add.

6   Browse to the output geodatabase in **\Gistutorial\MaricopaCounty**, then click **MaricopaCountyIncome.mdb**, Add, and OK. When the import process completes, click Close, then close ArcToolbox.

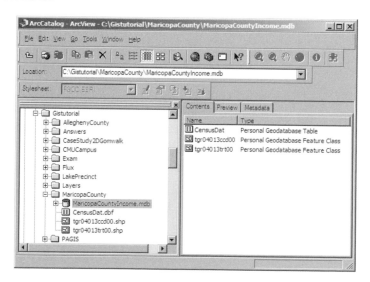

Add layers to ArcMap

1   On the Windows taskbar, click the **Tutorial4-1.mxd** button  to activate ArcMap.

2   Click the Add Data button.

3   Browse to the **\Gistutorial\MaricopaCounty** folder, double-click **MaricopaCountyIncome.mdb**, hold down the Shift key, click both feature classes **tgr04013ccd00** and **tgr04013trt00**, and click Add.

Change layer properties

1   Right-click tgr04013trt00 in the table of contents, click Properties, click the General tab, and change the Layer Name to Tracts. Click OK.

2   Right-click tgr04013ccd00, click Properties, and change its Layer Name to Cities. Click OK.

3   If necessary, click and hold the Cities (tgr04013ccd00) layer in the table of contents, drag it above Tracts (tgr04013trt00), and release.

4   Right-click the Cities layer and click Properties.

5   Click the Symbology tab for the Cities layer, then click the Symbol button. In the Symbol Selector, click the Hollow color patch, make the Outline Width 2, and click OK.

6   Click the Labels tab, check the Label Features in this layer box. In the Text Symbol frame, click the Symbol button, change the font Size to 12, set the Style to bold, and click OK twice.

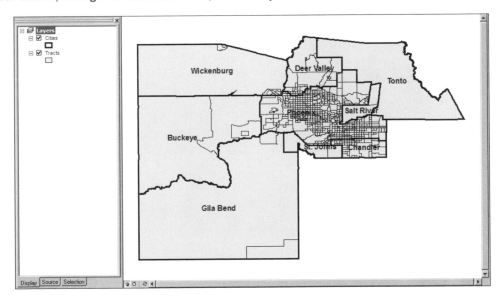

Modify a geodatabase

Examine and modify Layer Attribute Tables

1   In ArcMap, right-click Tracts in the table of contents and click Open Attribute Table.

You will delete some unneeded columns, but before you can do that, you will have to close ArcCatalog. Otherwise, you will get a message that the file is already in use and cannot be modified.

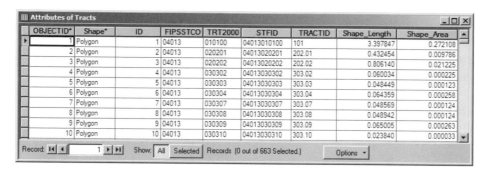

2   Close ArcCatalog.

3   In ArcMap, right-click the column heading for the ID field, click Delete Field, and Yes.

ID is an extra key identifier (or candidate primary key) that we do not need. The key identifier, or primary key, that we will retain is STFID, which is unique for every census tract in the United States.

4   Delete the FIPSSTCO, TRT2000, and TractID fields from the Attributes of Tracts table.

5   Close the Attributes of Tracts table.

YOUR TURN

Delete the following fields from the Cities layer: ID, County, SubMCD, and SubName.

Important note: You must complete this task in order to perform later steps of this tutorial.

Modify a primary key

1   Click the Add Data button.

2   Browse to **\Gistutorial\MaricopaCounty** and double-click **CensusDat.dbf.**

The Table of Contents tab automatically switches to the Source tab (bottom left of screen) to show that the table has been added to Tutorial4-1.mxd and shows the paths of all data sources.

3   Right-click the **CensusDat** icon in the table of contents and click Open.

4   Right-click Tracts in the table of contents and click Open Attribute Table.

The STFID column of the Attributes of Tracts and the Geo_ID column of the Attributes of CensusDat are the unique identifiers of each table (primary keys with no duplicates or null values). The values of each primary key would match, but Geo_ID has the extra characters "14000US" at the beginning of each value. Next, you will use a string function, Mid([Geo_ID], 8,11), that extracts an 11-character string from Geo_ID starting at position 8 and creates a new column in Attributes of CensusDat to match STFID of Attributes of Tracts.

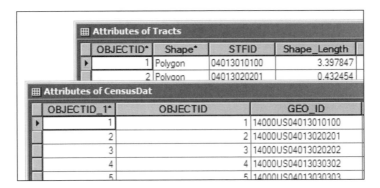

5   In the Attributes of CensusDat table, click Options and Add Field.

6   In the Add Field dialog box, type STFID in the Name field, change the Type to Text, and click OK.

7   Scroll to the right in Attributes of CensusDat, right-click the STFID column heading, click Calculate Values, then click Yes.

8   In the Field Calculator window, click the String radio button for Type, double-click the Mid() function, and in the STFID= box, modify the Mid() function to read Mid([Geo_ID], 8,11), and click OK.

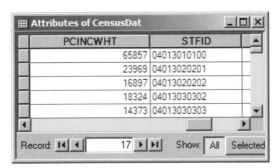

Calculate a new column

1   In the Attributes of CensusDat table, click Options, Add Field.

2   In the Add Field window, type **RNatWht** in the Name field, change the Type to Float, and click OK.

The new column will contain the Ratio of Native American per capita income to White per capita income. Next you must select only records where PCIncWht is greater than zero, because PCIncWht is the divisor for this ratio and will be used to calculate values for RNatWht.

3   In the Attributes of CensusDat table, click Options, Select by Attributes.

4   In the Select by Attributes window, scroll down in the Fields list, double-click PCINCWHT to add it to the lower Select box, click the > symbol button, click Get Unique Values, double-click O in the Unique Values list, then click Apply and Close.

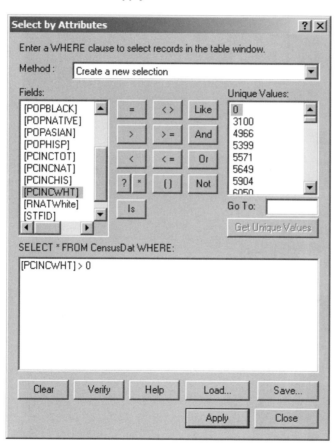

5   Right-click the RNatWht column heading, click Calculate Values, then click Yes. Delete any
     expressions that may be in the RNATWhite= box. In the Fields list, click PCINCNAT, click the /
     button, then click PCINCWHT in the Fields list. When you finish setting up the expression,
     click OK.

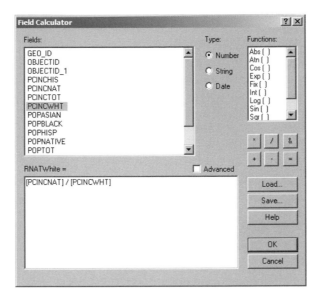

6   In the Attributes of CensusDat table, click Options, Clear Selections, and close the table.

YOUR TURN

Repeat the previous steps to calculate a new column in the Attributes of CensusDat table called
RHisWht, which is the ratio of PCINCHIS divided by PCINCWHT. This is the ratio of per capita
income of Hispanics divided by the per capita income of whites.

Minimize both attribute tables when you are finished.

Join tables

Data comes from a variety of sources, and you may want to display information on your map that is not directly stored with your geographic data. For instance, you might obtain data from other departments in your organization, purchase commercially available data, or download data from the Internet. If this information is stored in a table such as a dBASE, INFO, or geodatabase table, you can join it to your geographic features and display the data on your map.

Join a table to a map

This task allows you to join information from the CensusDat table to the polygon shapefile for the Census Tracts.

1   **In the ArcMap table of contents, right-click the Tracts layer, then click Joins and Relates, Join. In the Join Data dialog, make sure that Join attributes from a table is chosen from the drop-down list at the top of the dialog box.**

2   **For step 1, choose the STFID field from the drop-down list.**

3   **For step 2, choose the CensusDat table from the drop-down list.**

4   **For step 3, choose the STFID field, click OK, then click Yes if prompted to create an index. (An attribute index increases the speed with which attributes can be searched and queried.)**

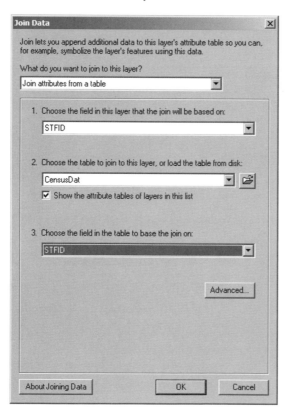

5   Right-click the Tracts layer in the table of contents, click Open Attribute Table, scroll to the right in the table, and verify that your CensusDat table has been joined to the Attributes of Tracts table.

This is an on-the-fly join that is not permanent, but will always be active when your Tutorial4-1.mxd project is open.

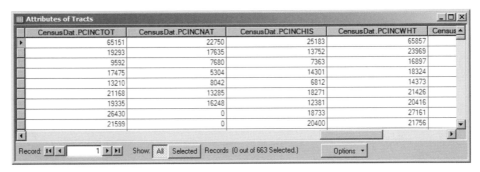

6   Close the Attributes of Tracts table.

Symbolize a map

Now that the CensusDat data is joined to the census tracts, the information can be symbolized using the census polygons.

1 Right-click the Tracts layer in the table of contents, click Properties then click the Symbology tab.

2 Under Show, click Quantities, Graduated Colors. Under Fields, change Value to CensusDat.RNatWht, then click Classify.

3 In the Classification dialog box, change the Classes to 7, change the Method to Manual, and in the Break Values box change the existing values to the following: 0.2, 0.4, 0.6, 0.8, 1.0, 1.2, 99999 and click OK.

4 In the Symbol column, double-click each color chip and change colors to dark reds for the lower values and bright green for the higher values, then click OK.

5 Right-click anywhere in the Label column and click Format Labels. In the Rounding panel of the Number Format dialog, make sure that the Number of decimal places option is selected, then change the number of decimal places to 2, and click OK.

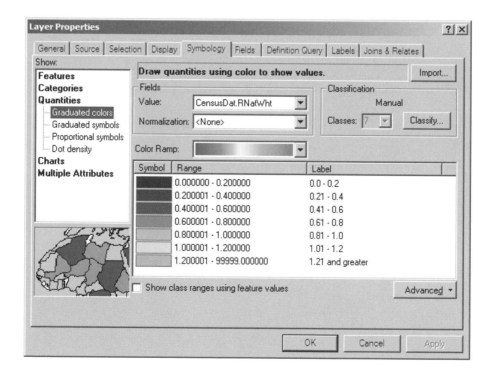

The resulting map shows that Native Americans generally have less per capita income than whites except in some urban areas.

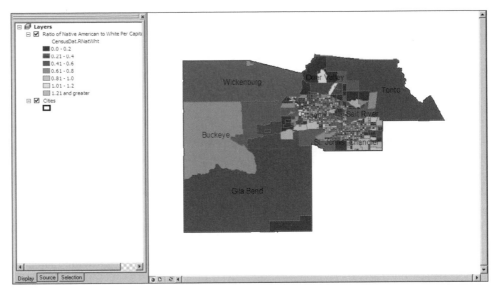

YOUR TURN

Save the Tracts layer as a layer file and add it again to get a second copy in the table of contents.

Change the name of one of the layers to Ratio of Native American to White Per Capita Income.

Change the name and symbolize the other layer to show the Ratio of Hispanic to White Per Capita Income.

When finished, save and close Tutorial4-1.mxd.

Aggregate data

The next part of this tutorial has you aggregate (count) points within police administrative areas (car beats) and then display the results on a map of the car beats. A car beat is the patrol area of a single unit or police car. The count of points per car beat can be displayed on a choropleth map. In this case, the end result will display those car beats that have the highest number of crime-prone businesses of a certain kind—eating and drinking places.

Examine tables to join

1   Close ArcCatalog if it is open. Start ArcMap and open **Tutorial4-2.mxd** from the **\Gistutorial** folder.

The map that opens displays police car beats in Rochester, New York, as polygons and all businesses (a list culled from an electronic yellow pages) as points.

2   Right-click the Businesses layer in the table of contents and click **Open Attribute Table.**

Notice that this table has latitude and longitude coordinates in it. As explained in the next tutorial, these coordinates allow the records in this table to be directly mapped as points. The SIC attribute is the Standard Industrial Code, a U.S. Census Bureau classification for all private sector enterprises.

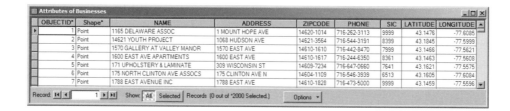

3   Click the Source tab at the bottom of the table of contents (you may need to move the Businesses table out of the way first), right-click SIC in the table of contents, and click **Open.**

This is a code table downloaded from the Internet that has a definition for each SIC value. Next you will join this table to the Attributes of Businesses table, so that we can see the nature of each business.

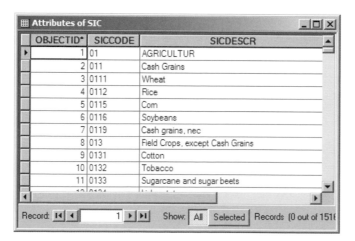

Join tables

1   Right-click the Businesses layer in the table of contents, click Properties, then click the Joins & Relates tab.

2   In the Joins box of the Joins & Relates tab, click Add. In the Join Data dialog box, make sure Join attributes from a table is chosen from the drop-down list at the top of the dialog box.

3   For step 1 in the Join Data window, choose SIC as the field in this layer on which the join will be based.

4   For step 2, choosing the table to join to this layer, choose SIC from the drop-down list.

5   For step 3, choose the SICCODE field, then click OK. Click Yes if prompted to create an index, then click OK to close the Layer Properties dialog.

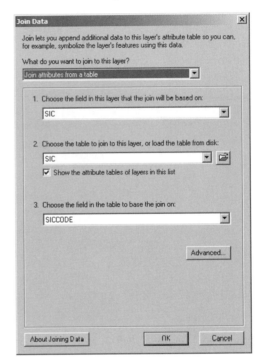

6   Scroll to the right in the Attributes of Businesses and see that the SIC code table has been joined to it.

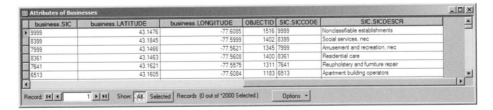

7   Scroll down this table and see that the yellow pages business names and independent code table values for SICDESCR match up reasonably well.

Extract a subset of points

Suppose that police just want to map all retail establishments, regardless of what is sold. These establishments have SIC code values 5200 through 5990. You will extract these next.

1   **From the ArcMap menu, click Selection, Select by Attributes.**

2   **In the Select By Attributes dialog, select Businesses from the Layer drop-down list.**

3   **In the Fields list, double-click SIC.SICCODE so that SIC.SICCODE is added to the expression box. Click the >= button, and in the expression box type '5200'. Click the And button, double-click SIC. SICCODE, click the <= button, and in the expression box type '5990'.**

Be sure to place single quotes (') around the numbers '5200' and '5990'. Without them, the query will not work.

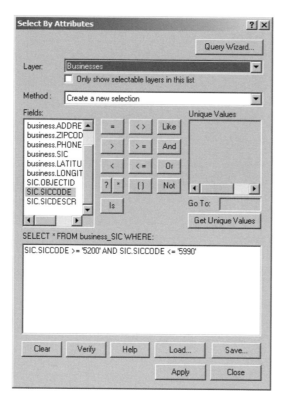

4   **Click Apply and Close.**

5   Right-click Businesses in the table of contents, click Selection, Create layer from Selected
    Features. In the table of contents, uncheck the Businesses layer to turn it off in the map display.

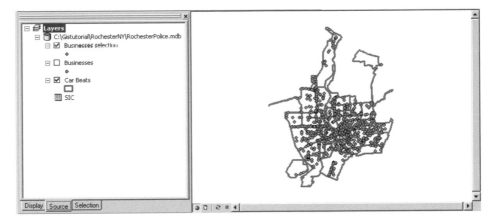

6   Right-click the Businesses selection layer, click Properties, click the General tab, and change the
    Layer name to Retail Businesses.

The resultant map will show only the retail businesses.

YOUR TURN

Extract a second set of businesses, those having to do with automobiles. You can use the following
query expression:

SIC.SICDESCR LIKE 'auto*'

This expression includes any business record that has its SIC description starting with the string
'auto'. The * is a wild card representing zero, one, or other additional characters.

Spatially join point and polygon layers

Now that you have a layer of retail businesses, you can assign each of these points the Car Beat identifier that it is covered by. To do this you will use a spatial join. Once you have joined the Car Beat identifier to each retail business, you will be able to summarize how many retail businesses are in each car beat.

1   **Right-click the Retail Businesses layer in the table of contents, click Joins and Relates, and click Join.**

2   **In the Join Data window, from the What do you want to join to this layer? drop-down list, choose Join data from another layer based on spatial location.**

3   **For step 1, choose the Car Beats layer from the drop-down list.**

4   **For step 2, click the it falls inside radio button.**

5   **For step 3, click the Browse button. In the Saving Data dialog, choose Personal Geodatabase feature classes from the Save as type drop-down list. Then browse to your Gistutorial\ RochesterNY folder and double-click the RochesterPolice.mdb. Name the output BusinessesJoined, click Save, then click OK.**

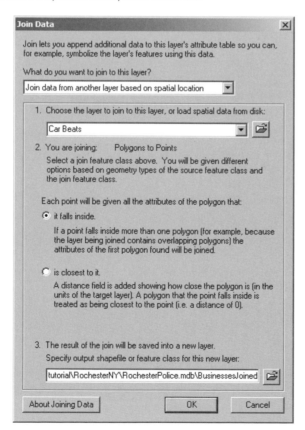

6   **Right-click BusinessesJoined, click Open Attribute Table, and verify that each business has been assigned a car beat number (field 'BEAT').**

Count points by polygon ID

Now you can summarize the number of retail businesses by car beat.

1   Right-click the BusinessesJoined layer in the table of contents and click Open Attribute Table (if not already open).

2   In the Attributes of BusinessesJoined table, scroll to the right, right-click the column heading of the BEAT column, and click Summarize.

3   In the Summarize dialog box, do not make any changes to options 1 or 2. For option 3, change the output table name from Sum_Output to BusCount, save it in your **\Gistutorial\ RochesterNY** folder, click OK, and click Yes to add the table to the map.

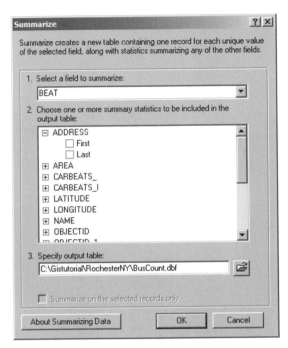

4   Right-click the BusCount table in the table of contents, click Open, and, after viewing the table, close it.

The Count_BEAT field contains the total number of retail business points in each police beat polygon.

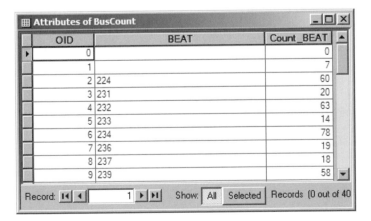

Join a count table to a polygon map

1   Right-click Car Beats in the table of contents, click Joins and Relates, Join.

2   In the Join Data window, click the What do you want to join to this layer? drop-down list and choose Join attributes from a table.

3   For step 1, choose BEAT.

4   For step 2, choose BusCount.

5   For step 3, choose BEAT and click OK. Click Yes if prompted to create an index.

6   Right-click the Car Beats layer in the table of contents, click Open Attribute Table, scroll to the right in the table, and verify that each beat has a count of retail businesses.

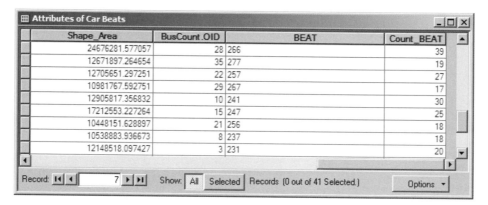

7   Close the Attributes of Car Beats table.

YOUR TURN

Starting with the Auto Businesses layer that you created in the previous Your Turn, carry out the following steps:

Spatially join the Car Beat polygons to the Auto Businesses.

Summarize Auto Businesses by Car Beat ID.

Join the count table to a new copy of the Car Beat layer added to the project.

When finished, click the new Car Beat layer off.

Note: Null values appear in several records of AutoCount.

Symbolize the choropleth map

With aggregate data on retail business points now available as counts per car beat, you are ready to create a car beat choropleth map. The resulting map will provide a good means for scanning the entire city for areas with high concentrations of retail businesses. Then the user can zoom to see details of the businesses.

1   Right-click Car Beats in the table of contents and click Properties. In the Layer Properties dialog box, click the Labels tab, and check the Label Features in this layer box.

2   Click the Symbology tab. In the Show box, click Quantities, then choose Graduated Colors.

3   Change the Value field to Count_BEAT, choose a monochromatic color ramp, and click Classify.

4   In the Classification window, choose 7 classes, set the Method drop-down list to Quantile, and click OK twice.

5   Turn off all the layers except the Car Beats.

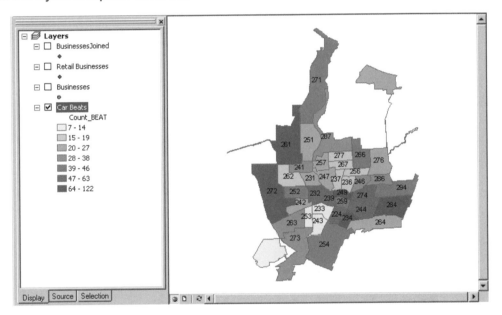

Symbolize the point map for drill down

1   Click the Add Data button, browse to **\Gistutorial\RochesterNY\RochesterPolice.mdb**, click streets, and click Add, then OK.

2   In the table of contents, right-click the line symbol just below the streets layer and choose a light gray color from the drop-down color palette.

3   Click the Zoom In button and zoom to the center of the city.

4   Turn on the Retail Businesses layer.

5   Right-click the Retail Businesses layer, click Properties, click the Labels tab, check the Label features in this layer box, choose SIC.SICDESCR from the Label field drop-down list, and click OK.

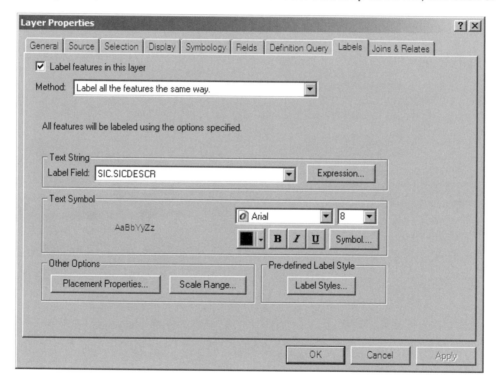

6   Right-click the Streets layer and click Visible Scale Range, Set Minimum Scale.

7   Right-click the Retail Businesses layer, click Visible Scale Range, and click Set Minimum Scale.

The map will show the businesses when zoomed to a scale larger than your current scale.

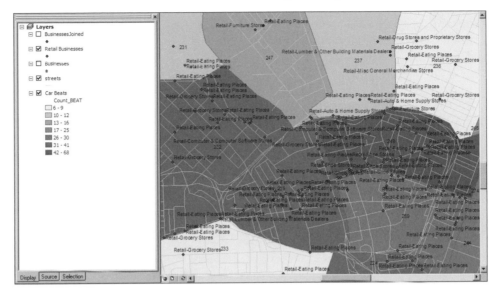

8   **Click the Zoom to Full Extent button.**

9   **Click File, Save, and close ArcMap.**

YOUR TURN

Following up on your work in the two previous Your Turn exercises:

Symbolize the Car Beat polygons for the count of Auto Businesses.

Symbolize the Auto Businesses point map for drill down.

Hint: You can copy and paste the value you set for minimum scale on the Retail Businesses layer by opening the Properties for that layer and selecting the General tab.

Export data from a geodatabase

Sometimes you will need to send another GIS user a map layer or data file that you have in a geodatabase. One way to do this is to use ArcCatalog to export the geodatabase tables as dBASE tables and the feature classes as shapefiles.

Export a table from a personal geodatabase

1   Start ArcCatalog by clicking Start, Programs, ArcGIS, ArcCatalog.

2   In the catalog tree, navigate to and expand the **Gistutorial\RochesterNY\RochesterPolice.mdb**.

3   Right-click the SIC table in the RochesterPolice geodatabase, click Export, To dBase (single).

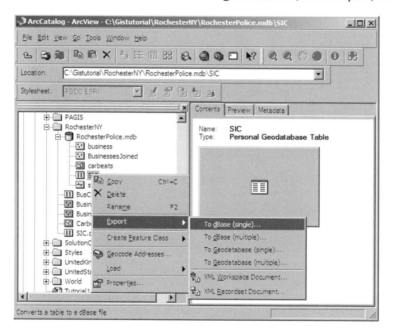

4   In the Table To Table dialog box, browse to **\Gistutorial\RochesterNY** for the Output Location, change the output table name from SIC to **SIC2**, and click OK. Click Close when the process completes.

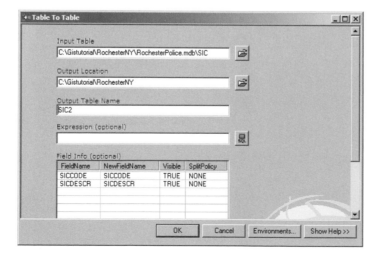

Export a layer from a personal geodatabase

1   If necessary, navigate to **\Gistutorial\RochesterNY** and expand the RochesterPolice geodatabase.

2   In the RochesterPolice geodatabase, right-click the BusinessesJoined layer and click Export, To Shapefile (single).

3   In the Feature Class to Feature Class dialog box, click the Browse button to the right of the Output Location box. Browse to your **\Gistutorial** folder, click the RochesterNY subfolder, then click Add.

4   Name the Output Feature Class **BusinessesJoined** and click OK. Click Close when the process completes.

Your new shapefile is added to the RochesterNY folder.

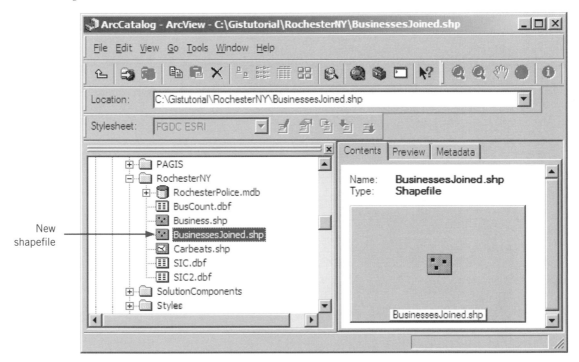

5   In ArcCatalog, right-click the new BusinessesJoined shapefile, click Properties, click the Fields tab, scroll down, see that the spatially joined attributes for car beats have been included in the shapefile, and click Cancel.

The Car Beat attributes that were joined to the Retail Businesses layer are now a permanent part of the new shapefile. This is another reason for exporting: to make a spatial join permanent. Then the shapefile can be imported back into the personal geodatabase.

Use ArcCatalog utilities

Many of the file maintenance tasks for which you would normally use My Computer or Windows Explorer must be done using ArcCatalog. This is because a change in a single layer often affects several tables in the geodatabase, and ArcCatalog will maintain these relationships.

Copy and paste geodatabase layers

1   If necessary, start ArcCatalog by clicking Start, Programs, ArcGIS, ArcCatalog.

2   In the catalog tree, navigate to **\Gistutorial\RochesterNY**, then expand the RochesterPolice geodatabase.

3   Right-click the carbeats layer that is inside the RochesterPolice geodatabase and click Copy.

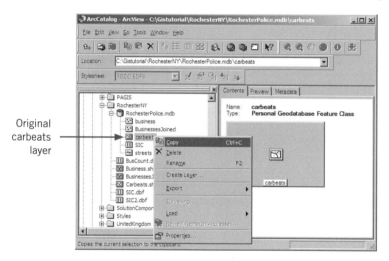

4   Right-click the RochesterPolice geodatabase, click Paste, and click OK.

You could have pasted this layer to any geodatabase on your computer. Now you have a copy of the carbeats layer called carbeats_1.

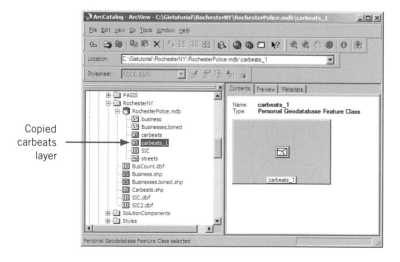

Rename and delete geodatabase layers

1   Right-click carbeats_1 in ArcCatalog, click Rename, and change the layer's name to **RochesterCarBeats**. (If ArcMap is open, you may need to close it for this step to work.)

2   Right-click RochesterCarBeats, Delete, and Yes.

Compact a geodatabase

1   Right-click the RochesterPolice geodatabase and click Compact Database.

To maintain a fast and efficient database, you should periodically compact it.

2   Close ArcCatalog.

Exercise Assignment 4-1

Compare county financial information in a map

Many cities across the nation are experiencing budget problems. Some regions are merging city and county governments to become "meaner and leaner." Others are merging some functions such as police and emergency rescue.

Allegheny County, Pennsylvania, consists of 130 different municipalities, each with its own administrative offices, police and fire departments, and so forth. An interesting GIS study would be to compare revenues, receipts, taxes, and other financial information for the 130 municipalities in Allegheny County. Although merging city and county functions might not be the ultimate solution, creating comparison maps would give a good indication of the financial state of each municipality. Subsequent maps could compare expenses for each political district.

In this assignment you will create a geodatabase and import a shapefile and database. You will then join revenue data that was downloaded from the Pennsylvania Department of Economic Development's Web site to the Allegheny County municipal boundary GIS layer, to create study maps of revenue information.

Start with the following:

Revenue Table
- **C:\Gistutorial\AlleghenyCounty\Revenue.dbf**—dBASE file of municipality revenue information from the State of Pennsylvania Department of Economic Development Web site, 1999.

Allegheny County Municipalities
- **C:\Gistutorial\AlleghenyCounty\Munic.shp**—polygon layer of Allegheny County municipality boundaries.

Join tables to create a map comparing county financial information

In ArcCatalog, create a new geodatabase called C:\Gistutorial\Answers\Assignment4\CountyFinancials.mdb with the Revenue table and Municipality shapefile imported into it.

In ArcMap, create a new map called C:\Gistutorial\Answers\Assignment4\Assignment4-1.mxd that includes a map layout comparing three variables: Total Revenue, Total Tax Revenue, and Total Revenue from Real Estate for Allegheny County municipalities. Label the top revenue-generating municipalities from each category (you choose which ones and how many to label), but be sure to label the municipality name and revenue for each category. See hints for creating the layout, joining, and classifying the revenue fields.

Export the layout to a PDF file called C:\Gistutorial\Answers\Assignment4\Assignment4-1.pdf.

Map hints
- Be sure to add the municipality layer and revenue table from the geodatabase (CountyFinancials.mdb) and not from their original location.
- You will need to create three separate data frames in order to compare each of the variables for Total Revenue, Total Tax Revenue, and Total Revenue from Real Estate. You can create one data frame with the joins, and copy and paste it into a layout to create the other data frames.

Joining hints
- You will need to join the two tables based on the municipality name. This requires you to edit the two tables to be sure the values you join on are exactly the same in both tables, otherwise you will have <null> values for some municipalities. You will notice that in the municipalities attribute table the municipality name and type are in one field, and in the revenue database they are in two fields. Also, the spelling of some names is different in both tables.
  1. Open the Revenue table and create a new field called NAME that combines fields MUNICIPA_1 and MUNICIPA_2. You can combine two fields by using the following expression with the calculator function: [MUNICIPA_1] & " " & [MUNICIPA_2]. Be sure to put a space between the quotation marks so a space will appear between the municipality name and municipality type.
  2. Open both tables and compare the names to be sure they are exactly the same. If they are not, edit the values in tables.
  Note: The Revenue.dbf file has data missing for PITCAIRN, MCDONALD, and TRAFFORD BOROUGHS. You can ignore these missing records for this assignment. MCDONALD and TRAFFORD are on the border of Allegheny County, and PITCAIRN is within the Monroeville municipality. For a complete map, you would need to contact a state or county official to obtain the missing data.

Classification on Number Fields hint
- Classifying data by quantities requires that the fields be number fields and the original revenue fields are text fields. In order to create choropleth maps using the revenue data, you will need to convert the REVENUE, TAXES, and REALESTATE fields to number fields. The easiest way to do this is to create three new long integer (number) fields in the Attribute of Revenue table and use the calculator to copy the values from the existing fields into the new fields.

  Note: You can also use Microsoft Excel or Microsoft Access to convert the fields from string to number fields *before* importing into your geodatabase.

Exercise Assignment 4-2

Map by census tract a count of schools and the number of K–12 students enrolled in schools

A unique task that GIS can complete is joining spatial data: that is, assigning counts and summarizations of point features (e.g., schools and number of students in schools) that are within polygon features (e.g., census tracts, neighborhoods, and counties).

In an earlier exercise, you studied the schools in the city of Pittsburgh by enrollment using a pin map. Another way to study the same data is to spatially join the school points to a polygon layer (census tract), and then count the number of students in each polygon (census tract). This will give you a count of the number of schools in each census tract as well as a summary of students enrolled in all of the schools located in each census tract.

After you create the map, study it to see if the number of schools in a census tract matches the enrollment numbers.

Start with the following:

- **C:\Gistutorial\PAGIS\PghTracts.shp**—polygon layer of Pittsburgh census tracts, 2000.
- **C:\Gistutorial\PAGIS\Schools.shp**—point layer of all schools with student enrollment data.

Create a map showing student enrollment

In ArcCatalog, create a personal geodatabase called C:\Gistutorial\Answers\Assignment4\SchoolStudy.mdb with the above layers imported.

In ArcMap, create a choropleth map that shows the census tract polygons shaded by the total number of students enrolled in school. Save this map as C:\Gistutorial\Assignments\Assignment4-2.mxd. Label each census tract with the number of schools. See hints for creating the map and spatial joins.

Export the layout to a PDF file called C:\Gistutorial\Answers\Assignment4-2.pdf.

Map hints:
- Be sure to add the PghTracts and Schools layers from the personal geodatabase (SchoolStudy.mdb) and not from their original location.
- Browse the attribute tables of both layers to see what fields are currently in each. Note that there is no school data in the PghTracts census polygon attribute table.
- After you spatially join the layers, some tracts will have no schools (and hence will have no enrolled students). A simple trick to remedy this problem is to include a second copy of the PghTract layer in your map with all tracts shown as an outline and have your second copy, with enrollment data, drawn on top of this layer.

Spatial joining tip

Below is a shortcut to spatially joining points to polygons that automatically counts and summarizes data.

1. Right-click the PghTracts layer and click Joins and Relates, Join....
2. Spatially join the Schools point layer to the PghTracts layer.
3. Click Sum in the join dialog box to summarize the number of students in each school. This will summarize all of the fields in the Schools point layer including the field ENROLL95.
4. Save the new layer in your personal geodatabase called TractSchoolJoin.
5. Open the attribute table of the new TractSchoolJoin layer and look at the fields that were created by joining the points to the polygons. Of particular interest will be the fields "COUNT_", which is the number of schools (points) in each census polygon and "SUM_ENROLL95" which is a summary of the number of students enrolled in each school. Remember, some fields will be <null> because those census tracts have no schools or student enrollment.

What to turn in

If you are working in a classroom setting with an instructor, you may be required to submit the exercises you created in tutorial 4. Below are the files you are required to turn in. Be sure to use a compression program such as PKZIP or WinZip to include all three files as one .zip document for review and grading. Include your name and assignment number in the .zip document (YourNameAssn4.zip).

ArcMap projects

C:\Gistutorial\Answers\Assignment4\Assignment4-1.mxd
C:\Gistutorial\Answers\Assignment4\Assignment4-2.mxd

Exported maps

C:\Gistutorial\Answers\Assignment4\Assignment4-1.pdf
C:\Gistutorial\Answers\Assignment4\Assignment4-2.pdf

Personal geodatabases and all files imported into them

Note: Before turning in the personal geodatabases, compact them in ArcCatalog by right-clicking and choosing Compact Database. This will reduce the file size.
C:\Gistutorial\Answers\Assignment4\CountyRevenue.mdb
C:\Gistutorial\Answers\Assignment4\SchoolStudy.mdb

OBJECTIVES

Familiarize yourself with sources of maps and data
Learn vector spatial data formats
Identify projections and learn how and when to change them
Store metadata on projections
Prepare attribute data

GIS Tutorial 5

Importing Spatial and Attribute Data

This tutorial will serve as a guide to obtaining GIS data sources, including free resources on the Internet. This, however, is only a small sample of resources for downloading GIS data. You will find local government agencies to be a great resource as well. This chapter compares the various file types used to create GIS basemaps, including ArcView and ArcMap shapefiles, ArcInfo coverages, CAD files, and aerial photographs. You will learn how to import and export files to and from other applications. Since file formats and map projections are not always the same, you will learn how to manipulate them.

Sources of maps and data

ESRI Web site

ESRI, the world's leader in GIS and mapping software, maintains a Web site that is a useful resource for obtaining information and data used to create GIS maps.

Note: If you have trouble downloading the tutorial files for this section, they are available in the \Gistutorial\ SolutionsComponents\Tutorial5 folder.

1 Open your Web browser.

2 Go to *www.esri.com*.

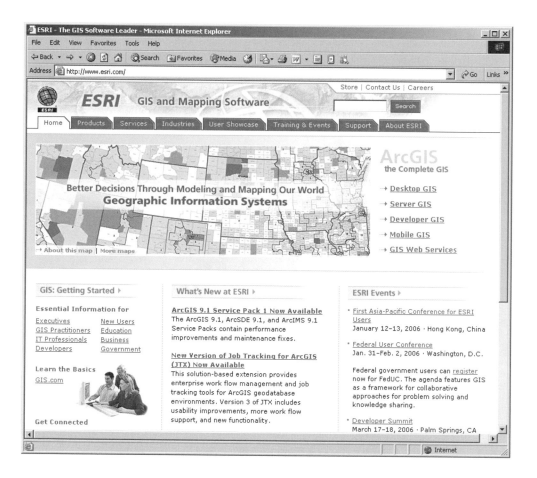

Navigate to free ESRI data

1   On the ESRI home page, click the Products tab and then Data & Maps.

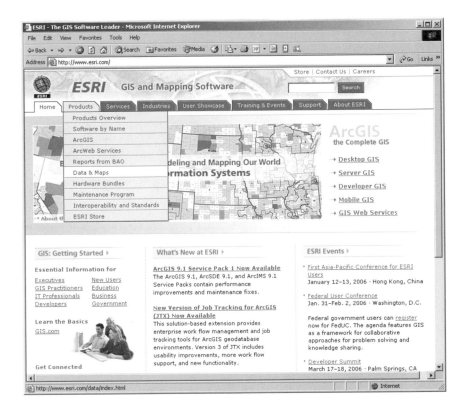

2   Click the Data Portals link from the menu on the left side of the page.

3   Click the ESRI World Basemap Data link from the Featured Data section.

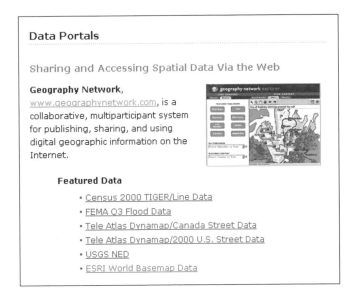

Download ESRI basemaps

1   Click Preview and Download.

The Data Downloader window appears. Data can be downloaded by zooming to the area to download or by typing the area to download.

2   Use the Zoom In button **to zoom to an area in Western Europe.**

3   Zoom in again to the area surrounding the United Kingdom and click Next.

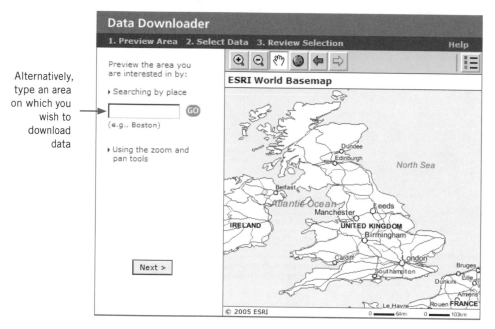

Three size selections will appear to help you choose the geographic range.

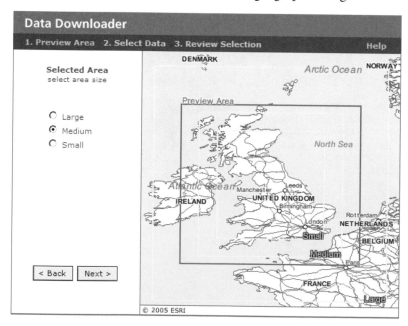

4   Click the radio button for Medium area and click Next.

5   From the Data Downloader window, select All
    Layers (all the other boxes will automatically be
    checked too).

6   Click Select.

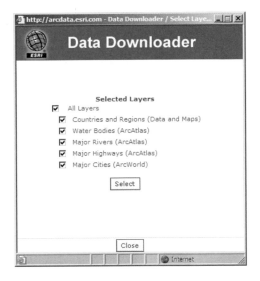

7   From the Data Downloader window, click Generate File.

8   Click Download File when your data file is ready.

9   Click Save to save the data on your local machine.

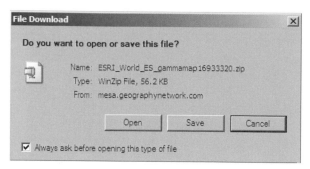

10   Create a folder called **\Gistutorial\UnitedKingdom** and save the downloaded file here.

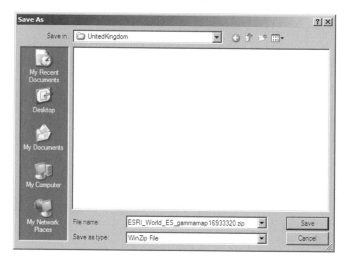

You will see a message indicating that the data has been downloaded. The files are stored in one .zip file that needs to be unzipped.

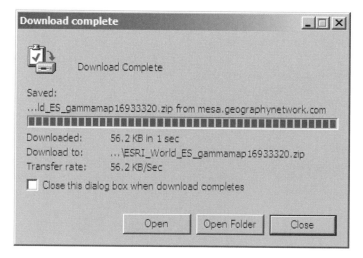

11   Close your Web browser, then unzip the files to the **\Gistutorial\UnitedKingdom** folder.

Add the data in ArcMap

1   Start ArcMap and open **\Gistutorial\Tutorial5-1.mxd**.

2   Click the Add Data button to add all the shapefiles from the **\Gistutorial\UnitedKingdom** folder.

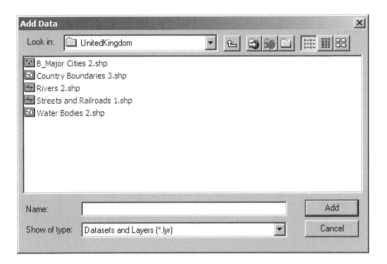

3   Change the symbology of the layers in the map to your liking.

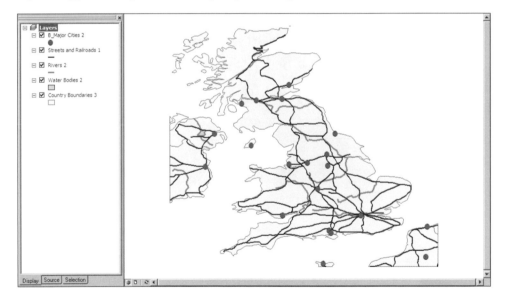

4   From the File menu, click Save, then close ArcMap.

YOUR TURN

Download another area of the world using other data from *www.esri.com*.

Geography Network

The Geography Network is another valuable resource for free and inexpensive GIS data. The Geography Network is managed and maintained by ESRI. ESRI sponsors the Geography Network to promote the sharing and discovery of geographic information and services.

1 **Open your Web browser.**

2 **Use the Web browser to go to *www.geographynetwork.com/freeresources.html*.**

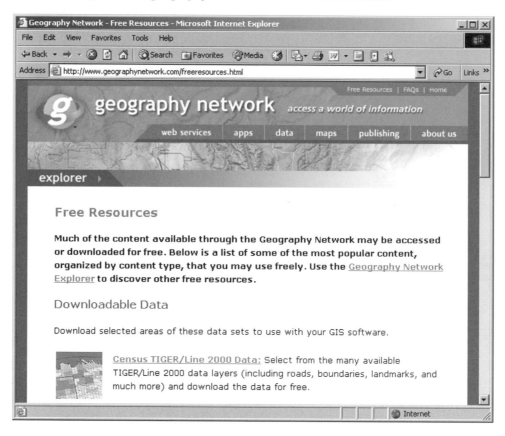

Download Census TIGER/Line Data

1   From the Geography Network–Free Resources page, click Census TIGER/Line 2000 Data.

2   On the Census 2000 TIGER/Line Data page, click Download Data.

3   Click the state of Illinois, or click it from the drop-down list and click Submit Selection.

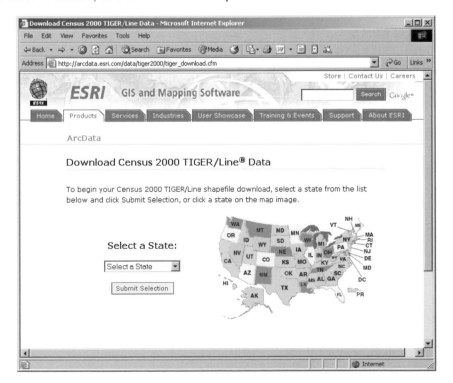

Download census tracts and data for a county

1 From the Select by County drop-down list, choose Cook, then click Submit Selection.

2 Check **Census Tracts 2000** in the Available data layers list.

<table>
<tr><td colspan="2"><u>Available data layers</u></td><td><u>File Size</u></td></tr>
<tr><td>☐</td><td>Block Groups 1990</td><td>726.9 KB</td></tr>
<tr><td>☐</td><td>Block Groups 2000</td><td>698.1 KB</td></tr>
<tr><td>☐</td><td>CMSA/MSA Polygons 2000</td><td>14.3 KB</td></tr>
<tr><td>☐</td><td>Census 2000 Collection Blocks</td><td>3.0 MB</td></tr>
<tr><td>☐</td><td>Census Blocks 1990</td><td>5.9 MB</td></tr>
<tr><td>☐</td><td>Census Blocks 2000</td><td>3.5 MB</td></tr>
<tr><td>☐</td><td>Census Tracts 1990</td><td>382.6 KB</td></tr>
<tr><td>☑</td><td>Census Tracts 2000</td><td>392.2 KB</td></tr>
<tr><td>☐</td><td>Congressional Districts - 106th</td><td>84.1 KB</td></tr>
<tr><td>☐</td><td>Congressional Districts - Current</td><td>84.0 KB</td></tr>
<tr><td>☐</td><td>County 1990</td><td>14.4 KB</td></tr>
</table>

Census tracts →

3 Scroll down to see the Available Statewide Layers and check Census Tract Demographics (SF1) from the list.

<table>
<tr><td colspan="2"><u>Available Statewide Layers</u></td><td><u>File Size</u></td></tr>
<tr><td colspan="2"><u>Census Block Demographics (PL94)</u></td><td>35.6 MB</td></tr>
<tr><td>☐</td><td>Census Block Demographics (SF1)</td><td>12.6 MB</td></tr>
<tr><td>☐</td><td>Census Block Group Demographics (SF1)</td><td>738.2 KB</td></tr>
<tr><td>☐</td><td>Census County Demographics (PL94)</td><td>26.0 KB</td></tr>
<tr><td>☐</td><td>Census County Demographics (SF1)</td><td>11.4 KB</td></tr>
<tr><td>☐</td><td>Census Place Demographics (PL94)</td><td>218.4 KB</td></tr>
<tr><td>☐</td><td>Census Place Demographics (SF1)</td><td>109.4 KB</td></tr>
<tr><td>☐</td><td>Census State Demographics (PL94)</td><td>1.6 KB</td></tr>
<tr><td>☐</td><td>Census State Demographics (SF1)</td><td>665.0 bytes</td></tr>
<tr><td>☐</td><td>Census Tract Demographics (PL94)</td><td>535.7 KB</td></tr>
<tr><td>☑</td><td>Census Tract Demographics (SF1)</td><td>251.8 KB</td></tr>
</table>

SF1 data table →

[Proceed to Download]

4 Click Proceed to Download.

You will see a message indicating that your data file is ready.

5 Click Download File.

6 Click Save to save the file to your computer.

7 Create a folder called **\Gistutorial\UnitedStates\Illinois\CookCounty** and save the file there. Close your Web browser.

Extract files

1   Use your zip program to extract the zipped files to your **\Gistutorial\Illinois\CookCounty** folder. (You will need to unzip a total of three files because the file you downloaded contains two zipped files.)

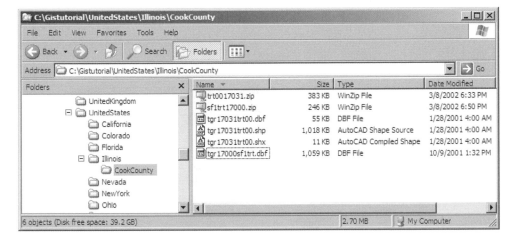

2   Launch ArcMap and add the files to a new, empty map.

3   Open the attribute tables for the table and the layer and explore their contents.

If you were going to join these tables, which field would you use, and what type of processing would you perform on the data before the join could be established?

4   Save map as **\Gistutorial\Tutorial5-2.mxd.**

U.S. Census Bureau

The U.S. Census Bureau Web site is a wonderful resource for census information. Data tables showing census attributes are especially useful to download. Census information can be downloaded here or from the American FactFinder site directly *(factfinder.census.gov)*. Census information can also be downloaded from many sites providing links to GIS shapefiles and databases (e.g., *www.esri.com*).

1 **Start your Web browser and go to *www.census.gov*.**

2 **From the U.S. Census home page, click TIGER in the Geography section.**

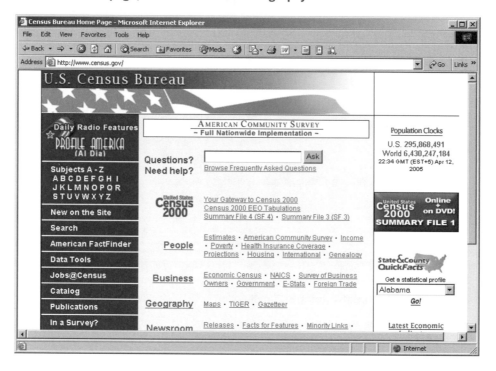

3 **Click Cartographic Boundary Files and follow the links to download any of the TIGER files (in shapefile format) that you would like to use in ArcMap.**

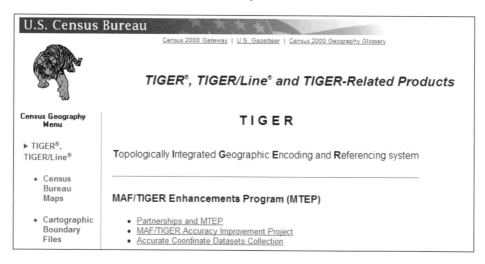

American FactFinder

You can use American FactFinder to view, print, and download statistics about population, housing, industry, and business. Using FactFinder, you can also find U.S. Census Bureau products, create reference and thematic maps, and search for specific data. It is an especially useful site for downloading data tables to join to ESRI maps.

1   Use your Web browser to go to *factfinder.census.gov.*

2   Click DATA SETS in the left panel.

In this exercise, you will download a text file that can be joined to a GIS map.

Data sets ———

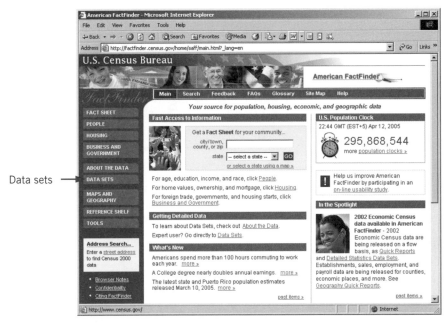

Create and download American FactFinder data tables

The census SF 1, SF 2, SF 3, and SF 4 data tables can be downloaded and joined to existing shapefiles. Visit the Census and FactFinder's Web sites to learn more about each table.

1   From the American FactFinder Data Sets page, click Census 2000 Summary File 3 (SF 3) - Sample Data.

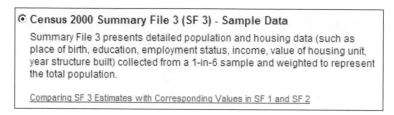

2   Click Geographic Comparison Tables.

3   From the geographic type drop-down list, click County.

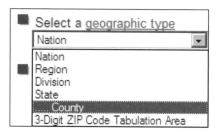

4   Click Arizona as the state, Maricopa as the county, and County -- Census Tract as the table format, then click Next.

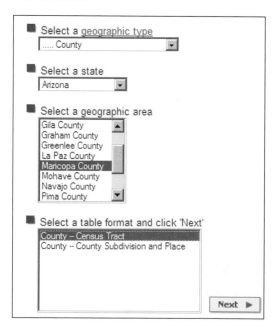

5   Choose Employment Status and Commuting to Work: 2000, then click Show Result.

The resulting table (at right) shows information for each census tract.

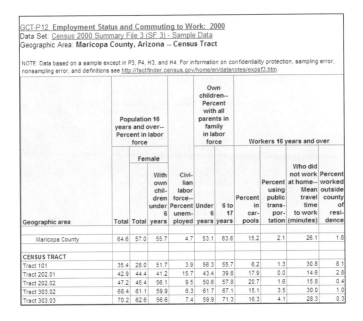

GCT-P12. Employment Status and Commuting to Work: 2000
Data Set: Census 2000 Summary File 3 (SF 3) - Sample Data
Geographic Area: Maricopa County, Arizona -- Census Tract

NOTE: Data based on a sample except in P3, P4, H3, and H4. For information on confidentiality protection, sampling error, nonsampling error, and definitions see http://factfinder.census.gov/home/en/datanotes/expsf3.htm

Geographic area	Population 16 years and over-- Percent in labor force			Civilian labor force-- Percent unemployed	Own children-- Percent with all parents in family in labor force		Workers 16 years and over			
	Total	Female			Under 6 years	6 to 17 years	Percent in carpools	Percent using public transportation	Who did not work at home-- Mean travel time to work (minutes)	Percent worked outside county of residence
		Total	With own children under 6 years							
Maricopa County	64.6	57.0	55.7	4.7	53.1	63.6	15.2	2.1	26.1	1.8
CENSUS TRACT										
Tract 101	35.4	28.0	51.7	3.9	56.3	55.7	6.2	1.3	30.8	8.1
Tract 202.01	42.9	44.4	41.2	15.7	43.4	39.8	17.9	0.0	14.6	2.8
Tract 202.02	47.2	45.4	56.1	9.5	50.6	57.8	20.7	1.6	15.8	0.4
Tract 303.02	68.4	61.1	59.9	6.3	61.7	67.1	15.1	3.5	30.0	1.0
Tract 303.03	70.2	62.6	56.6	7.4	59.9	71.3	16.3	4.1	28.3	0.3

6   From the Print/Download menu, click Download.

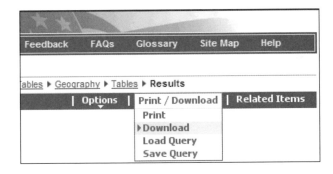

7   Click Microsoft Excel (.xls) and OK.

8   Save the file to **\Gistutorial\MaricopaCounty\output.zip**, then extract the Excel file to the same folder. This file can be joined to the Maricopa census tract polygons as described in the Maricopa County example of tutorial 4. Note: Sometimes it is best to download files from the same source. Census tracts can be downloaded from ESRI or *www.census.gov*.

YOUR TURN

Explore the other American FactFinder tables, including Detailed and Quick Tables.

Vector spatial data formats

Coverages

A coverage is a type of GIS vector data model used to store geographic features using ArcInfo software. Coverages typically store one or more feature classes that are topologically and thematically related. For example, in a cadastral dataset it is common for a coverage to store the parcel boundaries as polygons and the lot lines as arcs (lines). You can add coverage data to ArcMap and use it for analysis and presentation, but coverage data cannot be edited with ArcMap.

When browsing data within Windows Explorer, coverages will appear as folders containing several files. The graphic below shows four coverages within the EastLiberty folder; the contents of the Building coverage appear in the right-hand side of the window.

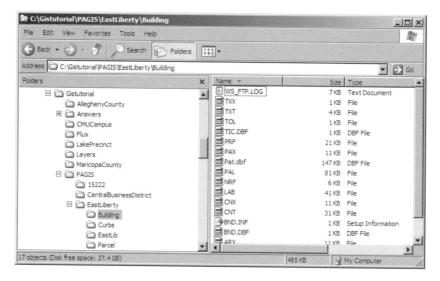

A better way to browse GIS data is with ArcCatalog. In fact, you should use only ArcCatalog to copy, move, or browse your GIS data because that's exactly its purpose—to help you manage your GIS data. The graphic shown (at right) contains an image of the same four coverages shown in the screen capture above, but this time they are being viewed with ArcCatalog. Notice that the coverage name appears beside a yellow icon of three stacked polygons, and that the feature classes inside the selected Parcel coverage appear in Contents tab of the Preview pane.

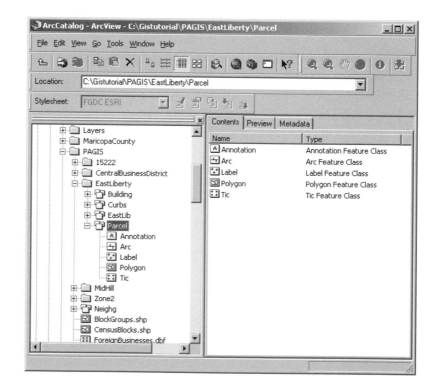

Add a coverage to ArcMap

1   If necessary, start ArcMap with a new, empty map, then click the Add Data button.

2   Navigate to **\Gistutorial\PAGIS\EastLiberty** and double-click Building.

3   Click the Polygon feature class, then click Add.

4   Click OK on the spatial reference warning message.

Convert a coverage to a shapefile

Since coverages cannot be edited in ArcMap, they must be exported as shapefiles or geodatabase feature classes before you can edit their geometry.

1   In the table of contents, right-click the Building Polygon layer and click Data, Export Data.

2   If necessary, select the radio button for Use the same Coordinate System as this layer's source data.

3   Navigate to the **\Gistutorial\PAGIS\EastLiberty** folder and name the output shapefile **Building.shp**.

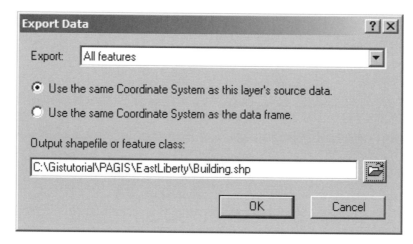

4   Click OK, then click Yes to add the exported data to the map as a layer.

The polygons in the new shapefile, Building.shp, can now be edited. You will learn about editing shapefiles in tutorial 6.

5   Save the map as **\Gistutorial\Tutorial5-3.mxd**.

Shapefiles

Shapefiles are another type of GIS vector data model used to store geographic features. Unlike coverages, which are made up of a collection of feature classes, a shapefile can only represent one feature class. For example, if you wanted to store parcel boundaries and lot lines using shapefiles, you would have to create two shapefiles—one to store the parcel boundaries as polygons and another to store the lots as lines. Shapefiles can be created, edited, and analyzed using ArcView 9, ArcEditor 9, or ArcInfo 9.

Shapefiles consist of at least three files: a .dbf file, a .shx file, and a .shp file. Each of these files is prefixed with the shapefile's name. The .dbf file stores the attributes, the .shp file stores the geometry of the features, and the .shx file stores an index of the spatial geometry. The graphic below shows a shapefile named Parks as it appears in Windows Explorer.

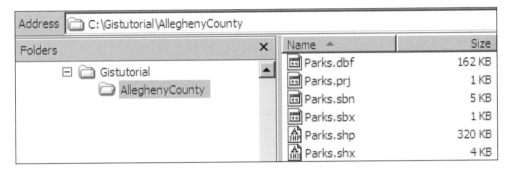

In the graphic below, the Parks shapefile (along with several other shapefiles and datasets) is shown in ArcCatalog. In ArcCatalog, shapefiles appear as one file and are represented with a green icon that indicates whether it is a point, line, or polygon shapefile.

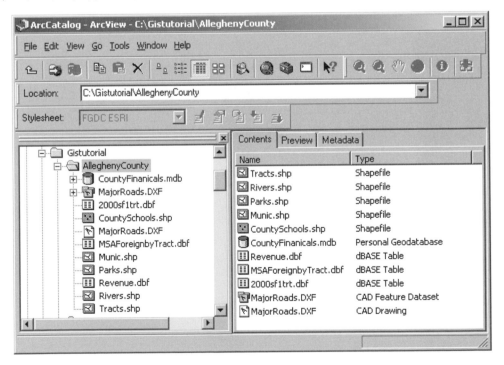

Add a shapefile in ArcMap

1   In ArcMap, create a new, empty map, then click the Add Data button.

2   Navigate to the **\Gistutorial\AlleghenyCounty** folder, hold the Ctrl key and click **munic.shp**, **parks.shp**, and **rivers.shp**, then click Add.

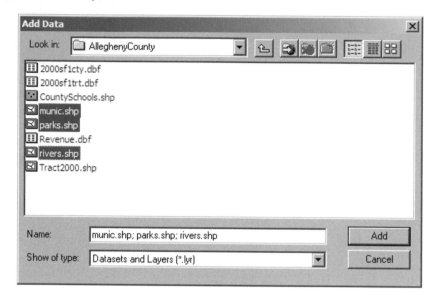

3   Save the map as **Gistutorial\Tutorial5-4mxd**.

Interchange (.e00) files

Many local planning agencies and GIS consultants provide their coverage data as interchange (.e00) files. Interchange files are the preferred method for sharing coverage data because all of the folders and files associated with the coverage are placed into one .e00 file during the export process. With ArcView, an interchange file can be converted back to a coverage by using the Import from Interchange File tool. In this example, you will import zip codes for Arizona that were originally downloaded from the U.S. Census Web site as an .e00 file.

Start ArcCatalog

1   If necessary, start ArcCatalog, then click View, Toolbars, ArcView 8x Tools.

2   Click Conversion Tools, Import from Interchange File.

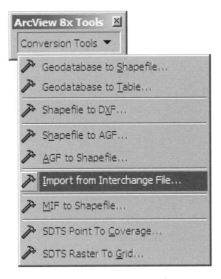

3   For the Input file, browse to **\Gistutorial\UnitedStates\Arizona**, then double-click **Zipcodes.e00**.

4   Name the output dataset Zipcodes and save it in the **\Gistutorial\UnitedStates\Arizona\Zipcodes** folder. When your input and output settings are made, click OK.

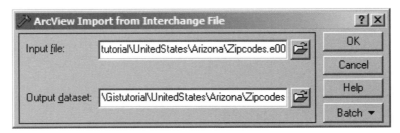

This creates a coverage that can then be added to ArcMap.

5   After the process is complete, use ArcCatalog to verify that the Zipcodes coverage now exists inside the folder into which you imported it.

Annotation layers

Labels are one option for placing text on an ArcGIS map. Labels are positioned on the map by the software based on a set of labeling properties defined in the Labels tab of the Layer Properties dialog. If you want full control over where labels are placed, you can convert them to annotation.

1　If necessary, start ArcMap. In a new, empty map, click the Add Data button.

2　Navigate to **\Gistutorial\PAGIS\CentralBusinessDistrict**, click the CBDStreets shapefile, click Add, then click OK on the spatial reference message.

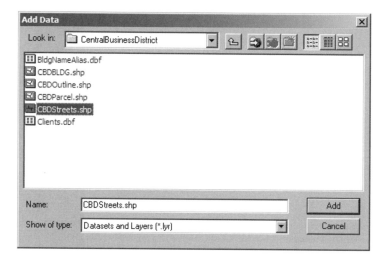

3　Zoom to the Full Extent of the layer.

4　Click the Fixed Zoom In button four times.

5　In the table of contents, right-click the CBDStreets layer and click Label Features.

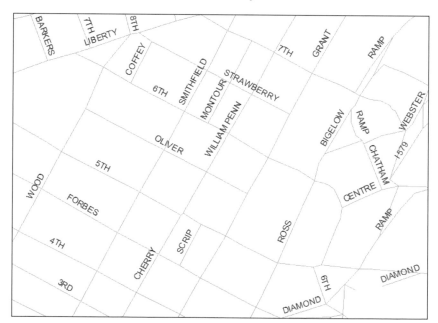

6   In the table of contents, right-click the **CBDStreets** layer and click **Convert Labels to Annotation.**

7   In the Store Annotation frame, click the In the map radio button.

8   Click in the Annotation Group field and type **StreetName.**

9   Click Convert.

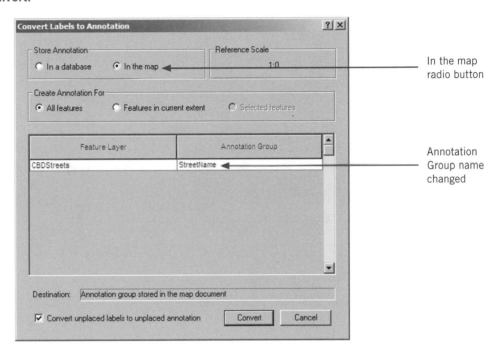

In the map radio button

Annotation Group name changed

After labels have been converted to geodatabase annotation, the annotation class is automatically added to the map. Annotation groups are listed in the Data Frame Properties dialog box on the Annotation Groups tab.

10   In the table of contents, right-click the Data Frame (Layers) and click Properties.

11   Click the Annotation Groups tab.

Annotation labels can be toggled on or off, and their properties can be changed in this dialog box.

12   Click the StreetName group and click the Properties button.

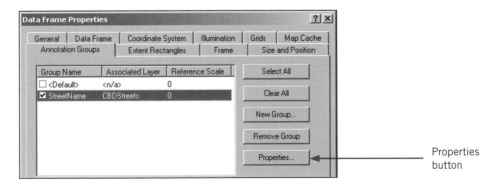

Properties button

13 Click the Associated Layer drop-down list and click <None>.

This allows you to turn the annotation street names on and off independently from the street centerlines.

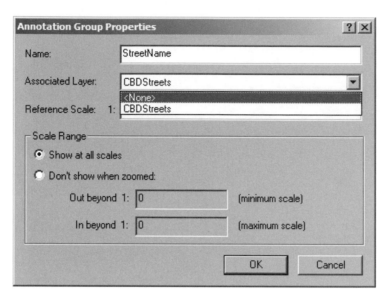

14 Click OK, then click OK again.

15 If necessary, close the Overflow Annotation dialog box.

16 In the table of contents, uncheck the CBDStreets layer to turn it off.

The labels remain on. This is because they are independent from the street layer.

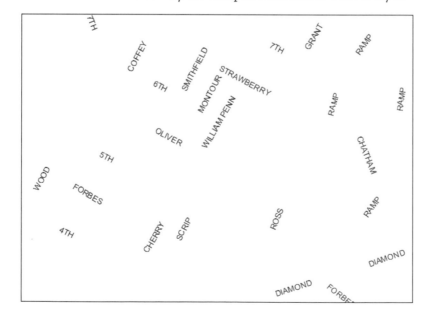

17 Save the map as \Gistutorial\Tutorial5-5.mxd.

CAD files

If an organization has existing CAD (computer-aided drafting) files, they can be added to ArcMap in their native format. Within ArcMap, CAD files can be viewed but not edited.

ArcMap can add CAD files in one of two formats: as native AutoCAD (.dwg) or as Drawing Exchange Files (.dxf) that can be created from most CAD applications.

When viewed in ArcCatalog, a CAD dataset will appear in the catalog tree with a light blue icon of three stacked polygons. By selecting the CAD dataset in the catalog tree, you can view its contents in the preview pane.

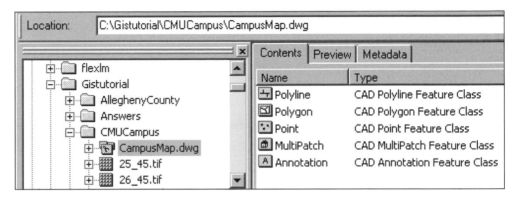

Add a CAD file as a layer for display

1 If necessary, start ArcMap, then create a new, empty map and click the Add Data button.

2 Navigate to **\Gistutorial\CMUCampus** and click the **CampusMap.dwg** with the white icon.

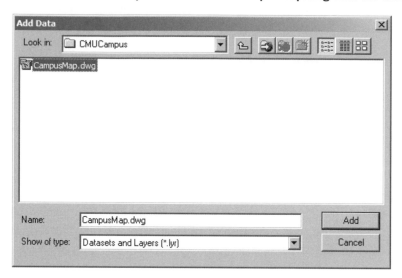

3 Click the Add button.

The following map of the Carnegie Mellon University campus appears in ArcMap. It contains many feature types, including lines, polygons, and text. Features on this map cannot be selected or edited. It is for display only. Next, you will add the other CAD file, which allows you to add specific feature types such as lines only.

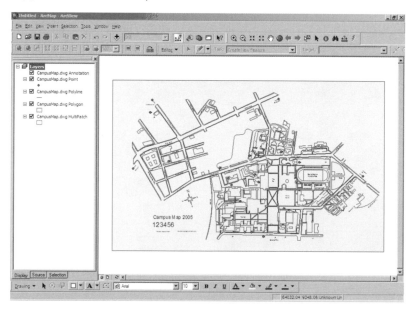

4 Save the map as **\Gistutorial\Tutorial5-6.mxd**. Leave ArcMap open.

Add a CAD file as a layer for edit and analysis

1   In the table of contents, turn off or remove the **CampusMap.dwg** layer.

2   Click the Add Data button.

3   Navigate to **\Gistutorial\CMUCampus**, double-click the **CampusMap.dwg** with the blue icon.

4   Click the Polyline feature class, then click the Add button.

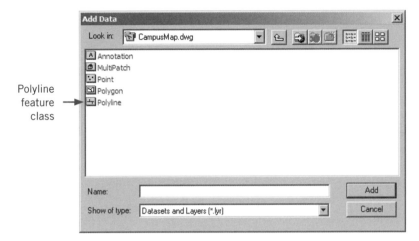

ArcMap adds the polyline feature class from the CAD dataset. The features in this layer can be selected and their properties manipulated, but they cannot be edited.

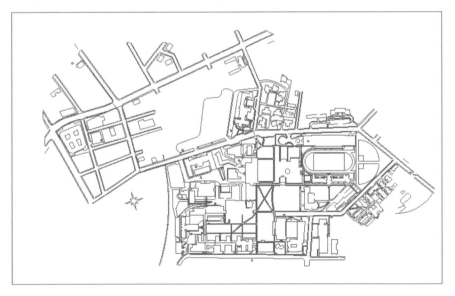

5   In the table of contents, double-click the **CampusMap.dwg** Polyline layer.

6   Click the Drawing Layers tab. Notice that you can turn the Drawing Layers on and off.

7　Click the Symbology tab. In the Show box, click Categories, then Unique Values.

8　From the Value Field drop-down list, choose Layer, then click Add All Values.

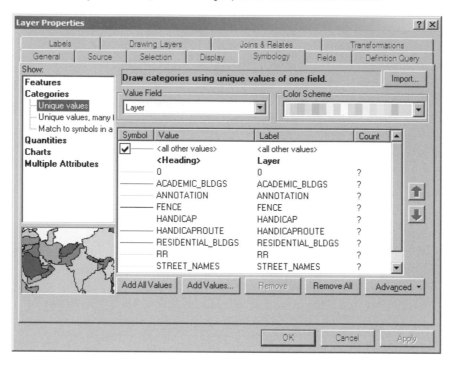

9　Click OK to apply your settings, and close the Layer Properties dialog box.

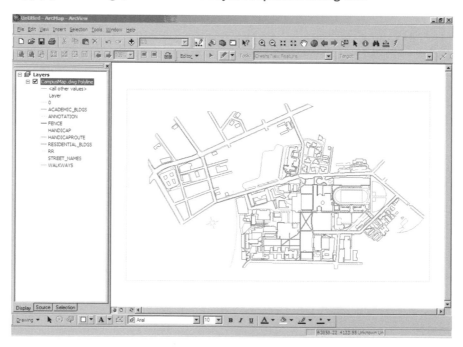

10　Save the map as **\Gistutorial\Tutorial5-7.mxd**.

Export shapefiles to CAD

Sometimes you may need to deliver shapefile data to a person working with CAD software. Using the Export tools in ArcCatalog, you can export shapefiles to .dxf format, which can then be opened by most commercial CAD applications.

Copy the shapefile to the root directory

1   If necessary, start **ArcCatalog.**

Note: CAD conversions cannot be done in a folder with more than eight characters in its name.

2   In the catalog tree, navigate to **C:\Gistutorial\PAGIS\CentralBusinessDistrict** and copy **CBDStreets.shp** to the **C:** drive. (To copy the shapefile, right-click it and choose Copy, then right-click **C:** and choose Paste.)

If you cannot write to the root directory on your machine, copy the files to another folder such as C:\TEMP—just be sure the name is fewer than eight characters.

3   Navigate to **C:** (or the directory where you copied your shapefile), right-click **CBDStreets.shp,** then click Export, Shapefile to DXF.

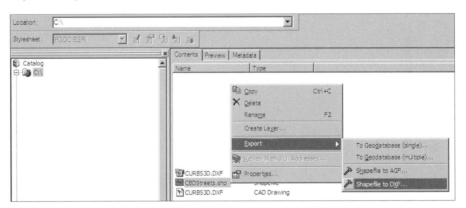

4   From the Decimals drop-down list, choose 6. (This is the number of decimal places used for the coordinates in the output.) Type **C:\CBDStreets.dxf** as the Output file name and click OK.

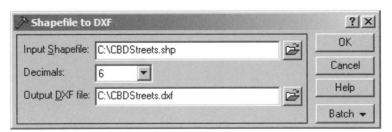

XY event files

In addition to data sources such as shapefiles, tabular data that contains geographic locations in the form of x,y coordinates can also be added to a map. These coordinates describe discrete locations on the earth's surface where point samples were collected. You can collect x,y coordinate data using a global positioning system (GPS) device.

In order to add a table of x,y coordinates to your map, the table must contain two fields—one for the x-coordinates and one for the y-coordinates. The values in the fields may represent any coordinate system and may be in units such as latitude and longitude or meters.

1   If necessary, start ArcMap. Create a new, empty map, then click the Add Data button.

2   Navigate to \Gistutorial\UnitedStates\California, and while holding down the Ctrl key, click **CACounties.shp** and **Earthquakes.dbf**, then click Add.

3   Right-click Earthquakes and click Open.

4   Scroll to the right to see the X and Y fields.

The x- and y-coordinates here represent latitude and longitude values for earthquake locations.

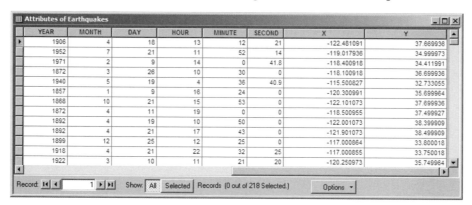

YEAR	MONTH	DAY	HOUR	MINUTE	SECOND	X	Y
1906	4	18	13	12	21	-122.481091	37.669936
1952	7	21	11	52	14	-119.017936	34.999973
1971	2	9	14	0	41.8	-118.400918	34.411991
1872	3	26	10	30	0	-118.100918	36.699936
1940	5	19	4	36	40.9	-115.500827	32.733055
1857	1	9	16	24	0	-120.300991	35.699964
1868	10	21	15	53	0	-122.101073	37.699936
1872	4	11	19	0	0	-118.500955	37.499927
1892	4	19	10	50	0	-122.001073	38.399909
1892	4	21	17	43	0	-121.901073	38.499909
1899	12	25	12	25	0	-117.000864	33.800018
1918	4	21	22	32	25	-117.000855	33.750018
1922	3	10	11	21	20	-120.250973	35.749964

Record: 1   Show: All Selected   Records (0 out of 218 Selected.)   Options ▼

5   Close the Attributes of Earthquakes table.

6   Right-click Earthquakes and click Display XY Data.

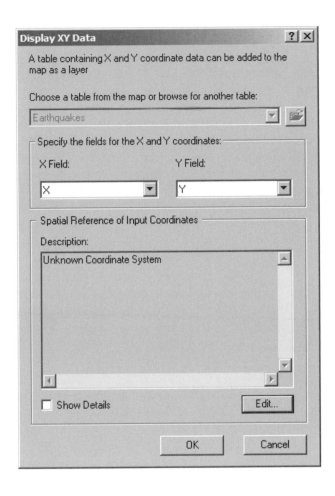

7   Click OK.

This will add point locations for the earthquakes in California as an Event layer.

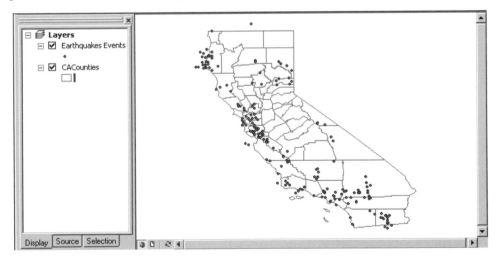

8   Save the map as C:\Gistutorial\Tutorial5-8.mxd.

World and U.S. projections

Features on a map reference the locations of the objects they represent in the real world. The positions of objects on the earth's spherical surface are measured in geographic coordinates.

There are two types of coordinate systems—*geographic and projected*. Geographic coordinate systems use latitude and longitude coordinates while **projected coordinate systems** use a mathematical conversion to transform latitude and longitude coordinates to a two-dimensional surface. Maps obtained from the U.S. Census are typically in geographic coordinates; U.S. maps obtained from local planning departments are typically projected coordinate systems (e.g., State Plane coordinates).

World projections

Since the earth is round and maps are flat, GIS applications require that a mathematical formulation be applied to the earth to represent it on a flat surface. This is called a map projection, and it will cause some distortions of distance, area, shape, or direction to your map data. Using ArcMap, you can apply different map projections to your data. In fact, ArcMap has over a hundred projections from which you may choose. Typically though, only a few projections are suitable for your data.

1   **If necessary, start ArcMap. In a new, empty map, click the Add Data button. Navigate to \Gistutorial\World and add the Country and Ocean shapefiles to the map.**

2   **Change the color of the layers to your liking. If necessary, move the Country layer to the top of the table of contents.**

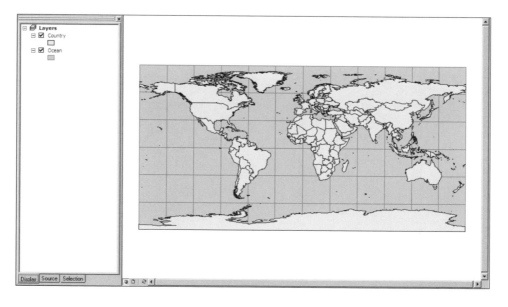

Change the map's projection to Mercator

1   **Right-click the Layers data frame and click Properties.**

2   **Click the Coordinate System tab.**

3   **In the Select a coordinate system box, expand the Predefined folder.**

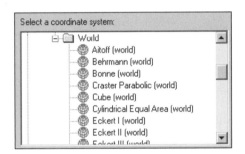

Plus sign clicked ──

4   **Expand the Projected Coordinate Systems folder, then expand the World folder.**

5   **Scroll down the coordinate systems, click Mercator, then click OK.**

The primary purpose of the Mercator projection is for navigation because straight lines on the projection are accurate compass bearings. It greatly distorts areas near the polar regions and distorts distances along all lines except the equator. The Mercator projection is a conformal projection, and thus it preserves small shapes and angular relationships.

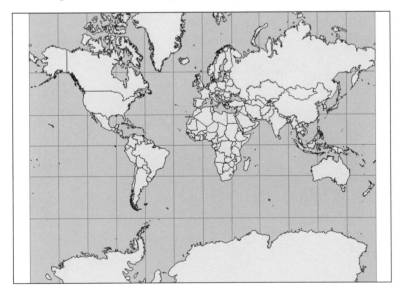

6   **Save the map as \Gistutorial\MercatorProjection.mxd.**

Change the map's projection to Hammer-Aitoff and then to Robinson

1   Repeat the previous six steps, but this time select the Hammer-Aitoff projection in the fifth step, then save your map as **Hammer-Aitoff.mxd**.

This projection is nearly the opposite of the Mercator. The Hammer-Aitoff is good for use on a world map, being an equal-area projection and preserving area. It distorts direction and distance. For more information on this projection, consult the ArcGIS Desktop Help.

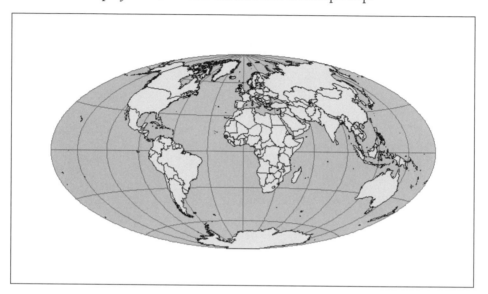

2   This time apply the Robinson projection to your map, then save the map as **Robinson.mxd**.

This projection minimizes distortions of many kinds, striking a balance between conformal and equal-area projections. Again, for more information on this or other projections, consult the ArcGIS Desktop Help.

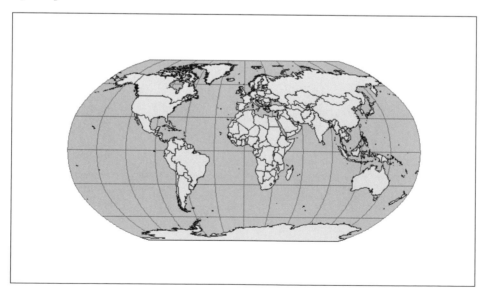

Projections of the USA

Albers equal area conic projection

1   In a new, empty map, click the Add Data button, navigate to **\Gistutorial\UnitedStates**, and add **States.shp** to the map.

2   Right-click the Layers data frame, then click Properties and the General tab. In the General tab, change the data frame name to **Albers Equal Area (Coterminous US)**.

3   Click the Coordinate System tab and click Predefined, Projected Coordinate Systems, Continental, North America, North America Albers Equal Area Conic.

4   Click OK.

5   Save the map as **\Gistutorial\USProjections.mxd**.

YOUR TURN

Experiment by applying a few other projections to the U.S. map such as North America equidistant.

State Plane coordinate system

The State Plane coordinate system is not a projection. It is a coordinate system that divides the fifty U.S. states, Puerto Rico, and the U.S. Virgin Islands into more than 120 numbered sections, referred to as zones. Used mostly by local government agencies such as counties, municipalities, and cities, the State Plane coordinate system was designed for large-scale mapping in the United States. It was developed in the 1930s by the U.S. Coast and Geodetic Survey to provide a common reference system for surveyors and mapmakers. Visit *www.ngs. noaa.gov/TOOLS/spc.html* to learn more or to determine the State Plane coordinates for your county.

Add a map without State Plane coordinates

1   **If necessary, start ArcMap. In a new, empty map, click the Add Data button, navigate to \Gistutorial\AlleghenyCounty, and add Tracts.shp to the map.**

This dataset was obtained from the U.S. Census Web site for census tracts in Allegheny County, Pennsylvania, for the year 2000. Notice the coordinate readout in the lower right corner of the display. The coordinates are reading as geographic latitude and longitude.

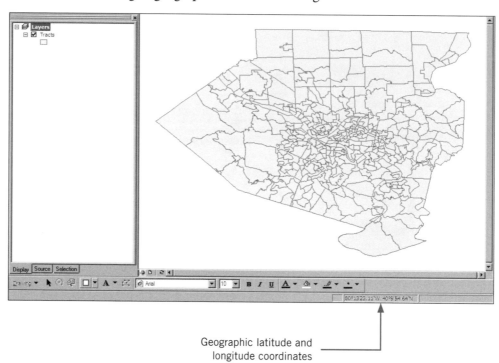

Geographic latitude and
longitude coordinates

Set the coordinate projection for the map

1   In the table of contents, right-click the data frame Layers and click Properties, or click View, Data Frame Properties.

2   Click the Coordinate System tab, and in the Select a coordinate system box, click the plus sign (+) next to Predefined.

Plus sign clicked →

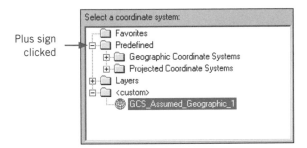

3   Click the plus signs (+) next to Projected Coordinate Systems to expand its contents, then expand the State Plane folder and the NAD 1983 (Feet) folder.

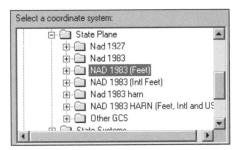

4   Scroll down the list of coordinate systems, click **NAD 1983 StatePlane Pennsylvania South FIPS 3702 (Feet)**, then click OK, and, if necessary, Yes in the Warning dialog box.

This system matches Allegheny County's coordinate system from the local agency. Data dictionaries from the local agencies will define what coordinate system the data uses.

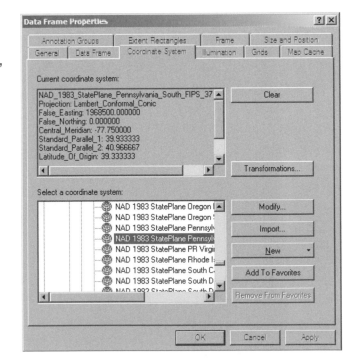

The coordinates appearing in the lower right corner of the display now appear in State Plane units. The origin of these coordinates (0,0) is the lower left corner of Pennsylvania.

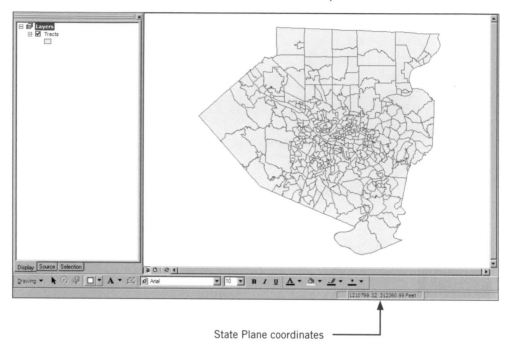

State Plane coordinates ⎯⎯⎯

Convert 2000 census tracts to a State Plane shapefile

1   In the table of contents, right-click the Tracts layer and click Data, Export Data.

2   Click Use the same Coordinate System as the data frame.

3   Change the name of the Output shapefile to **TractStatePlane.shp** and click OK.

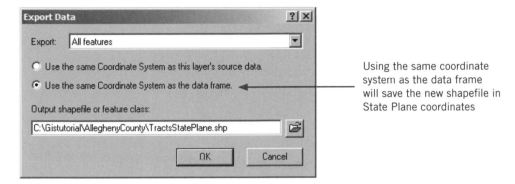

Using the same coordinate
system as the data frame
will save the new shapefile in
State Plane coordinates

4   Click Yes to add the exported data to the map.

5   Remove the Tracts layer from the map.

The new shapefile for the census tracts is now permanently in the State Plane coordinate system, Pennsylvania South 1983.

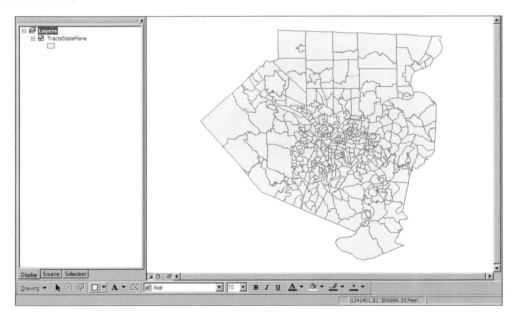

Add a map with State Plane coordinates

1   Click the Add Data button, navigate to the **\Gistutorial\AlleghenyCounty** folder, and add **munic.shp** to the map.

This dataset was obtained from the Southwestern Pennsylvania Commission and is already in State Plane Pennsylvania South coordinates.

2   Change the symbology of the Munic layer to a hollow fill with a black outline that has a width of 1.5.

The data layers will match boundaries now that they are both in the State Plane coordinate display.

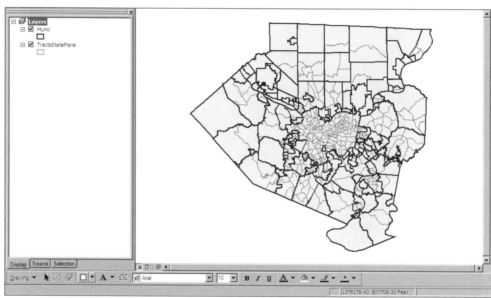

3   Save the map as **C:\Gistutorial\StatePlaneMap.mxd.**

Stored metadata

Metadata is often described as data about the data. In ArcGIS Desktop, ArcCatalog is used to create and view metadata. When creating metadata, some of the information, such as the spatial extent of the data, can be automatically created by the software, but much of the metadata must be entered manually.

Start ArcCatalog and view metadata

1   **If necessary, start ArcCatalog.**

2   **In the catalog tree, navigate to the Gistutorial\Allegheny County folder and click the Tracts.shp.**

3   **At the top of the preview pane, click the Preview tab.**

This will show a preview of the features in the selected shapefile.

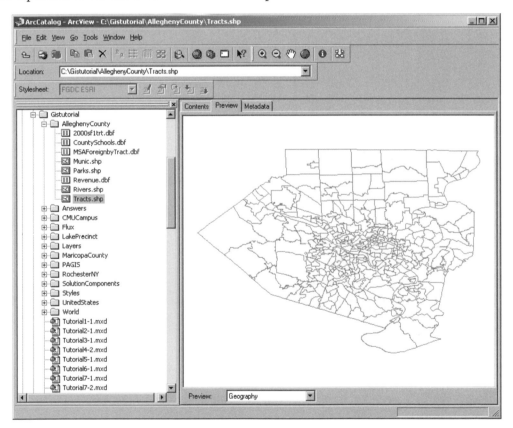

4   Click the Metadata tab.

5   From the Stylesheet drop-down list choose FGDC ESRI.

This metadata style sheet contains a Description tab, a Spatial tab, and an Attributes tab. The Description tab contains descriptive information about the dataset that must be manually entered. The Spatial tab contains information about the spatial properties of the dataset such as its projection and coordinate extent. The Attributes tab contains a list of all the attribute fields in the dataset and their properties. Currently, no metadata appears in the Description tab because metadata has not yet been entered into this section.

6   In the preview pane, click the Spatial tab.

Unlike the Description tab, much of the information in the Spatial tab already exists. This is because ArcCatalog reads the spatial properties directly from the dataset and automatically creates metadata from it.

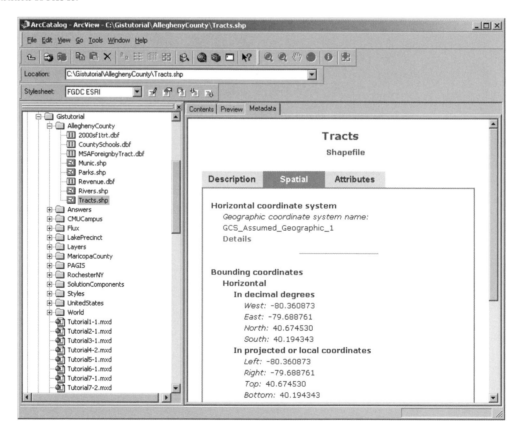

Attribute data

As you have seen in earlier exercises, stand-alone tables can also be added to ArcGIS and manipulated or joined to the attribute tables of other layers in a map. Sometimes data tables come in a standard delimited ASCII text format. ArcGIS (ArcCatalog and ArcMap) allows direct access to data in delimited text files, and the program works with them as tables. ArcCatalog and the Add Data dialog box in ArcMap list files with a .txt, .asc, .csv, .dbf, or .tab extension and assign them a file type of Text File.

Adding and opening .dbf (dBASE) files

1   If necessary, start ArcMap. In a new, empty map, click the Add Data button, navigate to the \Gistutorial\AlleghenyCounty folder, and add 2000sf1trt.dbf to the map.

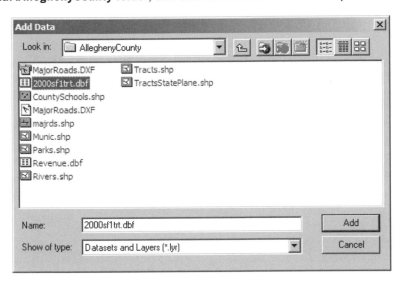

2   In the table of contents, right-click 2000sf1trt and click Open.

ArcMap opens the DBF table. This table contains detailed population information for Allegheny County Census Tracts. A common use for stand-alone tables like this one is to join them to other layers in your map.

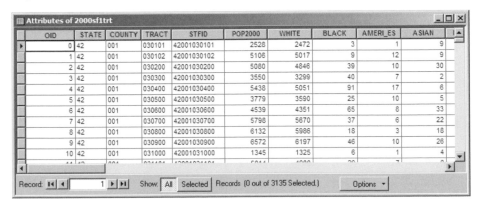

Adding and opening comma delimited .csv files

1   In ArcMap, click the Add Data button, navigate to the **\Gistutorial\UnitedStates\Pennsylvania** folder, and add **2000sf1county.csv** to the map.

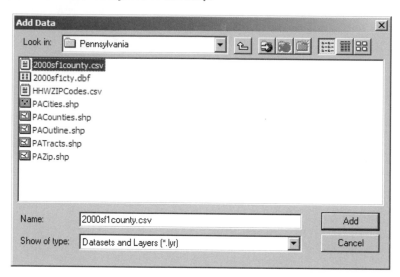

2   In the table of contents, right-click **2000sf1county.csv** and click Open.

ArcMap opens the CSV table. This table contains detailed population information for all Pennsylvania counties.

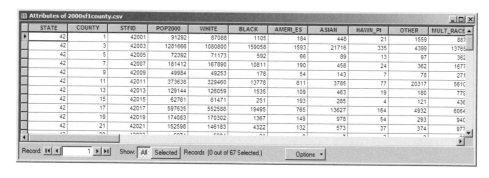

Microsoft Access tables

ArcGIS allows direct import of Microsoft Access tables into ArcMap. For more complicated connections to relational databases, ODBC connections must be made.

1   Click the Add Data button, navigate to the **\Gistutorial\Flux** folder, then double-click **FLUXEvent.mdb**.

2   Click the tAttendees table and click Add.

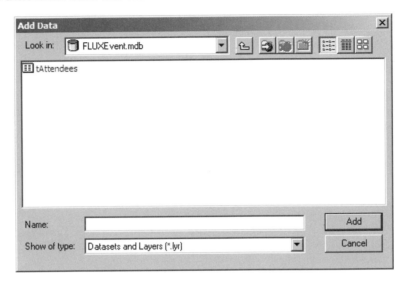

3   In the table of contents, right-click tAttendees and click Open.

ArcMap opens the tAttendees table. This table contains all the attendees of a recent FLUX event in Pittsburgh, Pennsylvania. You will geocode these addresses later in the tutorial.

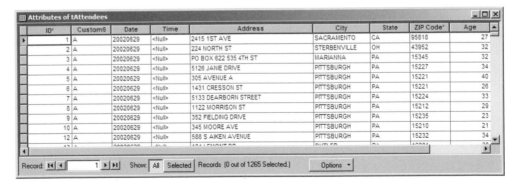

4   Close all the open tables, then save the map as **\Gistutorial\Table.mxd**.

EXERCISES

Exercise Assignment 5-1

Maps showing population changes for Florida counties

GIS is an excellent tool for visualizing census data that can be downloaded from a variety of Internet sites. Many sites provide GIS data as interchange (.e00) files that can be imported into ARC/INFO coverages and used in ArcMap.

In this exercise you will download a U.S. Census Cartographic Boundary file of Florida counties as an ARC/INFO interchange (.e00) file. After downloading the .e00 file, you will then create an ARC/INFO coverage using the import function found in ArcCatalog. The Cartographic Boundary files (and many of the spatial files that you download from various sites) do not contain much useful tabular data, so you need to join a table containing the supplementary data to them.

The tabular data for this exercise is stored in a Microsoft Excel spreadsheet that was already downloaded and compiled from the U.S. Census. This file contains data that measures Florida population growth and trends from 1900 to 2000. Because ArcMap cannot load an Excel spreadsheet directly, you need to save it as a dBASE or CSV file and then join it to the attribute table of the Florida Counties that you downloaded.

You will then be able to create choropleth color maps comparing Florida county populations for years 1970, 1980, 1990, and 2000. An alternative map could show a percentage change in population from 1970 to 2000.

Start with the following:

ArcInfo Export File

- **co12_d00.e00**—ArcInfo export file of Florida counties downloaded from *www.census.gov/ geo/www/cob/co2000.html*. Open the Florida county file called "Florida - co12_d00_e00.zip (275,924 bytes)" found under 2000 County and County Equivalent Areas in ARC/INFO Export (.e00) format.

Census table files

- **C:\Gistutorial\UnitedStates\Florida\FLCountyPopulation.dbf**—Florida county population spreadsheet.

Major cities

- **C:\Gistutorial\UnitedStates\Florida\MajorCities.shp**—point file of major cities in Florida.

Create a choropleth map showing population changes

Download the Florida Counties interchange file from the U.S. Census Bureau Web site.

In ArcCatalog, create an ARC/INFO coverage called C:\Gistutorial\Answers\Assignment5\FLCounties by importing the co12_d00.e00 interchange file. *Note: In addition to the FLCounties folder that is created as a coverage, a new folder will be created called INFO.*

In ArcCatalog, create a new geodatabase called C:\Gistutorial\Answers\Assignment5\FloridaPopulation.mdb and import the Florida Counties polygon coverage and the FLCountyPopulation dBASE file.

In ArcMap, create a new map called C:\Gistutorial\Assignments\Assignment5\Assignment5-1.mxd and add the coverage and table to the map. Join the tabular data (.dbf or .csv) to the attribute table of the Florida Counties coverage, taking care to edit the county names to be sure they are the same in both tables. In a layout, create a choropleth map comparing the Florida county populations for 1970, 1980, 1990, and 2000. Add and label the major cities in Florida for reference. Be sure to pay careful attention to the classifications and colors you choose to show the population changes. See hints below.

Export the layout to a JPEG file called C:\Gistutorial\Assignments\Assignment5\Assignment5-1.jpg.

Map and table hints
- Be sure to add the FLCounties feature class and FLCountyPopulation table from the geodatabase FloridaCounties.mdb, and not from their original locations.
- Because some counties are made up of multiple "islands" along the coastline, they have multiple polygons and records in the database. When you join the table to the polygons, there will be some county polygons with the same values. This is okay.

Questions
Create a Microsoft Word document called C:\Gistutorial\Answers\Assignment5\ Assignment5.doc with answers to the following questions.

1   **What are the general population trends in Florida counties from 1970 to 2000?**
2   **What Florida counties have the greatest increase in population from 1970 to 2000?**

Exercise Assignment 5-2

Create a voting district map for a local election

Many federal, state, and local candidates use GIS to help them in election campaigns. ESRI made news in the 2004 presidential campaign when they created maps for CBS News national election coverage. In addition to making maps for a campaign or election coverage, local election officials use GIS for a number of election tasks. One community that uses GIS for elections is Maricopa County, Arizona, one of the nation's fastest growing communities with 3.2 million residents and 1.5 million registered voters. Maricopa County uses GIS to ensure accurate voting boundaries, maintain voter lists, locate polling places, plan voting precincts, recruit poll workers, and deliver election supplies. Because elections in some counties are sometimes decided by only a few votes, these tasks must be very accurate.

A map that might help election officials determine if there are enough accessible polling sites is one showing major roads or bus routes compared to a choropleth map showing a count of polling places by voting districts. A summary count of schools by voting district (where many voting booths are located) can be created by spatially joining schools and voting districts, and additional points such as churches can be mapped to show these locations as well.

In this exercise, you will download from *www.esri.com* the voting district shapefile for Maricopa County, Arizona that is in a geographic projection. (This shapefile is also available on the U.S. Census Web site.) Then you will change its projection to match roads and schools layers whose coordinates are in Maricopa County's local State Plane coordinate system (NAD_1983_StatePlane_Arizona_Central_FIPS_0202_Feet). The voting district TIGER files must be converted to State Plane coordinates before a spatial join can be performed.

Start with the following:

- **Trg04013vot00.shp**—polygon shapefile of Maricopa County's voting districts downloaded from *www.esri.com* of Census 2000 TIGER/Line Data (free). This file is extracted from original .zip files called at_tigeresrixxxxxxxx.zip (the x's are random numbers generated when you download the file). Inside this file is the .zip file vote0004013.zip that contains the voting district shapefile.
- **C:\Gistutorial\MaricopaCounty\MajorRoads.dxf**—AutoCAD drawing of major roads in Maricopa County, Arizona, projected as NAD_1983_StatePlane_Arizona_Central_FIPS_0202_Feet.
- **C:\Gistutorial\MaricopaCounty\CountySchools.dbf**—event file of Maricopa County's schools whose X,Y coordinates are in NAD_1983_StatePlane_Arizona_Central_FIPS_0202_Feet. Add this file after you project the voting district layer in State Plane coordinates.

Create a map showing voting districts and major roads

Download the Voting District shapefile from *www.esri.com*.

In ArcCatalog, create a new geodatabase called C:\Gistutorial\Answers\Assignment5\VotingDistricts.mdb and import the Major Roads polyline .dxf file, County Schools shapefile (created from XY event file), and joined voting districts and schools. See hints.

In ArcMap, create a new map called C:\Gistutorial\Answers\Assignment5\Assignment5-2.mxd with a layout showing a choropleth map of a summary count of schools in voting districts compared to the major roads. Add the schools point as a layer that only displays when zoomed below 500,000. Add a scale bar showing distance in miles. See hints.

Export the layout to a JPEG file called C:\Gistutorial\Assignments\Assignment5\Assignment5-2.jpg.

Projection hints

- In your map, begin by changing the projection of the data frame to State Plane NAD 1983 (Feet) for Arizona Central, then add the voting district layer to the map. Export the layer to a new shapefile using the same coordinate system as the data frame (now in Arizona Central State Plane coordinates). You can do this by right-clicking the layer and exporting it using the same projection as the data frame. Because this is a temporary layer you do not need to include it in your geodatabase.
- After adding the newly projected voting districts, add the CountySchools event file (using XY Data) and export it as a geodatabase feature class in State Plane NAD 1983 (Feet) for Arizona Central projection called C:\Gistutorial\Answers\Assignment5\VotingDistricts.mdb\SchoolsProjected so it can be spatially joined to the voting districts. Be sure to load it to your map from the geodatabase.

Spatial join hint

- Spatially join the schools to voting districts to create a new feature class in your geodatabase called C:\Gistutorial\Answers\Assignment5\VotingDistricts.mdb\JoinSchoolsVote. Be sure to add it to your map from here.

What to turn in

If you are working in a classroom setting with an instructor, you may be required to submit the exercises you created in tutorial 5. Below are the files you are required to turn in. Be sure to use a compression program such as PKZIP or WinZip to include all three files as one .zip document for review and grading. Include your name and assignment number in the .zip document (YourNameAssn5.zip). *Do not* turn in interim files that are not in your final map (for example, voting district original file, county schools event file, and so on).

ArcMap projects
C:\Gistutorial\Assignments\Assignment5\Assignment5-1.mxd
C:\Gistutorial\Assignments\Assignment5\Assignment5-2.mxd

Geodatabase
Note: Before turning in the geodatabases, compact them in ArcCatalog by right-clicking and choosing "Compact Database." This will reduce the file size.
C:\Gistutorial\Assignments\Assignment5\FloridaCounties.mdb (includes imported Florida counties coverage and county population database)
C:\Gistutorial\Answers\Assignment5\VotingDistrict.mdb (includes imported major roads .dxf, projected schools, and joined schools/voting district shapefile)

Exported maps
C:\Gistutorial\Assignments\Assignment5\Assignment5-1.jpg
C:\Gistutorial\Assignments\Assignment5\Assignment5-2.jpg

Microsoft Word document
C:\Gistutorial\Assignments\Assignment5\Assignment5.doc (answers to questions in assignment 5-1)

GIS Tutorial 6

Digitizing

Sometimes it is necessary to add spatial features such as points, lines, or polygons to existing data. This tutorial introduces you to editing your spatial data. Within the following exercises you will learn how to digitize new features and manually add attribute data to a table. You will also spatially adjust vector data to make it align with a georeferenced aerial photo.

Create a new polygon shapefile

There are a few different ways to create shapefiles with ArcGIS Desktop. A common method is to use ArcCatalog.

Create a new polygon shapefile

1   **If necessary, start ArcCatalog.**

2   **In the catalog tree, navigate to \Gistutorial\PAGIS and click the MidHill folder.**

This is the folder in which the new shapefile will be created.

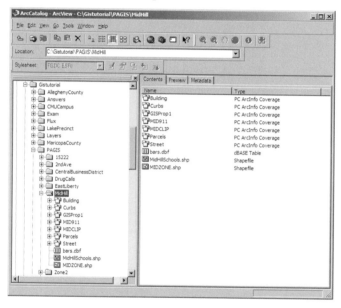

3   **Click File, New, Shapefile.**

4   **In the Name field, type CommercialZone.**

5   **From the Feature Type drop-down list, choose Polygon.**

6   **Click OK.**

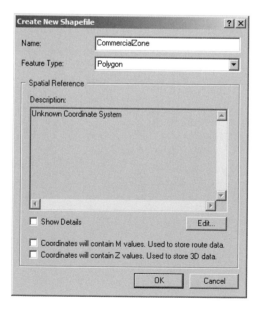

Start ArcMap: Open a map document

1   From the Windows taskbar, click Start, All Programs, ArcGIS, ArcMap.

2   Click the An existing map radio button in the ArcMap dialog box.

3   Click OK.

4   Browse to the drive on which the Gistutorial folder has been installed, select **Tutorial6-1.mxd**, and click Open.

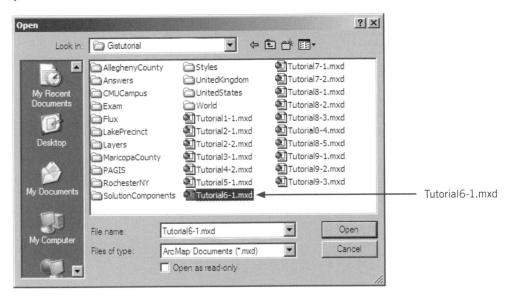

The Tutorial6-1 map document opens in ArcMap, showing a map of the Middle Hill Neighborhood of Pittsburgh, Pennsylvania.

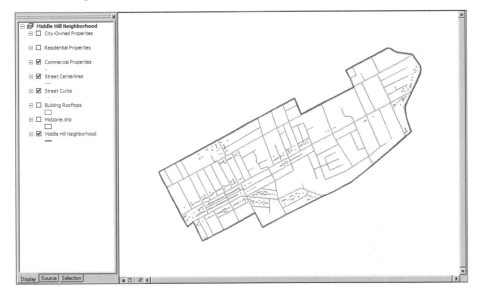

Add the shapefile to a map

1   Click the Add Data button.

2   Browse to **\Gistutorial\PAGIS\MidHill** in the Add Data dialog box.

3   Click the **CommercialZone.shp** shapefile.

4   Click Add.

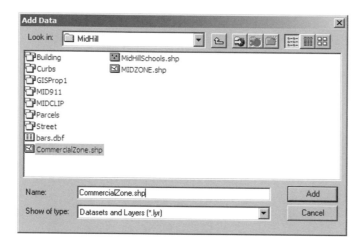

5   Click **OK** on the warning message about the layer's missing spatial reference.

The CommercialZone shapefile is added to the map, although there are no features in the shapefile yet.

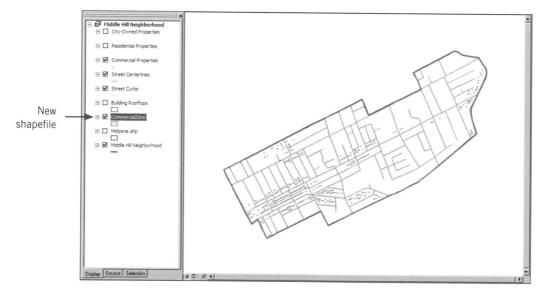

Digitize and edit the polygon layer

Open the Editor toolbar

1   Click Tools, Editor Toolbar.

The Editor toolbar appears. You can move it or dock it anywhere in ArcMap.

2   On the Editor toolbar, click Editor, Start Editing.

3   If necessary, click **\Gistutorial\PAGIS\MidHill** as the folder from which to edit the shapefile, then click OK.

The dialog box asking for the folder from which to edit the shapefile may not appear. If it doesn't, be sure to have the correct layer selected, as shown below.

On the Editor toolbar, the Target layer should be CommericalZone and the Task should be Create New Feature.

Task is
"Create New
Feature"

Commercial Zone
layer

Practice digitizing a polygon

1 From the Editor toolbar, click the Sketch tool.

2 Position the crosshair cursor anywhere on the map and click the left mouse button to place a vertex.

3 Move your mouse and click a series of vertices, one at a time to form a polygon (do not double-click!).

4 Double-click the last vertex, placing it just before the first vertex that you entered.

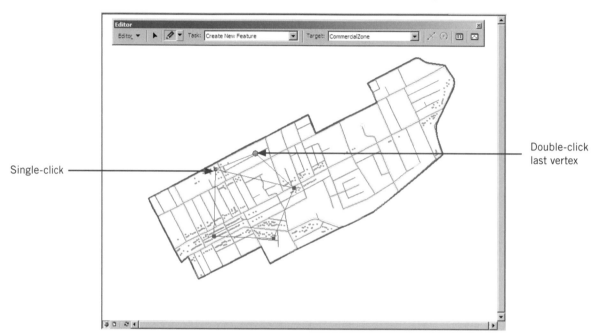

Single-click

Double-click last vertex

Practice editing a polygon

1   **From the Editor toolbar, click the Edit tool.**

2   **Click anywhere inside your new polygon and then grab the polygon by clicking and holding anywhere on its boundary.**

The cursor becomes a four-sided arrow when you are ready to grab the polygon.

3   **Drag the polygon a small distance and release.**

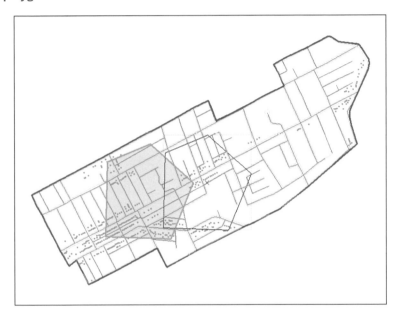

4   **Double-click the outline of the new polygon.**

Grab handles appear at the location of each vertex in the polygon. Next, you will see that you can edit the shape of a feature by moving a vertex.

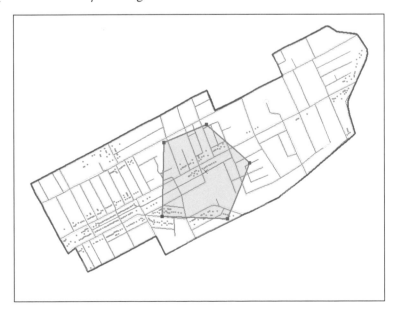

5   Position the cursor over one of the vertices.

6   Click and drag the vertex somewhere nearby and release.

The polygon's shape changes correspondingly.

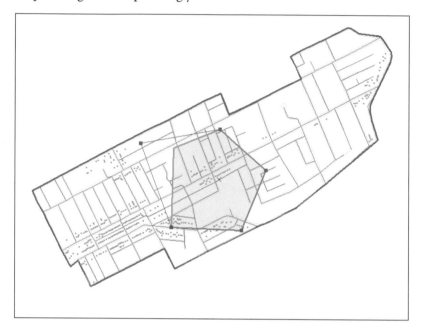

7   Click anywhere on the map or polygon to confirm the new shape.

8   Click the polygon shape again.

9   Press the Delete key to erase the polygon.

The polygon is erased. Next you will practice editing digitized polygons and learn how to add, delete, and move vertices.

Vertices

Move vertex points

It's good practice to learn how to work with vertices. Over the next several steps, you will move, add, and delete vertices from a new polygon.

1   **Zoom to a small area, then click the Sketch tool** **and draw another new polygon feature.**

2   **Click the Edit tool.**

3   **Double-click the new polygon.**

Square markers appear on the polygon at its vertex locations.

4   **Position the cursor over one of the vertices.**

5   **Click and drag the vertex somewhere nearby and release.**

The polygon's shape changes correspondingly.

6   **Click anywhere on the map or polygon to confirm the new shape.**

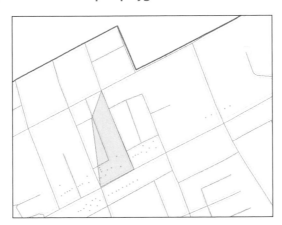

Add vertex points

1   **Double-click inside the polygon to make the vertex locations visible.**

2   **Move the mouse along the line between two vertices.**

3   **With your cursor directly over the line, right-click and choose Insert Vertex.**

A new vertex will be added at the location of the cursor when Insert Vertex is selected. This vertex can now be moved to change the polygon's shape.

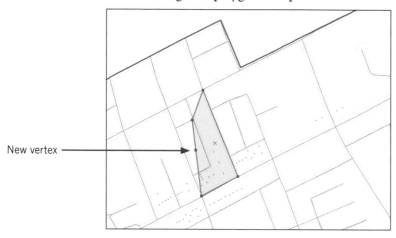

New vertex

Delete vertex points

1   **Place your mouse cursor over any vertex in the new polygon.**

2   **Right-click and choose Delete Vertex.**

YOUR TURN

Practice changing the shape of the new polygon by moving, adding, and deleting vertices.

Drawing and editing tips

This section covers some of ArcMap's advanced editing tools. You can explore the advanced editing tools now or come back to them at the end of the tutorial to edit the line and polygon shapefiles you will create.

Advanced Edit tools

1   If necessary, from the Editor toolbar, click Editor, Start Editing.

2   Click Editor, More Editing Tools, and Advanced Editing.

This opens the Advanced Editing toolbar.

3   Explore the various edit options on the Advanced Editing toolbar. Examples include drawing rectangles and circles.

Note: Some of the advanced editing tools are disabled when ArcMap is used with an ArcView license.

Precision snapping

The following function keys can be used to draw with better precision.

1   Press Ctrl + F5 to snap to line endpoints.

2   Press Ctrl + F6 to snap to polygon vertices.

3   Press Ctrl + F7 to snap to line midpoints.

4   Press Ctrl + F8 to snap to line edges.

Specify a segment length

1   Begin digitizing a polygon feature.

2   Right-click and click Length (or press Ctrl +L).

3   Type a segment length.

4   Click to choose the endpoint of the segment.

Edit tasks

The Task drop-down list on the Editor toolbar contains a set of editing tasks that affects how the Sketch tool functions.

1   Select a polygon in the CommercialZone layer. If there are no polygons currently in the layer, digitize one, then select it.

2   From the Editor toolbar, click the Tasks drop-down list.

The editing tasks are organized into four groups. Most of the tasks are used in conjunction with the Sketch tool. For example, to cut a polygon into two new polygons, select the polygon you want to cut, choose the Cut Polygon Features task, then use the Sketch tool to define the line along which you want to cut the selected polygon. For more information on how to use the editing tasks, refer to the ArcGIS Desktop Help.

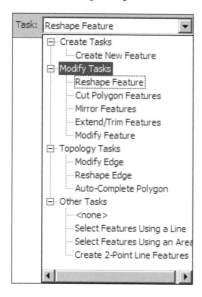

3   Experiment with the editing tasks by using them on the selected polygon.

Adding other graphics

In addition to the editing tools, ArcMap also has a set of tools on the Drawing toolbar used to draw graphics. Objects drawn with the drawing tools are stored in the map document as graphics, not as features in a feature class.

1   From the Drawing toolbar, click New Rectangle.

2   Click any of the drawing tools for adding graphics to the map.

Digitize the commercial zone polygons

1 Delete any of the practice polygons you may have created in the previous steps.

2 Zoom to the cluster of commercial centroids on the top left of the map.

3 Click the Sketch tool and roughly digitize the first polygon, seen below, by clicking one vertex at a time and double-clicking to finish.

Where possible, use street centerlines as a guide for digitizing your arcs.

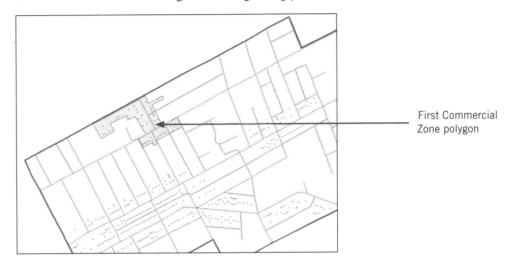

First Commercial Zone polygon

4 Click Editor, Stop Editing to close the edit session.

5 Click Yes to save your edits.

YOUR TURN

Click the Full Extent button. Repeat step 2 to roughly digitize polygons around the remaining seven commercial polygons. After completing each polygon, click Editor, Save Edits. When you complete the final polygon, close your edit session.

Note: You must complete this Your Turn *before moving on in the exercises.*

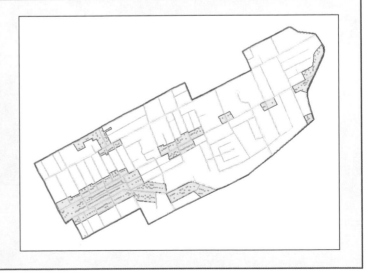

Add feature attribute data

Now that you have digitized the commercial polygons, you will assign zone numbers to them.

1 **Right-click the CommercialZone layer in the table of contents.**

2 **Click Open Attribute Table.**

The Attributes of CommercialZone table has three columns named FID, Shape, and ID, all of which were created by ArcMap.

3 **In the Attributes of CommercialZone, click Options, Add Field.**

If you are unable to select this option, go back to the Editor toolbar, click Stop Editing, and then try again to add a field.

4 **In the Name field, type ZoneNumber, choose Short Integer from the Type drop-down list, then click OK.**

5 **Click Editor, Start Editing, click in the top cell of the ZoneNumber field, type 1, and press Enter.**

Pressing Enter will not take you to the next cell. To activate the next cell for data entry, place your mouse cursor over it and click.

6 **In sequential order, continue numbering the remaining cells in the ZoneNumber field.**

7 **Click Editor, Stop Editing.**

8 **Click Yes to save your edits.**

Label the commercial zones

1 In the table of contents, right-click the CommercialZone layer and click Properties.

2 Click the Labels tab.

3 In the Text String frame, choose ZoneNumber from the Label Field drop-down list.

4 In the Text Symbol frame, set the font's type to Arial, the size to 12, and the style to Bold.

5 Click OK.

6 Right-click the CommercialZone layer and click Label Features.

Your label numbers may not match those below, depending on your order of digitizing.

7 Save the map as **\Gistutorial\Tutorial6-2.mxd**.

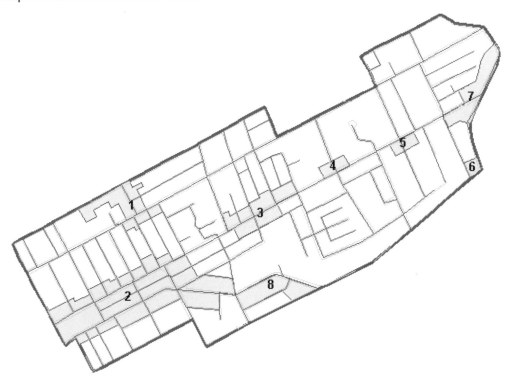

Digitize a point layer

Many local agencies use GIS for homeland security. Two GIS layers common to emergency preparedness applications are evacuation routes and shelter facilities. In this exercise, you will digitize shelter locations as points.

Create a point layer for evacuation shelters

1   If necessary, start ArcCatalog.

2   In the catalog tree, navigate to **\Gistutorial\PAGIS**, then click the **MidHill** folder.

3   Click File, New, Shapefile.

4   In the Name field, type **EvacShelter**.

5   From the Feature Type drop-down list, choose Point.

6   Click OK.

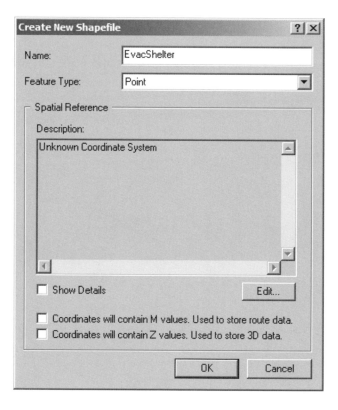

Add evacuation shelter points

1 If necessary, start ArcMap and open **Tutorial6-2.mxd** from the **\Gistutorial** folder.

2 Click the Add Data button, navigate to **\Gistutorial\MidHill**, and add **EvacShelter.shp** to the map.

3 In the table of contents, check EvacShelters.shp, Building Rooftops, Street Centerlines, and Middle Hill Neighborhood to turn them on. Turn off all other layers in the map.

4 In the table of contents, click the legend symbol for the EvacShelters layer.

5 Change the symbol to Square 2, the color to Ultra blue, and the size to 12.

6 Click OK.

7 From the Editor toolbar, click Editor, Start Editing.

8 If prompted, click **\Gistutorial\PAGIS\MidHill** as the folder from which to edit the shapefile.

Be sure the Target layer is EvacShelter.

9 Click the Sketch tool.

10 The blue squares in the map below represent the shelter locations. Using the Sketch tool, click the corresponding locations in your map to add the shelter points to the EvacShelters shapefile.

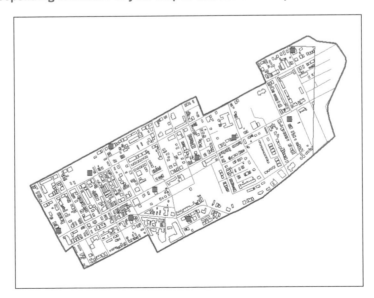

11 When you are finished adding the evacuation shelter points, click Editor, Stop Editing.

12 Click Yes to save edits to **EvacShelter.shp**.

Add a name field to the EvacShelter attribute table

1   In the table of contents, right-click the **EvacShelter.shp** layer.

2   Click Open Attribute Table.

3   In the Attributes of EvacShelter, click Options, Add Field.

4   In the Name field, type **Name**. From the Type drop-down list choose Text, then click OK.

Add name attributes to the EvacShelter records

1   From the Editor toolbar, click Editor, Start Editing.

2   If prompted, click **\Gistutorial\PAGIS\MidHill** as the folder from which to edit the shapefile.

If the dialog box asking for the layer does not appear, make sure that the EvacShelter is the Target layer on the Editor toolbar.

3   In the Attributes of EvacShelter table, click the small gray box to the left of the first record in the table.

This will highlight the record in the table and the related feature in the map.

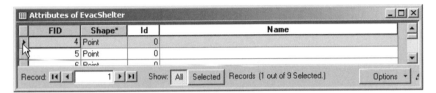

4   Using the map and table shown below as your key, add the Id and Name attributes to the selected record, then repeat the process to add the Id and Name attributes to the remaining records.

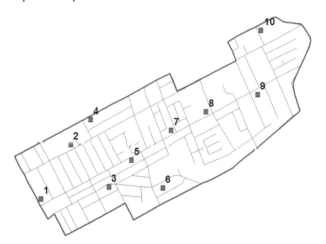

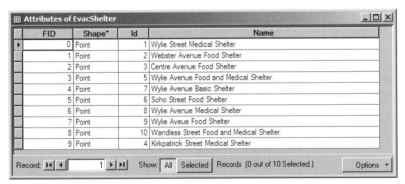

5   When you are finished adding the attributes, from the Edit menu choose Stop Editing, then click Yes to save your edits. Leave ArcMap open.

Digitize a line layer

An evacuation route can now be created to and from the evacuation shelters. This is accomplished by digitizing a line feature.

Create a line shapefile for an evacuation route

1 If necessary, start ArcCatalog.

2 In the catalog tree, navigate to **\Gistutorial\PAGIS,** then click the **MidHill** folder.

3 Click File, New, Shapefile.

4 In the Name field, type **EvacRoute**.

5 From the Feature Type drop-down list, choose Polyline.

6 Click OK.

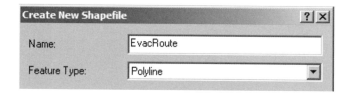

Change the line symbol for the evacuation route

1 In ArcMap, add **EvacRoute.shp** to the map.

2 In the table of contents, click EvacRoute's line symbol to open the Symbol Selector.

3 In the Symbol Selector, scroll down the list of line symbols to find and select the Arrow at End symbol.

4 Change the Color to Mars Red and Width to 2.

5 Click OK.

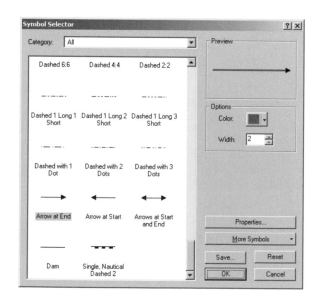

Prepare area for digitizing

1   If they are not already off, turn off all the layers in the map except Middle Hill Neighborhood, Street Centerlines, EvacShelters, and EvacRoute.

2   Click the Zoom In button, then use it to zoom to the western half of the Middle Hill neighborhood.

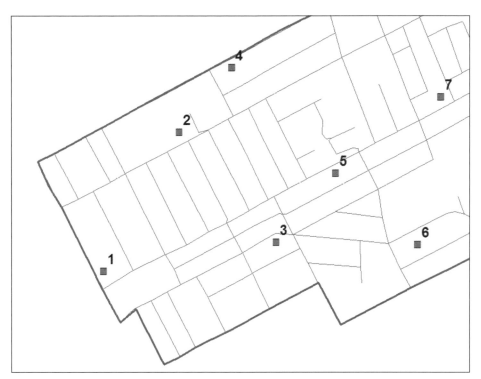

Start editing

1   From the Editor toolbar, click Editor, Start Editing.

2   If the Start Editing dialog box appears, click the **\Gistutorial\PAGIS\MidHill** folder that will allow you to edit the EvacRoute layer, then click OK.

Make sure the Target layer is EvacRoute and the Task is Create New Feature.

Digitize by snapping to features

When digitizing, you can snap the vertices you're adding to existing features. Snapping is used to reduce digitizing errors by ensuring that the features which must be connected actually *are* connected. Within ArcMap you can snap to vertices, or endpoints, anywhere along a line or polygon boundary (called edge snapping), or to the midpoint of a line.

1　**Click the Sketch tool.**　

2　**Click Evacuation Shelter 1 to add the route's starting point.**

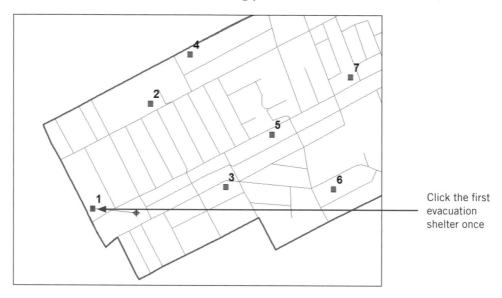

Click the first
evacuation
shelter once

3　**Move the cursor to the nearest street centerline, Center Avenue, right-click, and click Perpendicular (Ctrl + E) from the context menu.**

4　**Click Center Avenue once to place a vertex there.**

ArcMap will force the line to be perpendicular with the street centerline.

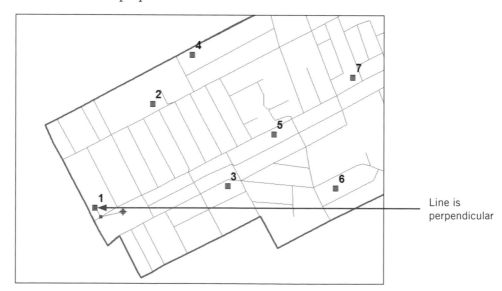

Line is
perpendicular

5   Move the cursor to the first intersection on the street centerline, right-click, and click Snap to Feature, Endpoint.

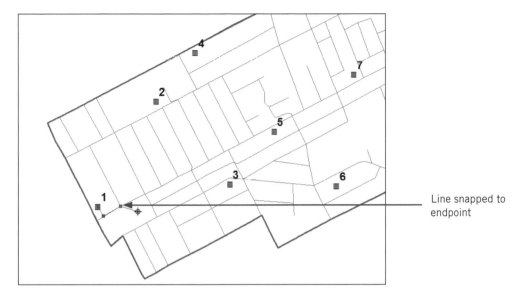

Line snapped to endpoint

6   Continue snapping to street intersections along the evacuation route shown below. Double-click to finish the route at Evacuation Shelter 2. (If necessary, use other snapping options from the Snap to Feature context menu.)

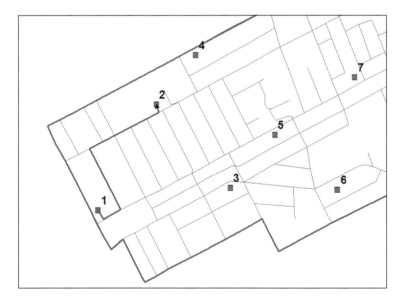

Save your edits and the map

1   From the Editor toolbar, click Editor, Stop Editing.

2   Click Yes to save your edits.

3   Save your map as **\Gistutorial\Tutorial6-2.mxd**.

YOUR TURN

Use the Sketch tool to digitize the remaining line segments connecting the evacuation shelters.

Use snapping tools for Endpoints, Midpoints, Edges, and Vertices.

Use the function key shortcuts for faster digitizing.

Use the Undo button if you make a mistake.

Label the evacuation shelters by name instead of number.

Save the edits and map as Tutorial6-2 when you are finished.

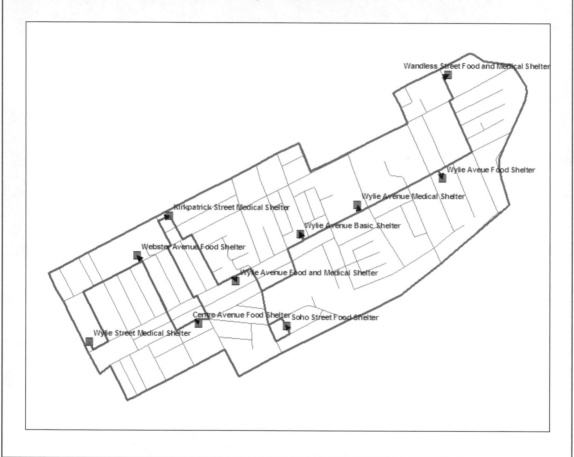

Spatial adjustment

The ArcMap spatial adjustment tools are used to transform, rubber sheet, and edge match features in a shapefile or geodatabase feature class. In this exercise, you will transform an outline of a building so that it correctly overlays an aerial photograph.

Add aerial photos to a map

1　If necessary, start ArcMap. In a new, empty map, click the Add Data button.

2　Browse to the **\Gistutorial\CMUCampus** folder and add **25_45.tif** and **26_45.tif** to the map.

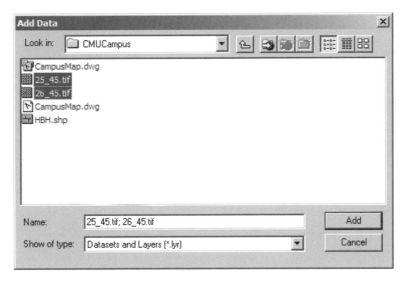

The two images you just added to ArcMap were obtained from the Southwestern Pennsylvania Commission *(spcregion.org)* 2000–2001 Aerial Photography program. Both aerial photos are georeferenced to State Plane South NAD 1983.

Adjust the transparency values of the aerial photos

1 In the table of contents, right-click **25_45.tif** and click Properties.

2 Click the Display tab.

3 In the Transparent field, type **20**.

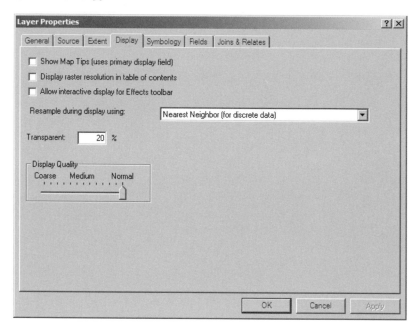

4 Using the same method outlined in the previous three steps, set the transparency value of the 26_45.tif layer to 20%.

5 In the map display, zoom to the Carnegie Mellon University (CMU) campus as shown below.

Add a building outline

1   Click the Add Data button.

2   Browse to the **\Gistutorial\CMUCampus** folder and add **HBH.shp** to the map.

3   Rename the HBH layer **Hamburg Hall**.

4   Change Hamburg Hall's symbol color to Mars Red and its symbol width to 1.5.

The Hamburg Hall layer contains the outline of one of the buildings on the CMU campus. The drawing originated as a CAD drawing from the university's facilities management department. As you can probably tell by looking at the map, the Hamburg Hall layer is not in proper alignment or scale with the buildings shown on the aerial photos. Like the aerial photos, the Hamburg Hall layer should be in state plane coordinates. In the next steps, you will adjust the Hamburg Hall layer so that it properly aligns with the aerial photo.

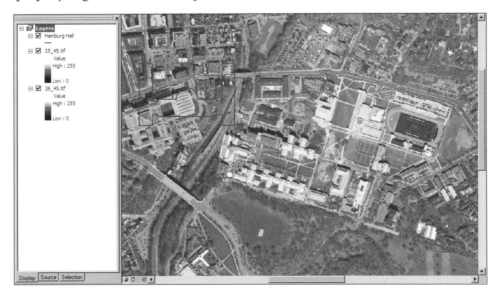

Move the building

1 From the Editor toolbar, click Editor, Start Editing.

2 Click the Edit tool.

3 Click the Hamburg Hall building.

Hamburg Hall in aerial photo

4 Place your mouse cursor directly over the outline of the Hamburg Hall feature so that the cursor icon changes to a four-headed arrow.

5 Click and drag the Hamburg Hall feature to the location shown above.

6 Zoom in to the building feature, as shown below.

Rotate the building

1   From the Editor toolbar, click the Rotate tool.

2   Click the Hamburg Hall feature and, while holding down the mouse button, rotate it
    180 degrees, as shown below.

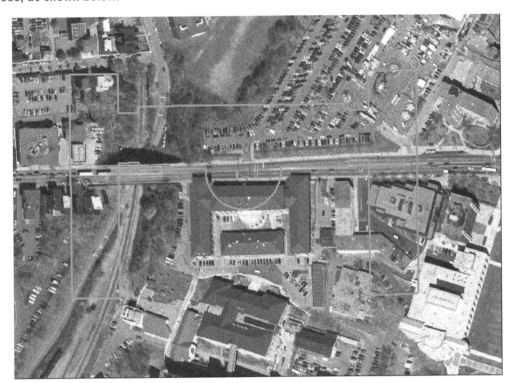

Transform the building to the aerial photo

Add displacement links

1   Click Editor, More Editing Tools, and Spatial Adjustment.

This opens the Spatial Adjustment toolbar.

2   Click Spatial Adjustment, Adjustment Methods, Transformation - Similarity.

3   Click the New Displacement Link button.

4   Click the upper left corner of the Hamburg Hall building feature.

Click here ——

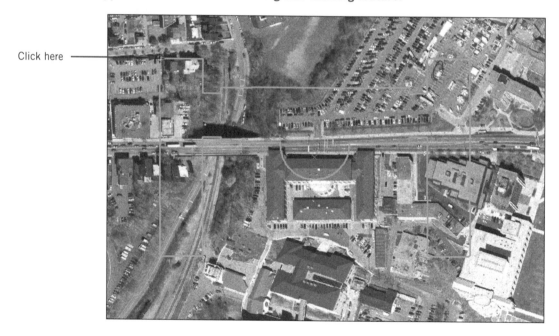

5 Click the corresponding location on the aerial photo.

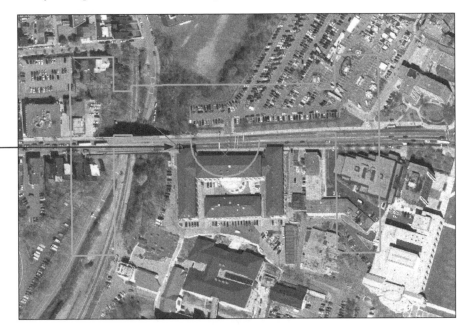

Click
corresponding
location on the
aerial photo

6 Continue adding displacement links to the building feature and the aerial photo, as shown below.

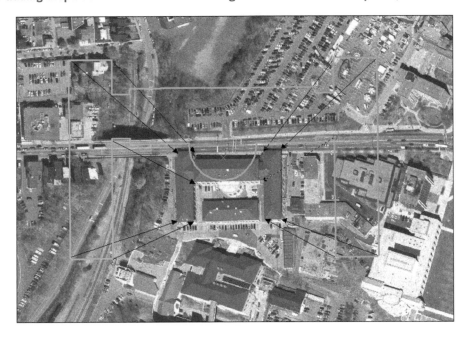

Edit displacement links

If you select the wrong position on the building or map, you can use the edit displacement tools to adjust your picks.

1   From the Spatial Adjustment toolbar, click the Select Elements button.

2   Click one of the displacement links.

3   Click the Modify Links button.

4   Click and drag the link to a new position.

5   Drag the link back to its original location, if necessary.

Link edited ——————

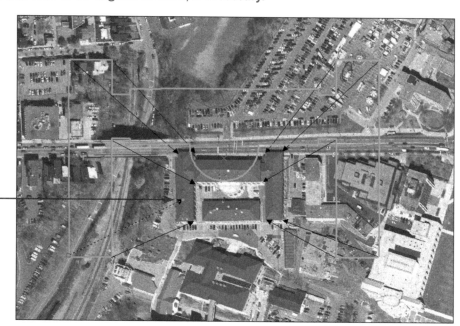

Adjust the building

1   From the Spatial Adjustment toolbar, click Spatial Adjustment, Adjust.

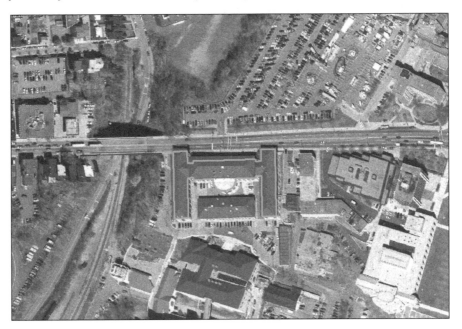

Based on the displacement links you set, the geometry of the Hamburg Hall feature is scaled down in size and moved to match the geometry of the feature in the aerial photo. If the resulting match is not very good, select the Hamburg Hall feature, redefine new displacement links, and run the Adjust command again.

2   Stop editing and save your edits.

3   Save your map as **\Gistutorial\Tutorial6-3.mxd**.

Exercise Assignment 6-1

Digitizing police beats

Community-oriented police officers are responsible for preventing crime and solving underlying community problems related to crime. These officers, among other activities, walk "beats," which are small networks of streets that define areas. Often the beats are designed in cooperation with community leaders who help set policing priorities. Beats change as problems are solved and priorities change. Hence, it is good to have the capability to digitize and modify police beats.

In this exercise, you will digitize two new polyline police beats for the City of Pittsburgh Zone2 Police District based on street centerlines that make up these beats.

Start with the following:

- **C:\Gistutorial\PAGIS\Zone2\StreetsZone2.shp**—TIGER streets for Zone 2 Police District.
- **C:\Gistutorial\PAGIS\Zone2\Zone2.shp**—polygon layer for boundary of Zone 2 Police District.

Note: You are only referencing these two shapefiles, so it is not necessary to include them in your geodatabase.

Create a police beat map

In ArcCatalog, create two new polyline shapefiles called Beat1.shp and Beat2.shp. See the guidelines on the next page for what streets should make up the beats.

In ArcCatalog, create a new geodatabase called C:\Gistutorial\Answers\Assignment6\PoliceBeats.mdb that includes the two newly digitized line shapefiles for police beats 1 and 2 imported into it. See hints about importing new shapefiles into a geodatabase.

In ArcMap, create a new map called C:\Gistutorial\Answers\Assignment6\Assignment6-1.mxd with a layout showing a map with an overview of Police Zone 2 and the newly digitized beats and maps zoomed into beats 1 and 2. Show the beats with thick line widths and bright, distinctive colors, and streets as lighter "ground" features. In the overview map, label the beats "Beat #1" and "Beat #2" and label the streets (see list on next page) in the detailed maps. Include a scale bar in feet. (Note: These are fictional beats.) See hints for digitizing.

Export your map to a PDF file called C:\Gistutorial\Answers\Assignment6\Assignment6-1.pdf.

Geodatabase hint

You cannot import into a geodatabase a shapefile that does not yet have existing features, so you will have to digitize the beats *first,* then import them into the geodatabase. You can then add them from the geodatabase and delete the shapefiles from their original location. Be sure the final symbolized shapefiles are the ones added from the geodatabase and not the original location.

Street centerline guides for Beat #1

There will be twenty-one street segments making up beat #1.

- 1 through 199—17th St (four segments)
- 1 through 99—18th St (two segments)
- 1 through 199—19th St (one segment)
- 1 through 199—20th St (four segments)
- 1 through 99—Colville St (one segment)
- 1700 through 1999—Liberty Ave (one segment)
- 1700 through 1999—Penn Ave (three segments)
- 1700 through 1999—Smallman St (four segments)
- 1700 through 1999—Spring Way (one segment)

Street centerline guides for Beat #2

There will be twenty street segments making up beat #2. See hints for selecting streets.

- 100 through 299—7th St (two segments)
- 1 through 299—8th St (three segments)
- 100 through 299—9th St (four segments)
- 800 through 899—Exchange Way (one segment)
- 700 through 899—Ft Duquesne Blvd (three segments)
- 700 through 899—Liberty Ave (three segments)
- 100 through 199—Maddock Pl (one segment)
- 700 through 899—Penn Ave (three segments)

Selecting streets hint

Open the feature attribute table for the streets. Move the table so you can see both the table and the streets on the map. Sort the table by field 'NAME' and make multiple selections for a given beat in the table by simultaneously holding down the Ctrl key and clicking rows corresponding to the beat's street segments. The streets layer is a TIGER file map with TIGER-style address number data, so look for street number ranges in the following fields: L_F_ADD, L_T_ADD, R_F_ADD, and R_T_ADD. With all streets for a beat selected, digitize the beat in the new line layers (beat 1 and beat 2). Some streets are made up of two segments (e.g., 700 to 899 Penn Avenue is made up of two streets); digitize one line for both street segments. You will learn more about this in the next chapter on geocoding streets.

Snapping hint

You want your new beats to match the street segments exactly. In order to do this, you need to use the ArcMap snapping functions. Use the snapping shortcut functions for Endpoint (e.g., [Ctrl + F5] and Finish Sketch [F2]) to snap to existing lines. You will only be able to snap to lines that are selected or lines within the existing beat shapefile (i.e., not to the underlying streets if they are not selected).

Digitizing in stages hint

It is a good idea first to rough your digitized lines in, being careful but knowing that you will edit your work to add more precision. After all lines are digitized, zoom in so that only part of your work fills the map. Use the Vertex tool to be sure your lines are snapped into the correct positions.

Exercise Assignment 6-2

Using GIS to track campus information

GIS is a good tool to create "way finding" information maps. These maps can be used in many organizations that have large campuses or complicated buildings (for example, airports, hospitals, office parks, colleges, and universities). For example, Carnegie Mellon University's campus can be confusing, especially to new students and visitors.

In this exercise, you will create a GIS campus map by spatially adjusting buildings to an aerial photo map of the campus. You will also digitize layers showing bus stop and parking lot locations. Additional layers could show routes around the campus that lead to various buildings.

Start with the following:

- **C:\Gistutorial\CMUCampus\25_45.tif and 26_45.tif**—digital orthographics of CMU Campus provided by Southwestern Pennsylvania Commission, Pennsylvania State Plane South NAD 1983 projection. *Note: These aerial photos are 80 MB in size. Do not include them in your geodatabase, just point to them in the map.*
- **C:\Gistutorial\CMUCampus\CMUCampus.dwg**—CAD drawing of CMU Campus provided by the CMU facilities management department.

Add to the campus map

In ArcCatalog, create a new polygon shapefile called **CMUParking.shp** and a new point shapefile called CMUBusStops.shp.

In ArcCatalog, create a geodatabase called C:\Gistutorial\Answers\Assignment6\CMUCampus.mdb with the newly created shapefiles from below imported. See hints.

In ArcMap, create a new map called C:\Gistutorial\Answers\Assignment6\Assignment6-2.mxd with a layout that shows the aerial photos of the CMU campus and the academic buildings spatially adjusted to match the buildings in the aerial photo. Digitize new shapefiles showing where parking lots and bus stops are located. Show the parking lots as semi-transparent polygons so you can see the parking lots in the aerial photo. Set the transparency of the aerial photos to 20 or 30 percent to better see the new shapefiles. See hints.

Export the finished map to a JPEG file called C:\Gistutorial\Answers\Assignment6\Assignment6-2.jpg.

CAD drawing and spatial adjustment hint

- Add the CMU Campus CAD drawing as polyline features. It is important to add the CAD file using polyline features so you can export selected layers. In the CAD drawing, turn on only the academic building drawing layers (found under Layer Properties...) and export them as a new shapefile called **AcademicBldgs.shp**.
- Use ArcMap's editing tools to move the buildings closer to the aerial image. Then use spatial adjustment tools and zooming functions to adjust the buildings to the aerial photo. Continue using editing tools, such as Move and Rotate, to adjust the buildings according to the aerial photo below.
- When you are happy with the spatial adjustments, stop editing and import the shapefile to your geodatabase (C:\Gistutorial\Answers\Assignment6\CMUCampus.mdb) and call it AcademicBldgs. Add it to your map from there and delete it from its original location.

Digitize new shapefiles hint

Digitize four separate parking lot polygon features in or around campus. You can see the parking lot locations because there are cars in the parking lots in the aerial photo. You can also visit the CMU Web site *(www.cmu. edu/home/visitors/map/visitor.html)* to see parking lot locations. Digitize at least four bus stops along Forbes Avenue (you can pick the locations). After you digitize the parking lots and bus stops, import them into your geodatabase and add them to your map from there. Delete them from their original location.

EXERCISES

What to turn in

If you are working in a classroom setting with an instructor, you may be required to submit the exercises you created in tutorial 6. Below are the files you are required to turn in. Be sure to use a compression program such as PKZIP or WinZip to include all three files as one .zip document for review and grading. Include your name and assignment number in the .zip document (YourNameAssn6.zip). *Do not* turn in interim files that are not in your final map.

ArcMap projects
C:\Gistutorial\Assignments\Assignment6\Assignment6-1.mxd
C:\Gistutorial\Assignments\Assignment6\\Assignment6-2.mxd

Geodatabases
Note: Before turning in the geodatabases, compact them in ArcCatalog by right-clicking and choosing "Compact Database." This will reduce the file size.
C:\Gistutorial\Assignments\Assignment6\PoliceBeats (with imported shapefiles Beat 1 and Beat 2)
C:\Gistutorial\Assignments\Assignment6\CMUCampus.mdb (with imported shapefiles for academic buildings, bus stops, and parking lots)

Exported maps
C:\Gistutorial\Assignments\Assignment6\Assignment6-1.pdf
C:\Gistutorial\Assignments\Assignment6\Assignment6-2.jpg
Reminder: *Do not* turn in the aerial photo for the campus. We are using it as a backdrop and not editing it.

OBJECTIVES

Geocode data by zip code
Geocode to streets
Prepare data and street maps
Interactively locate addresses
Perform batch geocoding
Correct street layer addresses
Use alias files

GIS Tutorial 7

Geocoding

The process used to plot address data as points on a map is referred to as address geocoding. You can geocode addresses to different levels such as the zip code level or the street level, depending on the type of addresses you want to map and the type of reference data you are matching your address records to. In this tutorial, you will learn to perform address geocoding using tables of address data, TIGER street centerlines, and zip code polygons obtained from the U.S. Census. You will also learn how to find and fix errors in the address data you use for geocoding.

Geocode data by zip code

Geocoding to zip codes is a common practice for many organizations. For example, many stores ask you for your zip code as you check out. This is a useful marketing method to learn where customers come from. It may also be desirable to match addresses by zip codes because less information is needed than for detailed street matching. The only information needed to geocode data at this level is a field with the data's postal zip code.

In this chapter, you will match attendees for an art event sponsored by an arts organization in Pittsburgh, Pennsylvania, called FLUX *(www.fluxpgh.com)*. The event planners of FLUX would like to know where those attending their functions come from. First you will geocode a table of FLUX attendees by zip code, and later in the chapter you will geocode the attendee data using their complete street address.

Map of Pennsylvania zip codes.

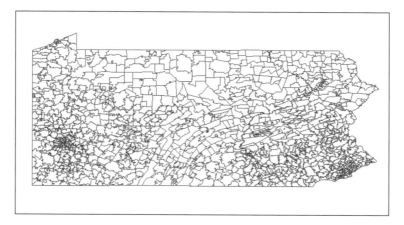

Database table of FLUX attendees.

	ID*	Custom6	Date	Address	City	State	ZIP Code*	Age	
	1	A	20020629	2415 1ST AVE	SACRAMENTO	CA	95818	27	
	2	A	20020629	224 NORTH ST	STERBENVILLE	OH	43952	32	
	3	A	20020629	PO BOX 622 535 4TH ST	MARIANNA	PA	15345	32	
	4	A	20020629	5126 JANIE DRIVE	PITTSBURGH	PA	15227	34	
	5	A	20020629	305 AVENUE A	PITTSBURGH	PA	15221	40	
	6	A	20020629	1431 CRESSON ST	PITTSBURGH	PA	15221	26	
	7	A	20020629	5133 DEARBORN STREET	PITTSBURGH	PA	15224	33	
	8	A	20020629	1122 MORRISON ST	PITTSBURGH	PA	15212	29	
	9	A	20020629	352 FIELDING DRIVE	PITTSBURGH	PA	15235	23	
	10	A	20020629	345 MOORE AVE	PITTSBURGH	PA	15210	21	
	12	A	20020629	588 S AIKEN AVENUE	PITTSBURGH	PA	15232	34	
	13	A	20020629	104 LEMONT DR	BUTLER	PA	16001	30	

Record: ◄◄ ◄ 0 ► ►◄   Show: All Selected   Records (0 out of 1265 Selected.)   Options ▾

Open the Pennsylvania zip code map

1   **Start ArcMap and open \Gistutorial\Tutorial7-1.mxd.**

Add the FLUX Attendee data file

1   Click the Add Data button.

2   Navigate to **\Gistutorial\Flux**, double-click **FluxEvent.mdb,** and click tAttendees.

3   Click Add.

4   In the table of contents, right-click the tAttendees table and click Open.

The attributes of tAttendees contains the addresses and ages of all the attendees of a recent FLUX event. In upcoming steps, you will geocode the records to the street level. For now, though, you will geocode them by their zip codes.

	ID*	Custom6	Date	Address	City	State	ZIP Code*	Age
▶	1	A	20020629	2415 1ST AVE	SACRAMENT	CA	95818	27
	2	A	20020629	224 NORTH ST	STERBENVIL	OH	43952	32
	3	A	20020629	PO BOX 622 535 4TH ST	MARIANNA	PA	15345	32
	4	A	20020629	5126 JANIE DRIVE	PITTSBURG	PA	15227	34
	5	A	20020629	305 AVENUE A	PITTSBURG	PA	15221	40
	6	A	20020629	1431 CRESSON ST	PITTSBURG	PA	15221	26
	7	A	20020629	5133 DEARBORN STREET	PITTSBURG	PA	15224	33
	8	A	20020629	1122 MORRISON ST	PITTSBURG	PA	15212	29
	9	A	20020629	352 FIELDING DRIVE	PITTSBURG	PA	15235	23
	10	A	20020629	345 MOORE AVE	PITTSBURG	PA	15210	21
	12	A	20020629	588 S AIKEN AVENUE	PITTSBURG	PA	15232	34
	13	A	20020629	104 LEMONT DR	BUTLER	PA	16001	30
	14	A	20020629	4025 WINDSOR STREET	PITTSBURG	PA	15217	29
	15	A	20020629	220 LYONS WAY	PITTSBURG	PA	15209	23
	16	A	20020629	7069 SPIN WAY	PITTSBURG	PA	15206	20
	17	A	20020629	510 HEMLOCK COURT	CORAOPOLI	PA	15108	37
	18	A	20020629	419 CALDWELL ST	CLAIRTON	PA	15025	23
	19	A	20020629	1419 CARNEGIE	MCKEESPOR	PA	15132	23
	20	A	20020629	708 3RD. AVENUE	BEAVER FAL	PA	15010	22
	21	A	20020629	11321 AZALEA DRIVE	PITTSBURG	PA	15235	19
	22	A	20020629	2622 NORWOOD ST	PITTSBURG	PA	15214	30

Record: ◄◄ ◄ 1 ► ►◄   Show: All   Selected   Records (0 out of 1265 Selected.)   Options ▾

5   Close the tAttendees table.

Build address locators for zip codes

1   From the ArcMap Standard toolbar, click the ArcCatalog button.

2   In the ArcCatalog catalog tree, expand the Address Locators folder by clicking the plus sign (+) next to it.

3   In the catalog tree, double-click Create New Address Locator.

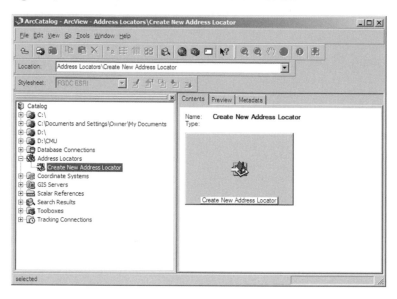

4   In the **Create New Address Locator** dialog box, scroll down the list of address locators, then locate and click ZIP 5Digit (File).

The reference data you will use to geocode the attendee data is the pazip (Pennsylvania zip codes) layer that's currently in your map. You selected this address locator style because the only address information contained in the pazip layer is zip codes.

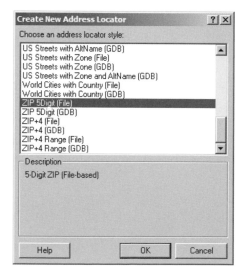

5   Click OK.

Specifying a reference table (zip codes)

The next step in the geocoding setup process is to specify the reference data to which the address records will be matched. The reference data, along with the addressing style and its properties that you choose, is referred to as the Address Locator. Once you have set up an Address Locator, it's stored inside ArcCatalog and can be applied to other address matching projects.

1   In the upper left corner of the New ZIP 5Digit (File) Address Locator dialog box, change the name of the new service to **PAZipCodes**.

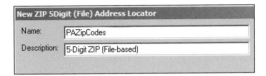

2   In the Primary table tab, click the Browse button.

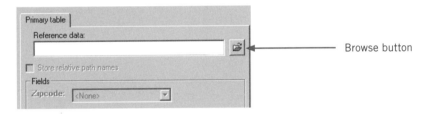

3   Navigate to **\Gistutorial\UnitedStates\Pennsylvania**, click **PAZIP.shp**, and Add.

4   Check the settings on your screen to be sure they match the settings below.

5   Click OK.

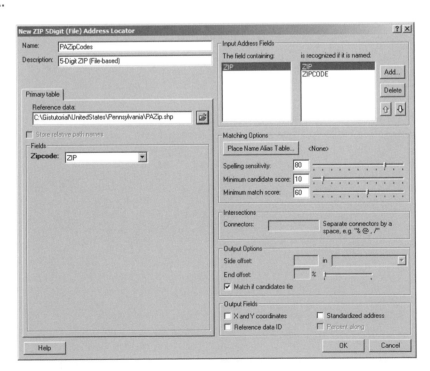

ArcCatalog creates the new Address Locator and prefixes it with the active user account name on your computer (for example, Owner.PAZipCodes). You can now use this address locator to address match any tables containing Pennsylvania zip codes in their records.

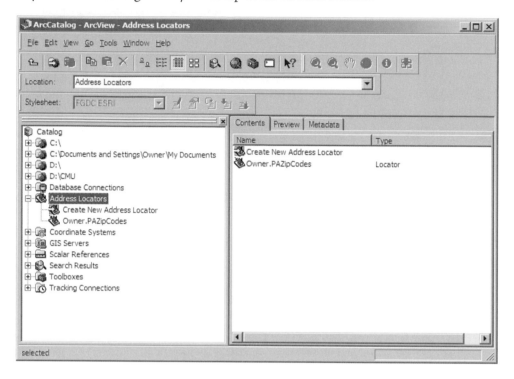

Add address locator to map

With the PAZipCodes address locator now built, you can use it to geocode the attendee data to the zip code level.

1   In ArcMap, click Tools, Geocoding, Address Locator Manager.

2   In the Address Locator Manager, click Add.

3   Click the Look in drop-down list, choose Address Locators, then click the name of the address locator you created in the previous steps (e.g., Owner.PAZipCodes).

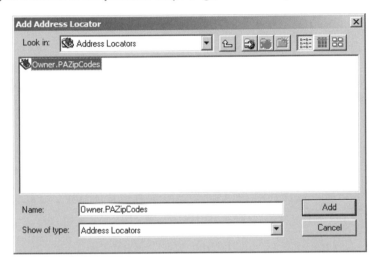

4   Click Add.

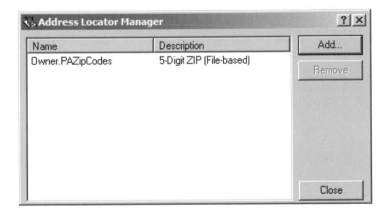

5   Click Close.

Batch match

The tAttendees table can now be address matched to the Pennsylvania zip codes.

Prepare table for geocoding

1 **In the ArcMap table of contents, right-click the tAttendees table.**

2 **Click Geocode Addresses.**

3 **Click the address locator you created for Pennsylvania zip codes (e.g., Owner.PAZipCodes), then click OK.**

4 **In the Address Input Fields frame, click the ZIP drop-down list and choose ZIP Code.**

5 **Name the output shapefile FluxAttendeeZIP.shp and save it in the \Gistutorial\Flux folder.**

6 **Make sure your settings match those in the graphic below, then click OK.**

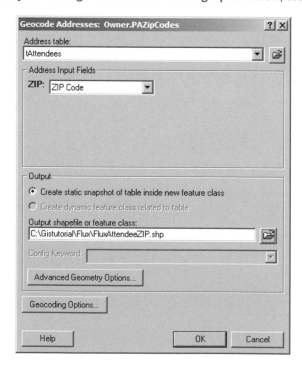

ArcView matches 1,089 attendees (86 percent) of the input records from the tAttendees table to the zip codes layer. ArcView was not able to match 176 (14 percent) of the records. You will look more at these results later.

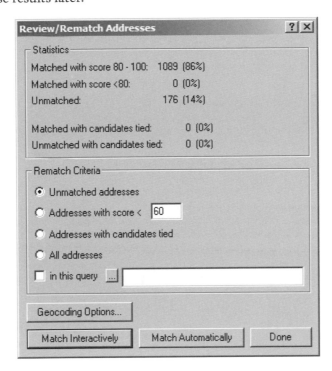

8 Click Done.

The map will display the new point shapefile of the addresses that successfully matched. Change the color and symbol to your liking.

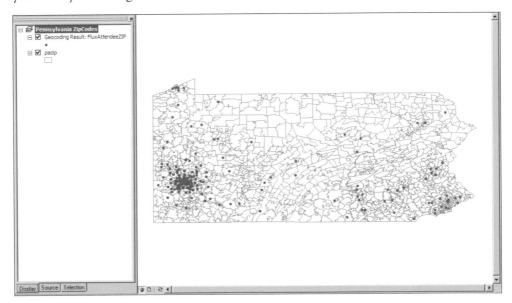

Review unmatched zip codes

There were 176 attendee records that were not matched with a Pennsylvania zip code. At this point, you will review these records to determine why they were not matched.

1   In the ArcMap table of contents, right-click Geocoding Result: FluxAttendeeZIP.

2   Click Open Attribute Table.

3   Right-click the Status field name and click Sort Descending.

Records with a Status value of U are unmatched. Most of these unmatched records are outside of Pennsylvania or have zip codes that are missing.

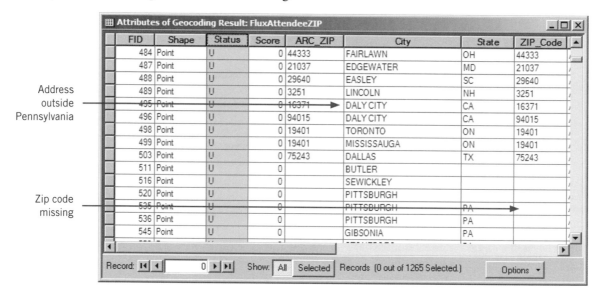

Address outside Pennsylvania

Zip code missing

Fix and rematch zip codes

1　If necessary, open the Editor Toolbar by clicking Tools, Editor Toolbar.

2　Click Editor, Start Editing.

3　In the Source column of the Start Editing dialog box, click the folder containing the Geocoding Result: FluxAttendeeZIP layer and click OK.

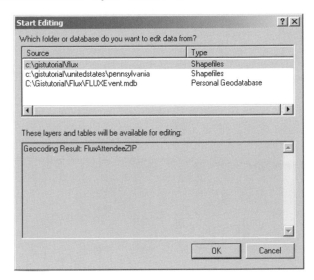

4　In the open attribute table, scroll to and select the record whose Address value is 414 SOUTH CRAIG STREET.

This record's ZIP_Code value was incorrectly entered as 15211 and should be changed to 15213.

5　Change the zip code to **15213**.

The erroneous zip code value has been corrected, and you can now rematch it using the geocoding tools.

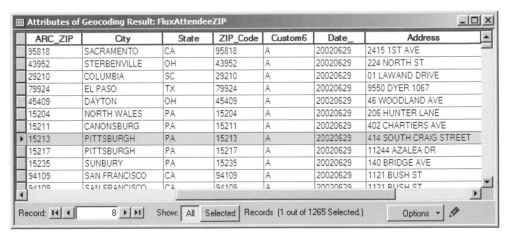

Rematch zip codes

Next you will rematch the record with the corrected zip code value.

1   Click Tools, Geocoding, Review/Rematch Addresses, Geocoding Result: FluxAttendeeZIP.

2   Click Match Automatically.

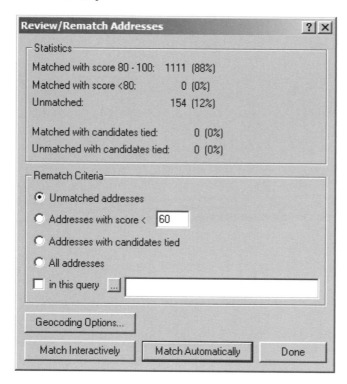

The matched score will increase and unmatched score will decrease.

3   Click Done.

4   Click Editor, Stop Editing. Click Yes to save your edits.

YOUR TURN

Many organizations like to see a summary map of geocoded data. Use the ArcMap spatial join functionality that you learned in chapter 4 to create a choropleth map showing the number of FLUX attendees by zip code.

Geocode to streets

In this exercise, you will again geocode the FLUX attendee records, but this time you will geocode them to the street level for Pittsburgh, Pennsylvania. Geocoding to the street level requires, at the least, that the records you wish to map contain attributes for the street name and house number. In this case, you will also incorporate the zip code value into the address locator, because some addresses may have the same house number and street name but exist in different zip codes.

When geocoding to the street level, you must have a properly constructed street layer to use as your reference data. For example, each street segment in the reference data must correspond to a specific block and be attributed with the correct address range values for both sides of the street.

When preparing to geocode addresses, it is important to obtain good and reliable datasets for both the input and the reference datasets. Before setting up the Address Locator and running the geocoding command, it's common practice to review and clean the involved datasets. For example, you could delete records outside of your study area or check fields to be sure the addresses were entered properly.

Street centerline map (reference data).

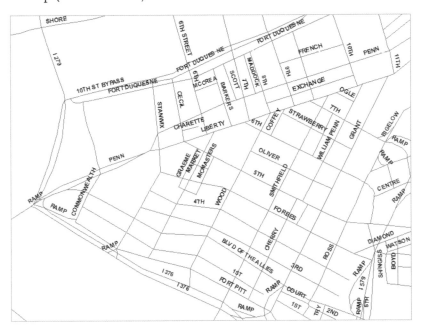

Database table of FLUX attendees (input data).

ID*	Custom6	Date	Address	City	State	ZIP Code*	Age
1	A	20020629	2415 1ST AVE	SACRAMENTO	CA	95818	27
2	A	20020629	224 NORTH ST	STERBENVILLE	OH	43952	32
3	A	20020629	PO BOX 622 535 4TH ST	MARIANNA	PA	15345	32
4	A	20020629	5126 JANIE DRIVE	PITTSBURGH	PA	15227	34
5	A	20020629	305 AVENUE A	PITTSBURGH	PA	15221	40
6	A	20020629	1431 CRESSON ST	PITTSBURGH	PA	15221	26
7	A	20020629	5133 DEARBORN STREET	PITTSBURGH	PA	15224	33
8	A	20020629	1122 MORRISON ST	PITTSBURGH	PA	15212	29
9	A	20020629	352 FIELDING DRIVE	PITTSBURGH	PA	15235	23
10	A	20020629	345 MOORE AVE	PITTSBURGH	PA	15210	21
12	A	20020629	588 S AIKEN AVENUE	PITTSBURGH	PA	15232	34
13	A	20020629	104 LEMONT DR	BUTLER	PA	16001	30

Record: 0 — Show: All Selected — Records (0 out of 1265 Selected.) — Options

Prepare data and street maps

Like you did in the previous exercise, you must define an address locator before you can geocode the data. Boiled down, the address locator acts as an interpreter that reads the address attributes in the input table, then translates them into a form that can be mapped to the reference data.

1 **If necessary, start ArcMap.**

2 **Open Tutorial7-2.mxd from the \Gistutorial folder.**

Tutorial7-2 contains a streets and neighborhoods layer for the city of Pittsburgh and the FLUX Attendees table. Click the Source tab below the table of contents if you are unable to see the tAttendees table.

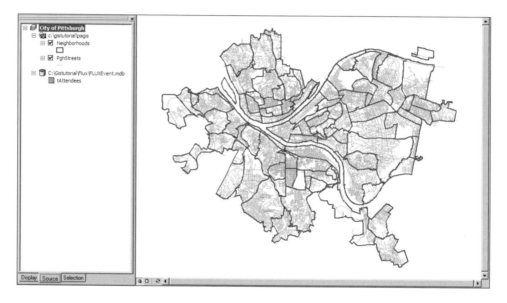

3 **Open the attribute tables for Pgh Streets and tAttendees and review their contents. Close the tables when you are finished reviewing them.**

Create an address locator for streets

1   If necessary, click the ArcCatalog button to open ArcCatalog.

2   In the catalog tree, click the plus (+) sign beside the Address Locators folder, then double-click Create New Address Locator.

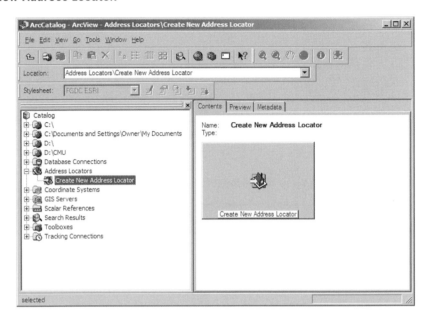

3   Scroll down the list of Address Locators, then locate and click US Streets with Zone (File).

This Address Locator will geocode records containing street addresses and zip codes (Zones).

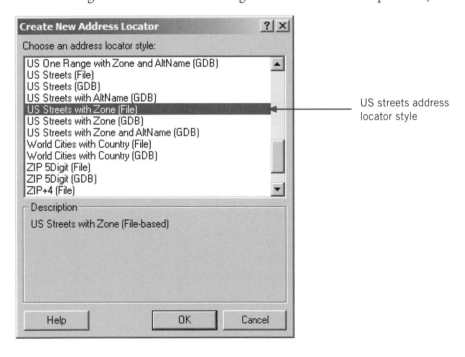

US streets address locator style

4   Click OK.

Specify a reference table (streets)

At this point, you need to define the properties associated with the US Streets with Zone (File) Address Locator. These properties include the name of the address locator, the reference data, and the fields from the reference data that store the address ranges.

1   Change the name of the new locator to **PittsburghStreets**.

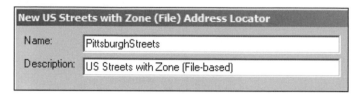

2   In the Primary tab, click the Browse button next to the Reference data box.

3   In the Choose Reference Data dialog box, navigate to the **\Gistutorial\PAGIS** folder, click **PghStreets.shp**, then click Add.

4   Use the graphic below to verify that the correct fields are chosen from their respective drop-down lists in the Fields frame. Correct any incorrect entries.

The Fields list automatically recognizes the correct address fields because the field names in the PghStreets shapefile conform to industry standards for address data.

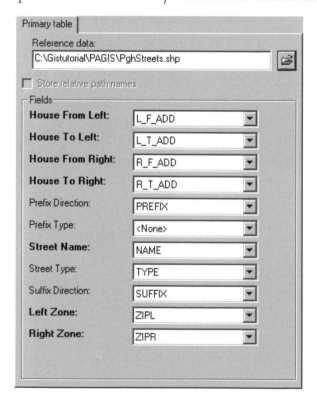

Create address locator

1   Verify that the settings in your dialog box match those in the graphic below, then click OK.

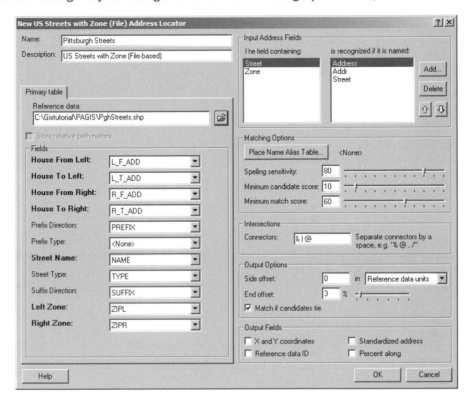

The Pittsburgh Streets Address Locator is now available for geocoding Pittsburgh addresses to Pittsburgh streets.

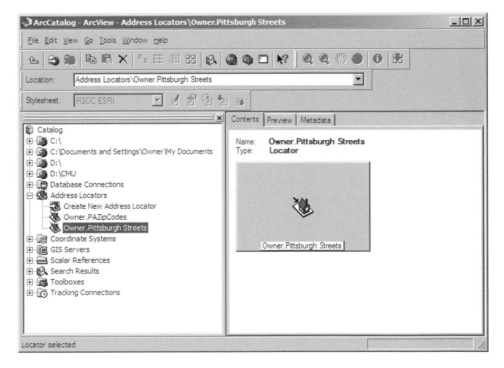

Add address locator to a map

Now that an Address Locator has been created for the streets, it can be used to geocode a batch of addresses from a table or to interactively locate addresses using the Find tool in ArcMap.

1   **In ArcMap click Tools, Geocoding, Address Locator Manager.**

2   **Click Add.**

3   **From the Look in drop-down list, choose Address Locators, then click the Pittsburgh Streets address locator.**

4   **Click Add.**

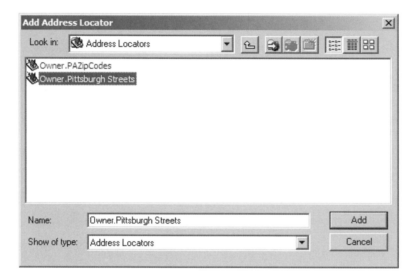

5   **In the Address Locator Manager, click Close.**

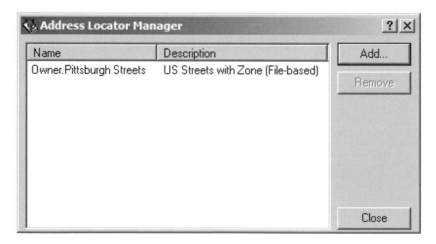

Interactively locate addresses

Before address matching the entire tAttendee database to the streets layer, use the Find tool in ArcMap to locate individual addresses.

1   **In ArcMap, click the Find button on the Tools toolbar.**

2   **In the Find dialog box, click the Addresses tab.**

3   **Type 3609 Penn Ave in the Street or Intersection box.**

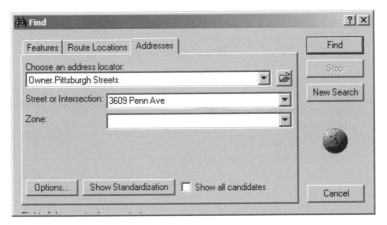

4   **Click Find.**

The found address will appear at the bottom of the Find dialog box.

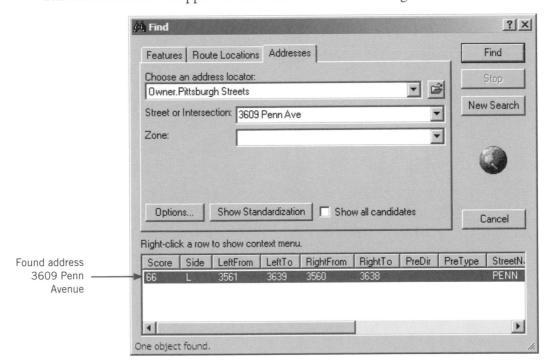

Found address
3609 Penn
Avenue

Show address on map

1 Right-click the potential address shown near the bottom of the Find dialog box.

2 Click Add as Graphic(s) to Map.

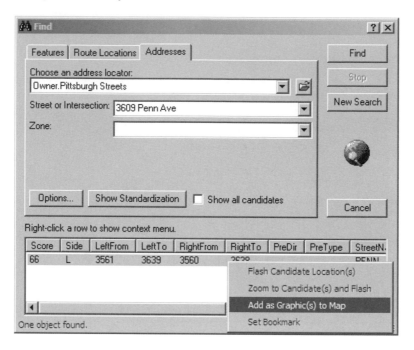

3 Close the Find window.

A graphic dot will appear on the map at the location of the address.

YOUR TURN

Using the Find tool, locate the following addresses:

- 1920 S 18th ST
- 255 Atwood ST
- 3527 Beechwood BLVD

Select the graphics and delete them before continuing.

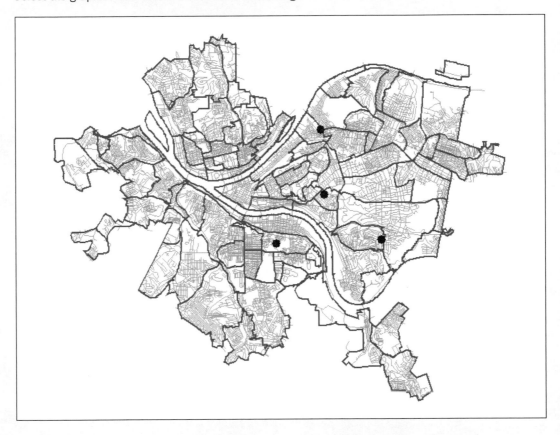

Perform batch geocoding

The entire tAttendees table can now be geocoded to the Pittsburgh Streets layer.

Prepare table for geocoding

1   In the ArcMap table of contents, right-click the tAttendees table.

2   Click Geocode Addresses.

3   Click Pittsburgh Streets address locator, then click OK.

4   In the Address Input Fields frame, click the Zone drop-down list and choose ZIP Code.

5   Name the Output **FluxAttendeeStreets.shp** and save it in the **\Gistutorial\Flux** folder.

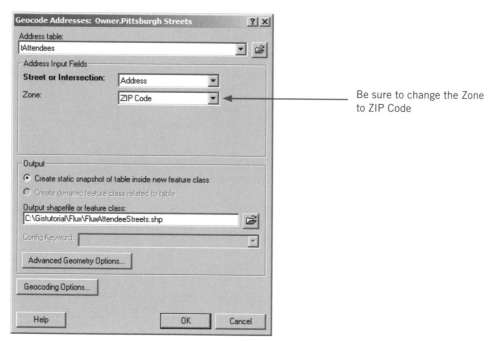

Be sure to change the Zone
to ZIP Code

6   Click Geocoding Options and change the Spelling sensitivity to 75.

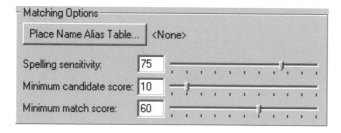

7   Click OK twice to geocode the addresses.

A total of 552 addresses (44 percent) in the tAttendees table were matched to the PghStreets layer. A total of 713 addresses (56 percent) were not matched. Although it appears that many did not match, most of the unmatched records actually exist outside of Pittsburgh. You will look more at these results later.

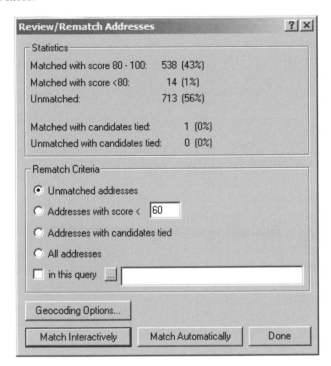

8 Click Done.

The map now displays the new point shapefile containing the addresses that were successfully matched. Change the point symbol to your liking.

New shapefile added to the map →

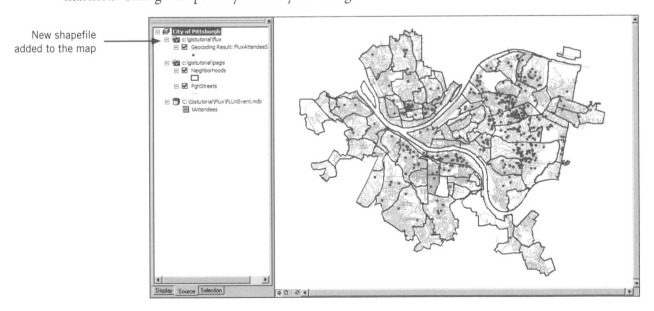

Correct addresses using interactive rematch

Many of the addresses in the tAttendees table were not matched to the PghStreets layer because they exist outside of Pittsburgh. Several others records did not match due to spelling errors or data omissions in either the input table (tAttendees) or the reference data (PghStreets). Resolving these types of errors requires a bit of investigation to identify the nature of the problem and make the necessary corrections. Making corrections to the address and street data mostly depends on the user's knowledge of the streets and access to the correct data. In this exercise, you will use an interactive review process to correct then match the unmatched records.

Match interactively

1   In ArcMap, click Tools, Geocoding, Review/Rematch Addresses, Geocoding Result: FluxAttendeeStreets. Click Yes to begin editing the workspace.

2   In the Review/Rematch Addresses dialog box, click Match Interactively.

This option shows each unmatched record individually in the Interactive Review dialog box, and allows you to manually edit the address values. Horizontally scroll the fields so you can see the Address, City, State, and Zip_Code fields. Notice that many of the unmatched records are outside of Pittsburgh. Some of the records that have "Pittsburgh" in the City field are not really within the city limits. This is a common problem in address matching.

3   In the Interactive Review dialog box, scroll down the list of unmatched records, then locate and click the record with an address value of 1741 ARLINGTON AVE (record 52).

4   In the Candidate list at the bottom of the Interactive Review dialog box, click the candidate with a LeftFrom address value of 1703.

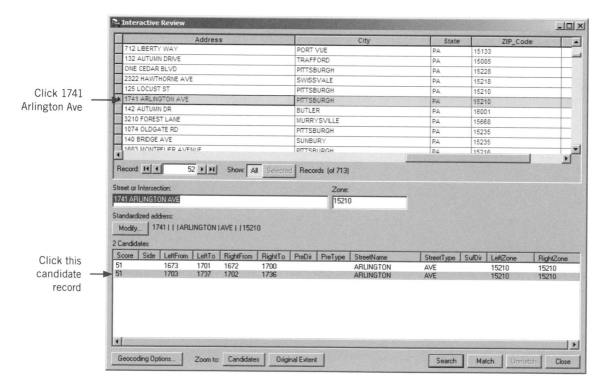

Click 1741 Arlington Ave

Click this candidate record

5 Click Match.

6 In the list of unmatched records, locate, then click the record with an Address value of **275 N.DITHRIDGE ST (record 283)**.

This record did not match due to the period after the "N" in N.DITHRIDGE ST. Removing this period will allow the record to find its match in the street data.

7 In the Street or Intersection box, remove the period from 275 **N.DITHRIDGE ST**, then press the Enter key.

8 In the Candidate list, click the candidate with a PreDir value of N, then click Match.

9 In the Interactive Review dialog box, click Close.

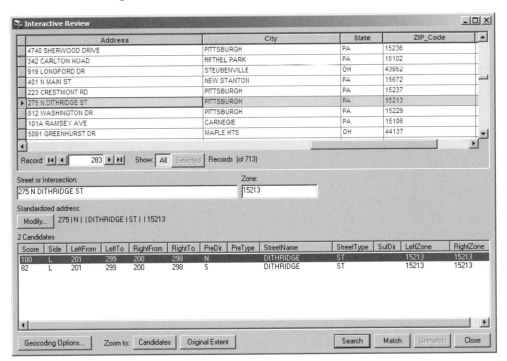

10 In the Review/Rematch Addresses dialog box, click Done.

New point features were created in the FluxAttendeeStreets shapefile at the two address locations that you rematched.

11 From the Editor menu, choose Stop Editing, then click Yes to save your changes.

12 Save your map.

Correct street layer addresses

In this exercise, you will learn how to find and fix an incorrect address in a streets layer used for geocoding. To do this, you will isolate unmatched user addresses, identify the streets the addresses are located along, then examine the attributes of the questionable street features to look for misspellings or data omissions.

Open a new map

1   If necessary, start ArcMap.

2   Open **Tutorial7-3.mxd** from the **\Gistutorial** folder.

3   If necessary, click the Source tab at the bottom of the table of contents.

Tutorial7-3 contains a fictitious dataset of clients and a layer containing the streets in Pittsburgh's Central Business District.

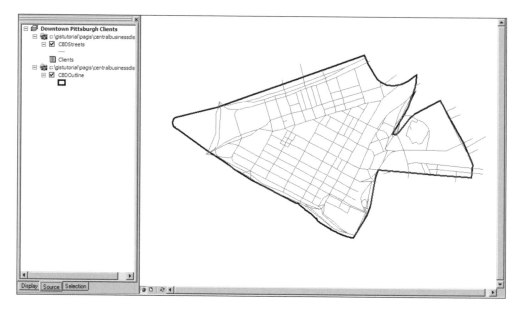

Create a new address locator

1   If necessary, start ArcCatalog.

2   Create a new address locator that uses the US Streets (File) style.

3   Name the address locator **Central Business District Streets**.

4   Set the address style's reference data to **Gistutorial\PAGIS\CentralBusinessDistrict\CBDStreets.shp**.

5   Verify that your settings match those in the graphic below, then click **OK**.

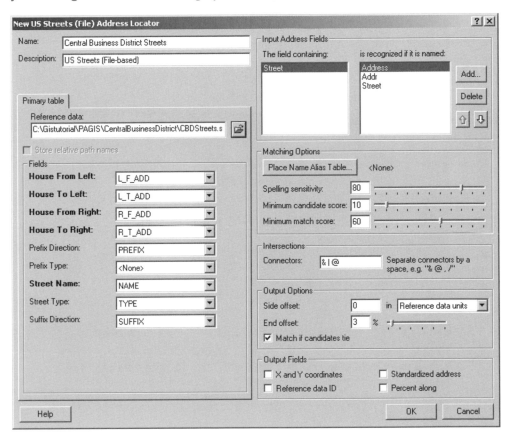

Geocode clients' addresses to CBD streets

1 In ArcMap, add the Central Business District Streets address locator to your map. (Hint: From the Tools menu, click Geocode Addresses, Address Locator Manager.)

2 Geocode the records in the Clients table based on their Address field. Name the output shapefile **CBDClients.shp** and save it in the **\Gistutorial\PAGIS\CentralBusinessDistrict** folder.

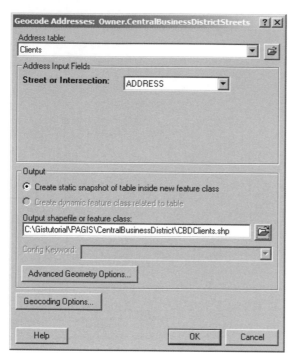

3 When your geocode settings are complete, click OK, then click Done.

4 Change the point symbology of the CBDClients layer to suite your preferences.

ArcView initially matched 15 (56 percent) of the 27 records, partially matched 1 (4 percent), and could not match 11 (41 percent).

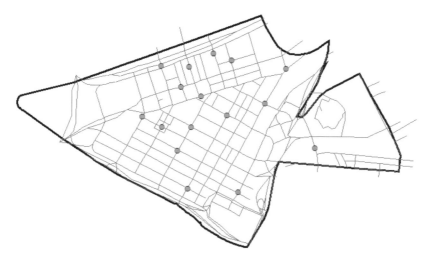

Identify and isolate streets for unmatched address

1   In the table of contents, right-click the Geocoding Results:CBDClients layer and choose Open Attribute table.

2   In the attribute table, right-click the Status field name and choose Sort Descending.

The unmatched addresses, coded with a Status value of "U", are now displayed at the top of the table. You will investigate why 490 Penn Ave was unmatched by taking a look at the street records with Penn as their name value.

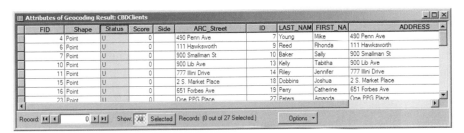

3   In the table of contents, right-click the CBDStreets layer and choose Open Attribute Table.

4   Click Options, Select By Attributes.

5   In the Select By Attributes dialog box, click the Layer drop-down list and choose CBDStreets. If necessary, click the Method drop-down list and choose Create a new selection.

6   In the Fields box of the Select by Attributes dialog box, double-click "Name", click the = button, click Get Unique Values, then, in the Unique Values box, double-click 'Penn'.

7   Verify that your settings match those in the following graphic, then click Apply and Close.

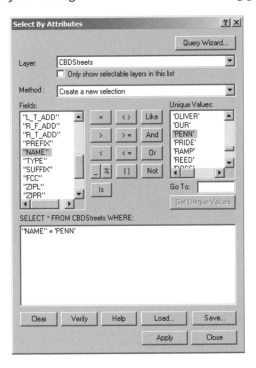

Identify and isolate unmatched streets

1   In the Attributes of CBDStreets table, click Selected.

All street segments whose name value is Penn are now highlighted, and these are the only records visible in the Attributes of CBDStreets table.

2   Scroll to the right in the Attributes of CBDStreets table until the L_F_ADD, L_T_ADD, R_F_ADD, and R_T_ADD are all visible at the same time.

3   Scroll down in the Attributes of CBDStreets table and search for a record with an address range that contains 490.

You will find that this record does not exist in the table. There is, however, a record with no address range values.

4   Click the small gray square directly to the left of the row with the missing range values.

The row you selected is highlighted in yellow, as is the corresponding feature in the map. Your next task is to explore this street segment in the map and determine whether or not you can infer its range values from the connecting street segments. In practice, you might have to check another map source or go into the actual streets to get the address ranges.

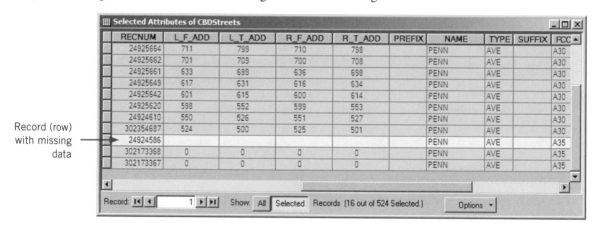

Record (row) with missing data —

RECNUM	L_F_ADD	L_T_ADD	R_F_ADD	R_T_ADD	PREFIX	NAME	TYPE	SUFFIX	FCC
24925664	711	799	710	798		PENN	AVE		A30
24925662	701	709	700	708		PENN	AVE		A30
24925661	633	699	636	698		PENN	AVE		A30
24925649	617	631	616	634		PENN	AVE		A30
24925642	601	615	600	614		PENN	AVE		A30
24925620	598	552	599	553		PENN	AVE		A30
24924610	550	526	551	527		PENN	AVE		A30
302354687	524	500	525	501		PENN	AVE		A30
24924586						PENN	AVE		A35
302173368	0	0	0	0		PENN	AVE		A35
302173367	0	0	0	0		PENN	AVE		A35

Selected Attributes of CBDStreets

Record: 1   Show: All | Selected   Records (16 out of 524 Selected.)   Options ▾

Modify the attributes of CBDStreets

1   Move or minimize the Attributes tables so you can see the map.

2   Click View, Zoom Data, Zoom to Selected Features.

3   Click the Identify button, then click the two street segments connected to the selected segment. (Hold down the Ctrl key while clicking the segments.)

Identify these
street segments →

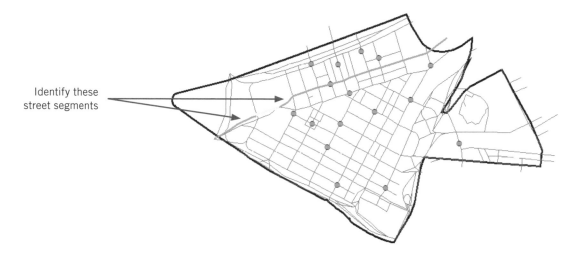

Note the values for L_F_ADD, L_T_ADD, R_F_ADD, and R_T_ADD. The segment to the west (left) contains zeros for the address range values, while the segment to the east (right) contains address values ranging from 500 to 525.

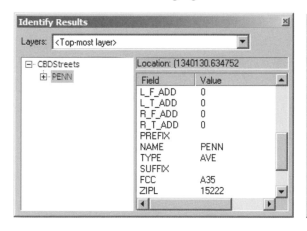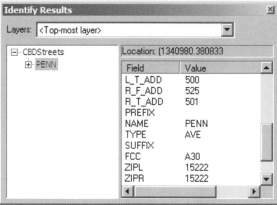

Hence, there is a gap corresponding to the segment without range values. Given that one adjacent segment contains all 0 values and many Penn Ave segments are addressed in increments of 25, we will assume that the following are valid numbers for the street segment's missing attributes: 498 to 474 on the left side and 499 to 475 on the right side.

4 Close the Identify Results window.

5 Activate the Attributes of CBDStreets table.

6 If necessary, click Tools, Editor to open the Editor toolbar.

7 Click Editor, Start Editing. In the Start Editing dialog box, click the source folder containing the CBDStreets shapefile and click OK.

Note: If you cannot edit the table, close ArcCatalog.

8 In the Attributes of CBDStreets table, add the following values to the record highlighted in yellow: L_F_ADD=498, L_T_ADD=474, R_F_ADD=499, AND R_T_ADD=475.

9 Click Selection, Clear Selected Features.

10 Click Editor, Stop Editing.

11 Click Yes to save your edits.

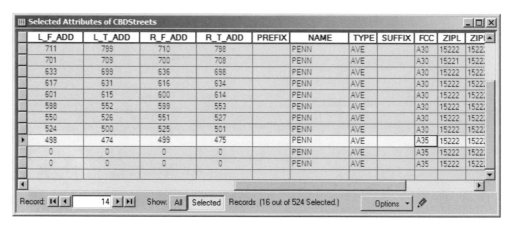

L_F_ADD	L_T_ADD	R_F_ADD	R_T_ADD	PREFIX	NAME	TYPE	SUFFIX	FCC	ZIPL	ZIP
711	799	710	798		PENN	AVE		A30	15222	1522
701	709	700	708		PENN	AVE		A30	15221	1522
633	699	636	698		PENN	AVE		A30	15222	1522
617	631	616	634		PENN	AVE		A30	15222	1522
601	615	600	614		PENN	AVE		A30	15222	1522
598	552	599	553		PENN	AVE		A30	15222	1522
550	526	551	527		PENN	AVE		A30	15222	1522
524	500	525	501		PENN	AVE		A30	15222	1522
498	474	499	475		PENN	AVE		A35	15222	1522
0	0	0	0		PENN	AVE		A35	15222	1522
0	0	0	0		PENN	AVE		A35	15222	1522

Record: 14 Show: All Selected Records (16 out of 524 Selected.) Options

12 In the map display, identify the selected record to see the updated address fields.

13 If you are continuing to the next exercise, leave ArcMap open. Otherwise save your map as \Gistutorial\Tutorial7-3.mxd.

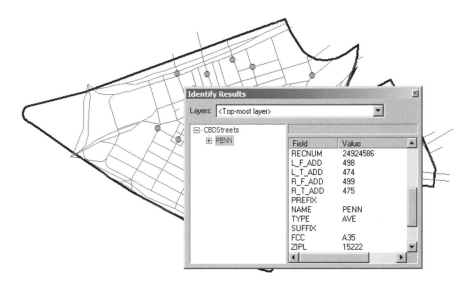

Now, 490 Penn Ave, one of the unmatched client addresses, will geocode the next time you attempt to rematch the addresses.

YOUR TURN

Use Web sites such as *www.mapquest.com*, *maps.yahoo.com*, and *www.usps.com* to try to determine other unmatched addresses on the map.

Use alias tables

Some locations are more commonly identified by their landmark name instead of their street address. For example, the White House may be listed in a table as "White House" instead of 1600 Pennsylvania Avenue NW Washington, D.C., 20500. In the following exercise, you will create an alias table to catch records that may be identified by their landmark name rather than their street address.

Add an alias table and rematch addresses

1   If necessary, start ArcMap and open the **Tutorial7-3.mxd** from the **\Gistutorial** folder.

2   Click the Add Data button and add the **BldgNameAlias.dbf** table from the **\Gistutorial\PAGIS\ CentralBusinessDistrict** folder.

3   In the table of contents, right-click BldgNameAlias and click Open.

Browse the information in the table. The table contains both the alias names and street address for each record.

4   Click Tools, Geocoding, Review/Rematch Addresses, Geocoding Result:CBDClients, and Yes to start editing.

5   Click Geocoding Options.

6   Click Place Name Alias Table.

7   From the Alias Table drop-down list, choose BldgNameAlias.

8   From the Alias field drop-down list, choose BLDGNAME.

9   Verify that your settings match those in the following graphic, and click OK.

10 **Click OK to close the Geocoding Options dialog box.**

11 **Click Match Automatically.**

ArcMap will match the records listed as
PPG Place and Gateway Center (building
names in downtown Pittsburgh). The
remaining unmatched addresses are outside
of Pittsburgh's central business district.

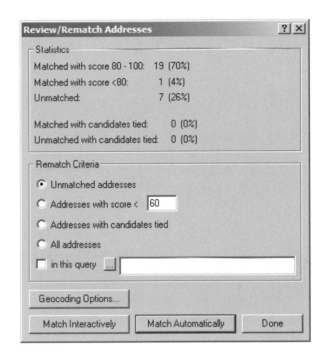

12 **Click Done.**

You will see newly added points on the map as a result of rematching.

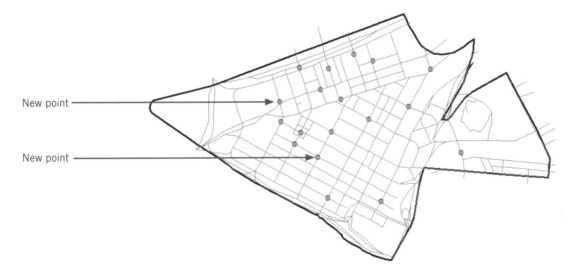

13 **Save your map as \Gistutorial\Tutorial7-3.mxd.**

YOUR TURN

Experiment with the rematch criteria while rematching addresses.

Exercise Assignment 7-1

Geocode household hazardous wastes participants to zip codes

Many county, city, and local environmental organizations receive inquiries from residents asking how they can dispose of materials that cannot be placed in regular trash or recycling collections. Homeowners continually search for environmentally responsible methods for disposing of common household products such as paint, solvents, automotive fluids, pesticides, insecticides, and cleaning chemicals. As a result of an exploratory meeting held at Carnegie Mellon University, the Southwestern PA Household Hazardous Waste Task Force *(www. cmu.edu/greenpractices/hhw.htm)* was formed to fill the need to secure funding, organize events, and create a partnership of individuals representing governmental, private, and public organizations.

The Pennsylvania Resources Council (PRC) *(www.prc.org),* a nonprofit organization dedicated to protecting the environment, serves as the map administrator. As the campaign's administrator, PRC's responsibilities include facilitating meetings, organizing collection events, spearheading fundraising and volunteer efforts, and developing education and outreach materials.

At each event, the PRC collects information about where the participants come from. This will help them in their efforts to coordinate future events. In this exercise, you will geocode participants by zip code information for the Allegheny County event held in 2004.

Start with the following:

- **C:\Gistutorial\UnitedStates\Pennsylvania\ HHWZIPCodes.dbf**—database of zip codes for the HHW Allegheny County event in May 2004 collected by Pennsylvania Resource Council.
- **C:\Gistutorial\UnitedStates\Pennsylvania\PAZIP.shp**—polygon layer of Pennsylvania zip codes used for address matching.
- **C:\Gistutorial\UnitedStates\Pennsylvania \PACounties.shp**—polygon layer of Pennsylvania counties.

Create a choropleth map of HHW participants by zip code

In ArcCatalog, create a new geodatabase called C:\Gistutorial\Answers\Assignment7\HHWParticipants.mdb and import the shapefile that you create as a result of geocoding and spatially joining HHW participants and zip codes. As with the previous exercises, you will need to import the final shapefile after geocoding and spatially joining the shapefiles.

In ArcCatalog, create an address locator to use when geocoding HHW participants to zip codes.

In ArcMap, create a new map called C:\Gistutorial\Answers\Assignment7\Assignment7-1.mxd that includes a choropleth map in a layout showing the number of Household Hazardous Waste participants by zip code in Pennsylvania. Add the PA County shapefile as a thick, dark outline to show what counties participants came from. Label counties with county names.

Export the layout to a file called C:\Gistutorial\Answers\Assignment7\Assignment7-1.pdf.

Geocoding and spatial joining hints

- Geocode the zip codes in HHWZIPCodes.csv to create a point layer of participants by zip code, called **GeocodedParticipants.shp.** You should match 1,464 (99 percent) and not match 14 (1 percent). Open the new participants table and look at the addresses that are unmatched. Browse the attribute table to see if you can rematch any of the 14 that didn't match.
- Spatially join the new geocoded points to the zip codes to create a polygon layer called C:\Gistutorial\ Answers\Assignment7\HHWParticipants.mdb\ZipCodeParticipants that shows a count of the number of participants in each zip code. Add this feature class from the geodatabase for the final map.

Questions

Create a Microsoft Word document called C:\Gistutorial\Answers\Assignment7\ Assignment7.doc and answer the following questions:

1 **Name some reasons why participant zip codes didn't match.**
2 **What zip code had the most participants?**
3 **What county has the most participants?**
4 **What is the POName of the zip code from Mercer County?**

EXERCISES

Exercise Assignment 7-2

Geocode ethnic businesses to Pittsburgh streets

As the 2000 Census attests to, immigrants are largely becoming one of the most salient indicators of growth and wealth in a region. By looking at the immigrants who live in a city and analyzing where they decide to set up their entrepreneurial businesses, a region may plug into clues that indicate why certain neighborhoods are more "immigrant-friendly" than others, and in turn, focus on the qualities that make a neighborhood open and diverse.

According to the 2000 Census, Pittsburgh, Pennsylvania, ranked twenty-fifth of all metropolitan areas in its immigrant population. GIS can geocode precisely where these immigrants create businesses and then aggregate this to neighborhoods. The data used in this exercise is a sample of businesses generated by CMU students that focused on foreign-run, high-tech firms, restaurants, and grocery stores. A more complete listing of businesses would need to be collected from a variety of sources. For more details on foreign businesses in the region, visit the Pittsburgh Regional Alliance at *www.pittsburghregion.org* and Global Pittsburgh at *www.globalpittsburgh.org*. In addition to mapping the businesses, an expansion of the project could be to download foreign-born population from the U.S. Census SF3 tables, aggregating this to neighborhoods as well.

Start with the following:

- **C:\Gistutorial\PAGIS\ForeignBusinesses.dbf**—sample database of Pittsburgh foreign owned businesses.
- **C:\Gistutorial\PAGIS\PghStreets.shp**—TIGER line layer of Pittsburgh street centerlines.
- **C:\Gistutorial\PAGIS\Neighborhoods.shp**—polygon layer of Pittsburgh neighborhoods.

Create a pin (point) map of geocoded foreign-owned businesses and choropleth map of businesses by neighborhood

In ArcCatalog, create a geodatabase called C:\Gistutorial\Answers\Assignment7\ForeignBusinessses.mdb and import the shapefile that you created as a result of geocoding. Also import the shapefile that you created as a result of spatially joining neighborhoods and businesses. As with the previous exercises, you will need to import the final shapefiles after geocoding and spatially joining them.

In ArcCatalog, create an address locator to use when geocoding foreign business locations to streets.

In ArcMap, create a new map called C:\Gistutorial\Answers\Assignment7\Assignment7-2.mxd that includes a layout showing a pin map of foreign business locations in Pittsburgh and a choropleth map showing a count of the number of businesses in each neighborhood. You can create these as comparison maps or together on the same map. Label the features to your liking.

Export the map as a file called C:\Gistutorial\Answers\Assignment7\Assignment7-2.jpg.

Geocoding hints
- Geocode the foreign businesses to Pittsburgh Streets, creating a file called GeocodedForeignBusinesses.shp. You may get a relatively small number of businesses to match initially (about 60 percent). There are a variety of reasons for this: some are outside of Pittsburgh, some have business locations that are not accurate street addresses (e.g., Four Gateway Center), and some are simply entered wrong.
- Use any of the following to help rematch addresses: alias tables, Pgh zip code polygons, Internet sites such as *www.usps.com,* or online mapping programs such as *YellowPages.com*. You should be able to rematch at least five additional locations. Keep a log of steps you took to try to rematch addresses; turn this in with your assignment.

Spatial join hint
- Spatially join the geocoded businesses to the neighborhoods in a new shapefile called C:\Gistutorial\ Answers\Assignment7\ForeignBusinessses.mdb\JoinNeighBusiness.

Questions
In the Word document that you created in exercise 7-1, add answers to the following questions:

5   What two neighborhoods have the most foreign-owned businesses?

6   Turn in a log of the steps you took to try to rematch addresses.

What to turn in
If you are working in a classroom setting with an instructor, you may be required to submit the exercises you created in tutorial 7. Below are the files you are required to turn in. Be sure to use a compression program such as PKZIP or WinZip to include all three files as one .zip document for review and grading. Include your name and assignment number in the .zip document (YourNameAssn7.zip). *Do not* turn in interim files that are not in your final map (e.g., HHW participants geocoded point shapefile).

ArcMap projects
C:\Gistutorial\Answers\Assignment7\Assignment7-1.mxd
C:\Gistutorial\Answers\Assignment7\Assignment7-2.mxd

Geodatabases
Note: Before turning in the geodatabases, compact them in ArcCatalog by right-clicking and choosing "Compact Database." This will reduce the file size.
C:\Gistutorial\Answers\Assignment7\HHWParticipants.mdb (includes imported zip code shapefile that is a result of spatially joining geocoded participants and zip codes)
C:\Gistutorial\Answers\Assignment7\ForeignBusinesses.mdb (includes imported foreign businesses geocoded shapefile and joined neighborhoods shapefile that is a result of spatially joining geocoded businesses and neighborhoods)

Exported maps
C:\Gistutorial\Answers\Assignment7\Assignment7-1.pdf
C:\Gistutorial\Answers\Assignment7\Assignment7-2.jpg

Word document
C:\Gistutorial\Answers\Assignment7\Assignment7.doc

Extract features to create a new shapefile
Clip streets to match a polygon boundary
Dissolve polygons based on their zip code value
Append several polygon layers into one new shapefile
Create a model that uses the Clip and Union tool

GIS Tutorial 8

Spatial Data Processing

Basemaps are available from many sources. Often, however, you will need to modify available maps for use in a specific project. In this tutorial, you will learn how to extract a subset of spatial features from a map using either attribute or spatial queries. You will also learn how to aggregate polygons and how to append two or more layers into a single layer. These functions are referred to as geoprocessing functions and are commonly strung together to perform different types of spatial analysis. One way to build, share, and document your GIS work flows is to create models, and within this tutorial you will learn how to create and run a simple GIS workflow model.

Launch ArcMap

1   **From the Windows taskbar, click Start, All Programs, ArcGIS, ArcMap.**

Depending on how ArcGIS and ArcMap have been installed, there may be a different navigation menu.

2   **Click the An existing map radio button in the ArcMap dialog box.**

3   **Click OK.**

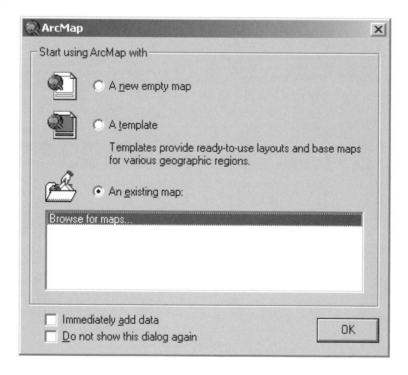

Open an existing map

1 Browse to the drive on which the Gistutorial folder has been installed (e.g., C:\Gistutorial), select the **Tutorial8-1.mxd**, and click the Open button.

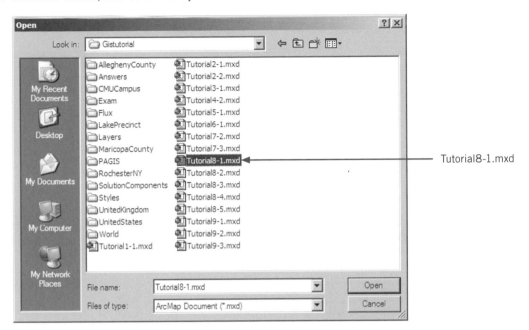

Tutorial8-1.mxd

The Tutorial8-1.mxd file opens in ArcMap showing a map of the New York City Metro Area including Manhattan, Brooklyn, the Bronx, Staten Island, and Queens.

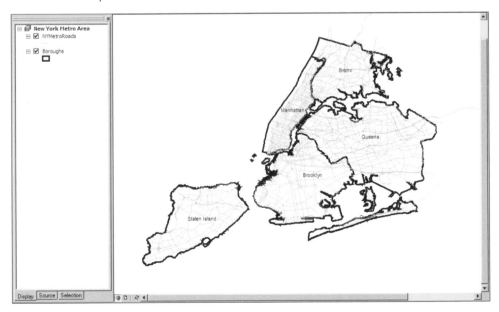

Use data queries to extract features

Use the ArcMap Select By Attributes dialog box

Here you will use ArcMap's Select By Attributes function to create a study area for Manhattan which will be extracted from the NY Boroughs layer.

1 **Click Selection, Select By Attributes.**

2 **From the Layer drop-down list, click Boroughs.**

3 **In the Fields box, double-click "NAME".**

4 **Click the = button.**

5 **Click the Get Unique Values button and then, in the Unique Values box, double-click 'Manhattan'.**

Based on this query expression, the Select by Attributes dialog box will select the Manhattan borough feature.

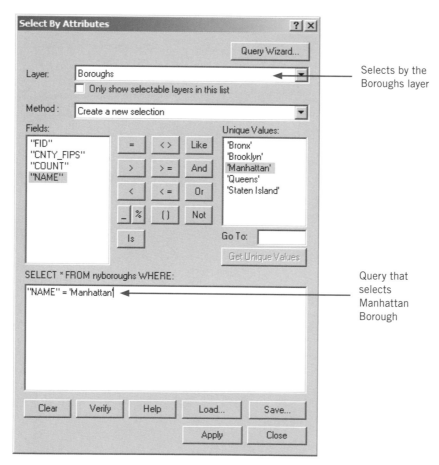

6 **Click Apply and Close.**

Show selected features and convert to shapefile

1   Click View, Zoom Data, Zoom to Selected Features.

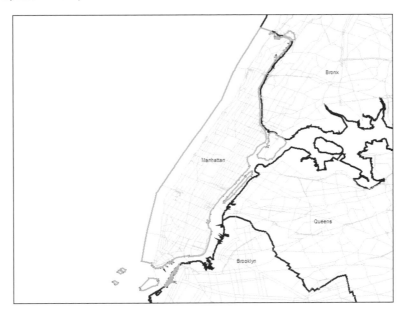

2   In the table of contents, right-click the Boroughs layer, click Data, Export Data.

3   Save the output shapefile as **\Gistutorial\UnitedStates\NewYork\Manhattan.shp**.

4   Click OK, then click Yes to add the layer to the map.

5   Drag the NY Metro Roads to the top of the table of contents.

Your map now contains a new shapefile containing only the borough of Manhattan.

Use the ArcMap Select Features tool

In the previous steps, you used an attribute query to select the feature you wanted to extract. Sometimes, however, it's easier to manually select the feature(s) you want to extract directly from the map display instead of building a query expression in the Select By Attributes dialog box.

1 Click the Full Extent button, then click the Select Features button.

2 Click once inside the polygon feature for Brooklyn.

3 In the table of contents, right-click the Boroughs layer, click Data, Export Data.

4 Save the output shapefile as **\Gistutorial\UnitedStates\NewYork\Brooklyn.shp**.

5 Click OK, then click Yes to add the layer to the map.

Your map now contains another new shapefile, this one containing only the borough of Brooklyn.

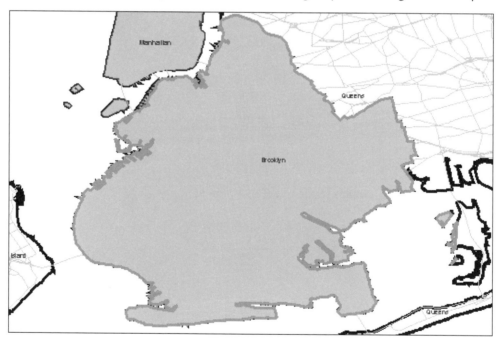

YOUR TURN

Use either the Select By Attributes dialog box or the Select Features tool to create study area shapefiles for Queens, the Bronx, and Staten Island.

Clip features

Use the ArcMap Select By Location tool

In the following steps, you will use the ArcMap Select By Location dialog box to select the roads in the Manhattan borough. After selecting the roads, you will create a new shapefile from them.

1 **Click Selection, Select by Location.**

2 **If necessary, click the I want to drop-down list and choose select features from.**

3 **Check NYMetroRoads as the layer from which to select features.**

4 **From the Selection Method (that) drop-down list, choose intersect.**

5 **From the third drop-down list in the dialog box, choose Manhattan.**

Once made, the settings in this dialog box can be read as a sentence. In this case the sentence reads as follows: "I want to select features from the NYMetroRoads layer that intersect the features in the Manhattan layer." The result of these settings will be the selection of all the roads contained by or crossing the boundary of the Manhattan borough.

Selection method ——————

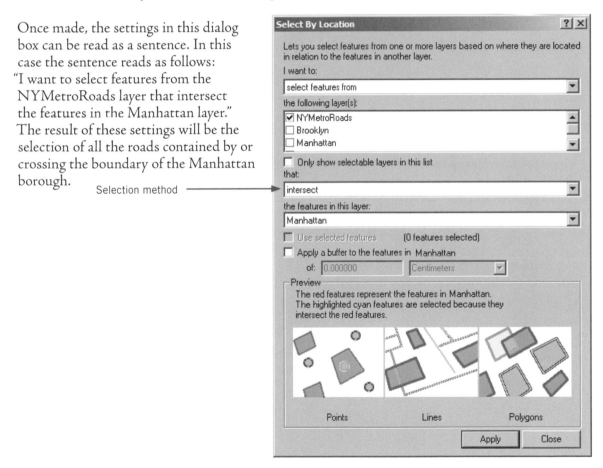

6 **Verify that your settings match those in the above dialog box, click Apply, then click Close.**

Show selected features and convert to shapefile

1   **Click View, Zoom Data, Zoom to Selected Features.**

The selected roads are only those within or those that intersect the Manhattan borough.

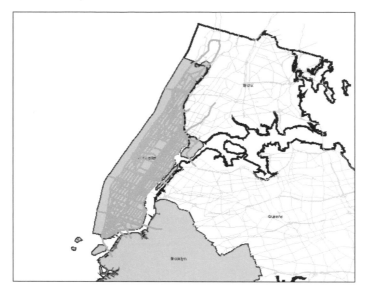

2   **In the table of contents, right-click the NYMetroRoads layer, click Data, Export Data.**

3   **Save the output shapefile as \Gistutorial\UnitedStates\NewYork\ManhattanRoads.shp.**

4   **Click OK, then click Yes to add the layer to the map.**

5   **Turn off the NYMetroRoads layer so the only roads visible in the map are those in the ManhattanRoads layer.**

Notice that some of the roads in the ManhattanRoads layer extend or "dangle" beyond the Manhattan borough outline.

Clip the Manhattan streets

Next, you will open the Clip tool from ArcToolbox and use it to cut off the street segments dangling outside the polygon that represents the borough of Manhattan. Once this is done, the streets in the ManhattanRoads layer will be clipped exactly to the edge of the Manhattan borough and saved within a new shapefile.

1   **Click the ArcToolbox button.**

2   **In ArcToolbox, click the plus (+) sign beside the Analysis Tools toolbox, then click the plus (+) sign to expand the Extract toolset.**

3   **In the Extract toolset, double-click the Clip tool to open its dialog box.**

4   **Click the Input Features drop-down list and choose NYMetroRoads.**

5   **Click the Clip Features drop-down list and choose Manhattan.**

6   **Save the Output Feature Class as \Gistutorial\UnitedStates\NewYork\ClippedManhattanRoads.shp.**

7   **Verify that your Clip settings match those in the graphic below, then click OK. Click Close when the process completes.**

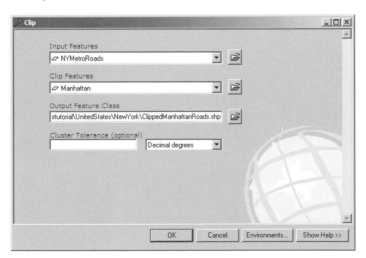

After the clip process completes, the output feature class is automatically added to your map.

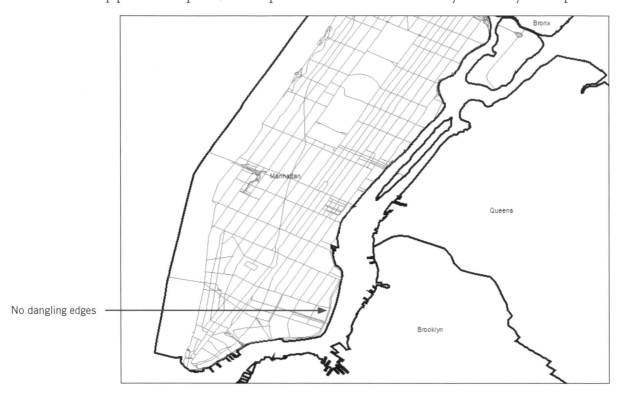

No dangling edges

8 **Turn on the ClippedManhattanRoads layer and turn off the ManhattanRoads layer.**

The streets in ClippedManhattanRoads layer do not cross the borough of Manhattan's boundary.

YOUR TURN

Using the Select By Location function in combination with the Clip tool, clip the NYMetroRoads roads to one of the other New York boroughs.

Dissolve features

It is often convenient or even necessary to form administrative or other types of boundaries by merging together polygons in a feature class that share a common attribute. This type of a merge is called a dissolve, and in this section you will use the Dissolve tool to dissolve zip code polygons based on their borough name.

Open an existing map

1   **If necessary, start ArcMap. In ArcMap, open Tutorial8-2.mxd from the \GISTutorial folder.**

Tutorial8-2 contains a map of the New York City Metro Area zip codes, including Manhattan, Brooklyn, Staten Island, the Bronx, and Queens.

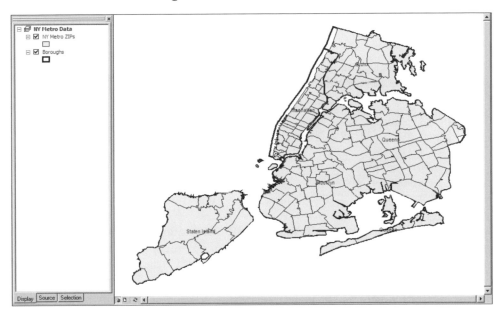

Dissolve zip codes using the ArcMap command line

In ArcToolbox, the Dissolve tool exists inside the Generalization toolset, which is inside the Data Management toolbox. All the geoprocessing tools, however, can be run from the Command Line window in ArcMap or ArcCatalog. Running a tool from the command line allows you to bypass opening the tool from ArcToolbox and interfacing with its dialog box. Instead, you type the name of the tool and its parameters as a string, then execute the tool by pressing Enter. This is a more direct route to a tool and its functionality, especially if you are already familiar with the tool and its parameter values.

1   Click Window, Command Line.

2   In the top half of the Command Line window, type **Dissolve.**

3   Press the space bar, choose NY Metro ZIPs from the pop-up list, then press Enter. This is your input feature class.

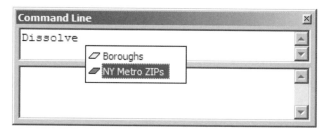

4   Press the space bar and type **C:\Gistutorial\UnitedStates\NewYork\DissolvedNYBoroughs.shp**. This is your output feature class. (If your Gistutorial folder is installed on a different drive or folder, change the path accordingly.)

5   Press the space bar and choose PO_NAME from the pop-up list. This is the field upon which the dissolve will be based.

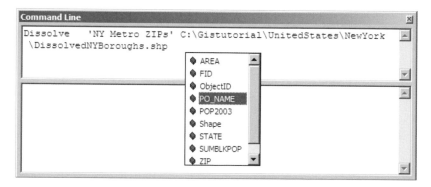

6 Press the space bar and choose POP2003.

This an optional setting. When the dissolve runs, the values in the POP2003 field will be summarized for each group of polygons with the same PO_NAME value. In other words, it will summarize the population for each new polygon feature.

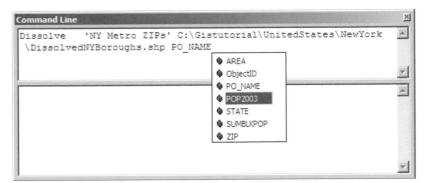

7 Type **SUM,** then place quotation marks around the last two parameter values so they read **"POP2003 SUM".**

The dissolve command should look like this →

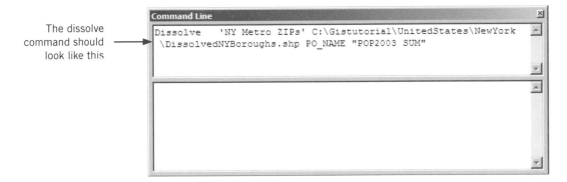

8 Press Enter.

The lower half of the Command Line window reports the status of the dissolve process and whether or not it successfully executes.

Once the dissolve process completes, the DissolvedNYBoroughs shapefile is automatically added to the map. This new shapefile contains the boundaries created from the dissolved zip codes polygons. The zip codes for the Queens borough were not dissolved, because the zip codes in that borough had unique values in the PO_NAME field.

9   **Use the Identify button** **to view the attribute information for each dissolved borough.**

In addition to the name of each borough, you will see a population value in the SUM_POP200 field, which was derived from the POP2003 values stored with the polygons that were dissolved.

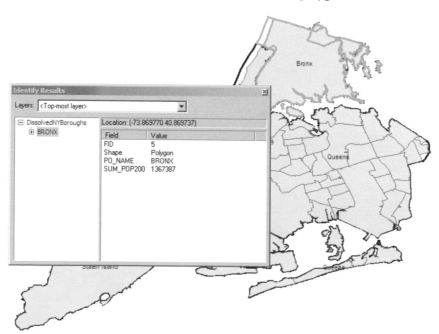

Append layers

Sometimes it is necessary to append (or merge) two or more separate layers into a single layer. For example, you may want to build a single soils layer for an environmental study that includes two adjacent counties, and you already have a soils layer for each county. Using the Append tool, you could merge these two soil layers into a single layer, then use the complete soil mosaic for further analysis. When running the Append command, input feature classes (layers) must have the same geometry type (point, line, or polygon). You can append feature classes that do not have identical attribute fields, but the differing fields will be dropped from the output.

Open an existing map

1   If necessary, start ArcMap, then open **Tutorial8-3.mxd** from your **\Gistutorial** folder.

Tutorial8-3.mxd contains a map of the New York City Metro Area's boroughs. Each borough in the map exists in a separate shapefile.

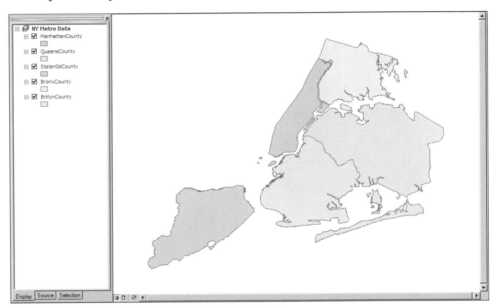

Create an empty polygon layer for appending

1   On the Standard toolbar, click the ArcCatalog button.

2   In ArcCatalog, create a new polygon shapefile named **AppendedNYBoroughs.shp** in the **\Gistutorial\UnitedStates\NewYork** folder.

3   Close ArcCatalog.

4   Add **AppendedNYBoroughs.shp** to ArcMap. (Click OK on the missing spatial reference message.)

Append several shapefiles into one shapefile

1   If necessary, open ArcToolbox in ArcMap by clicking the Show/Hide ArcToolbox button on the Standard toolbar.

2   In ArcToolbox, expand the Data Management Tools toolbox, then expand the General toolset.

3   Double-click Append.

4   Click the Input Features drop-down list and, one at a time, add all five New York Borough shapefiles to the Input Features list.

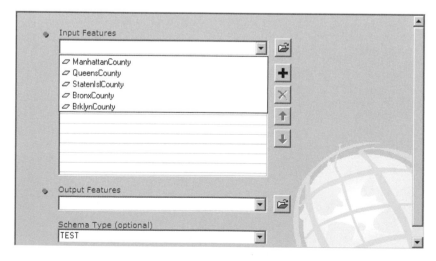

5   Click Output Features drop-down list and choose AppendedNYBoroughs.

6   Click the Schema Type drop-down list and choose NO_TEST.

7   Click OK. When the process is
     complete, click Close.

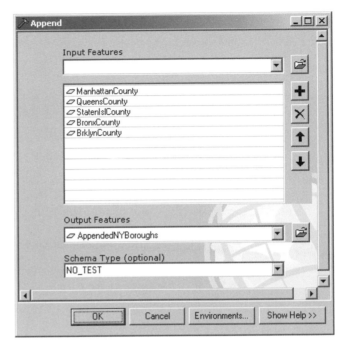

The AppendedNYBoroughs layer now contains all five boroughs of New York.

YOUR TURN

Practice using the Append tool by using it to append two New York boroughs.

Union layers

The Union tool performs a type of overlay in which the geometry and attributes of two input polygons layers are combined to generate a new output polygon layer. The output from a union contains polygon features derived from the geometric intersection of the input polygons; the output also contains the attributes from both inputs. For example, you could union a vegetation and soils layer, then query the output to find polygons with a specific vegetation and soil type.

In this example, you will union a layer containing the zip codes in the borough of Queens with a layer containing the boundary Queens. The output of the union will contain all the zip codes in Queens, and each zip code will have its borough name (Queens) assigned to it.

Open an existing map

1   If necessary, start ArcMap, then open **Tutorial8-4.mxd** from your **\Gistutorial** folder.

Tutorial8-4.mxd contains the borough of Queens and its zip codes.

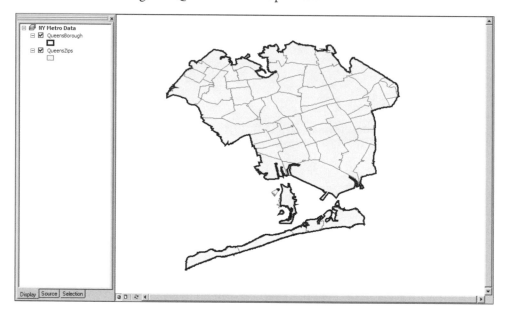

Union shapefiles

1   If necessary, open ArcToolbox.

2   In ArcToolbox, expand the Analysis Tools toolbox, then expand the Overlay toolset.

3   Double-click the Union tool.

4   From the Input Features drop-down list choose QueensBorough and QueensZips.

5   Save the Output Feature Class as **\Gistutorial\UnitedStates\NewYork\QueensBoroughZips_Union.shp**.

6   From the Join Attributes drop-down list, choose ALL.

7   Verify that your settings match those in the graphic below and click OK. Click Close when the
    process is complete.

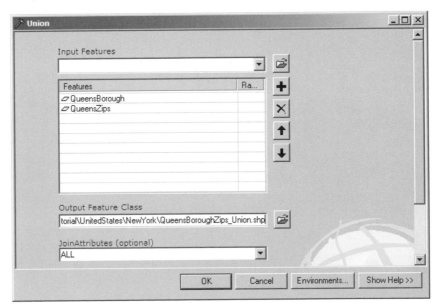

The output added to your map contains the zip code polygons with the borough name (Queens) now included in its attributes table.

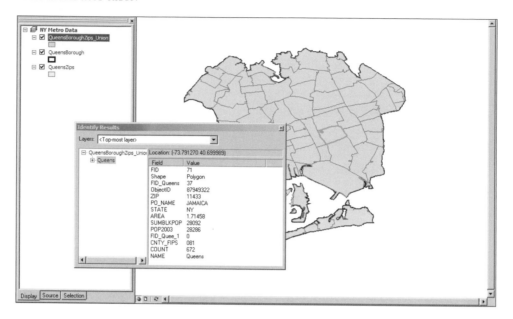

YOUR TURN

Look at the attribute table for the new layer you created. There are some features without a borough name. Why do you think this occurred, and how would you fix this using some of the techniques you learned in this tutorial?

Use the ArcMap Online Help to learn about Intersecting layers.

ModelBuilder

The geoprocessing tools in ArcGIS are often used together in sequence to perform spatial analysis. Sometimes there are many steps involved, making it difficult to keep track of the tools used, the datasets involved, and the parameters defined within the overall work flow.

ModelBuilder is an application within ArcView that you can use to document and automate your geoprocessing work flows. Within ModelBuilder, you construct model diagrams from the data and geoprocessing tools needed for your analysis or work flow. Once the model is built, you can run it once or save it and run it again using different input data parameters and tools.

ModelBuilder can be used to automate simple tasks which you frequently do, or it can be used to construct very complex analytical processes involving several data sources and geoprocessing tools. Either way, models are an excellent way to create and save a visual, shareable, and reusable GIS workflow model.

In this exercise, you will build a model that will clip then union a set of census tracts to a neighborhood layer.

Open an existing map

1   **If necessary, start ArcMap. Open the Tutorial8-5.mxd from your \Gistutorial folder.**

Tutorial8-5 contains the Pennsylvania census tracts and Pittsburgh neighborhoods. Although census tracts aggregate to neighborhoods, you will notice that some borders do not match exactly.

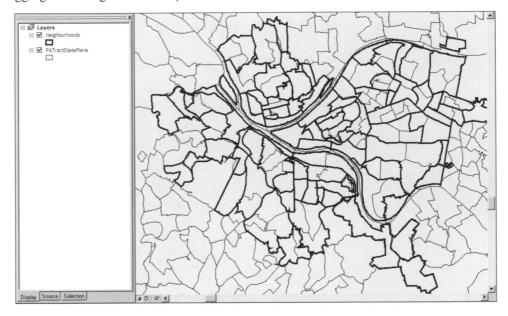

Create a new model

1   If necessary, open ArcToolbox.

2   Right-click any white space inside ArcToolbox, and choose New Toolbox.

3   Name the new toolbox ModelBuilder.

4   Right-click the ModelBuilder toolbox and click New, Model.

Choosing to create a new model automatically opens the Model window. You will use this window to create your model.

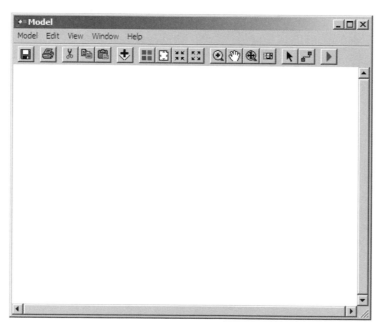

Add a Clip operation to the model

1   If necessary, position the Model window where you can see it simultaneously with ArcMap's table of contents. In ArcMap's table of contents, click the PATractStatePlane layer, then drag it into the Model window.

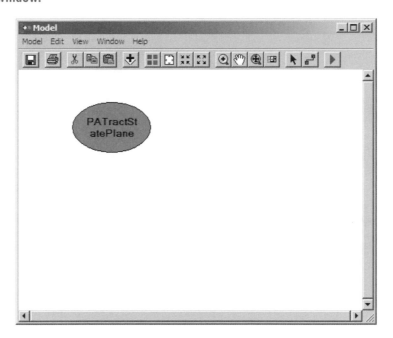

2   If necessary, position the Model window where you can see it and ArcToolbox at the same time. In ArcToolbox, expand the Analysis Tools toolbox, then expand the Extract toolset.

3   In the Extract toolset, click the Clip tool, then drag it into the Model window.

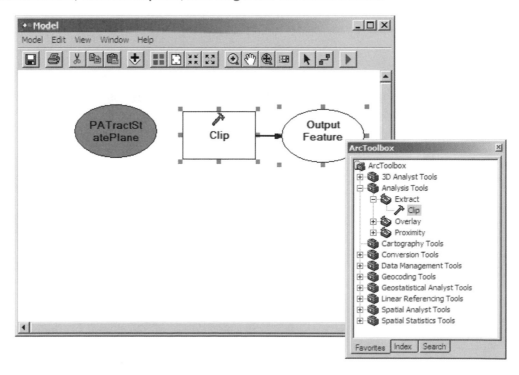

Connect PATractStatePlane layer to Clip tool

1   From the Model toolbar, click the Add Connection button.

2   In the Model window, click the PATractStatePlane layer and drag a line to the Clip tool.

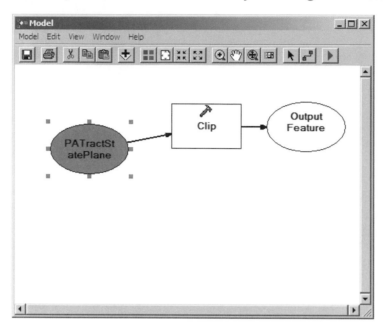

3   From the Model toolbar, click the Select button.

4   In the Model window, double-click the Clip tool.

The Clip tool's dialog box appears with the Input Features property already defined (PATractStatePlane).

5   From the Clip Features drop-down list, select the Neighborhoods layer.

6   Save the Output Feature Class as **\Gistutorial\UnitedStates\Pennsylvania\PATractStatePlane_Clip.shp**. (This will be the default path and name.)

7   Verify that your settings match those in the graphic shown at right, then click OK.

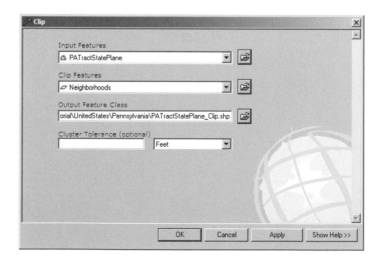

Connect Union function to layers

1   In ArcToolbox, expand the Analysis Tools toolbox, then expand the Overlay toolset.

2   In the Overlay toolset, click the Union tool, then drag it into the Model window.

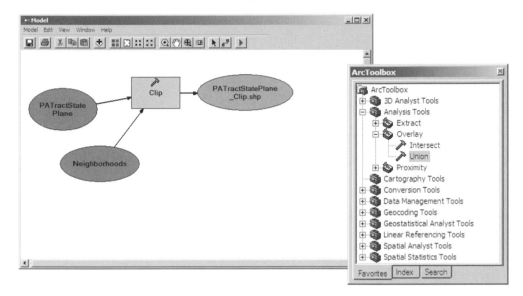

3   From the Model toolbar, click the Add Connection button.

4   In the Model window, click PATractStatePlane_Clip.shp and drag a line to the Union tool.

5   In the Model window, click Neighborhoods and drag a line to the Union tool.

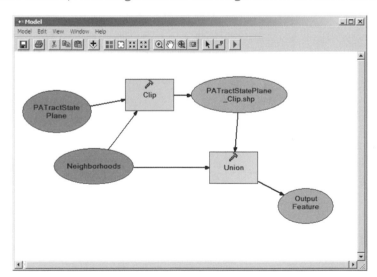

6   From the Model toolbar, click the Select button, then double-click the Union tool in the Model window.

7   Name the Output Feature Class **TractNeigh_Clip_Union.shp** and save it in the **\Gistutorial\ UnitedStates\Pennsylvania** folder.

8   Verify that your settings match those in the graphic below, then click OK.

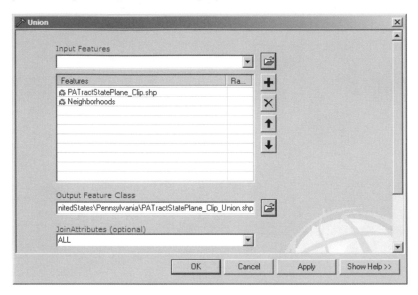

9   Open the Model toolbar, click the Auto Layout button, then click the Full Extent button.

Clicking the Auto Layout button followed by the Full Extent button is a good way to quickly organize and get a full view of your model.

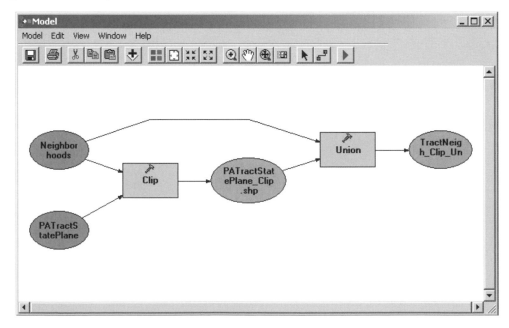

Run the model

1   From the Model menu, click Model, Run.

The functions will process and the following messages will appear, indicating that the model was successful.

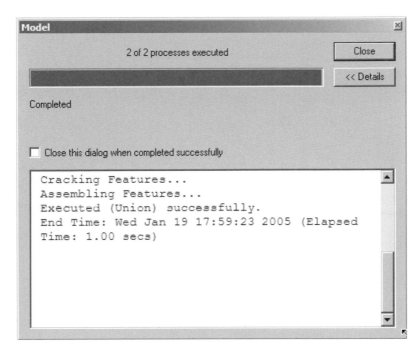

2   Click Close when the process is complete.

Display the new shapefile

1   In the Model window, right-click TractNeigh_Clip_Union.shp and choose Add to Display.

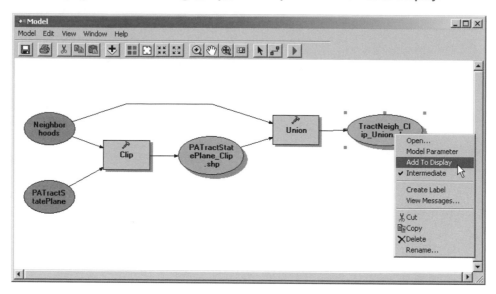

2   Close the Model window and save your changes to the model.

3   In the ArcMap table of contents, uncheck the Neighborhoods and PATractStatePlane layers.

The TractNeigh_Clip_Union layer contains the census tracts that exist within the boundaries defined by the neighborhoods layer. This new layer also contains all the attributes from the Neighborhoods and PATractStatePlane layers.

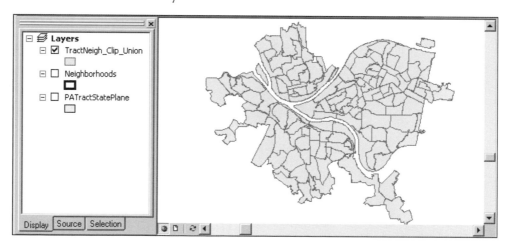

4   Use the Identify tool to view the neighborhood name and information for each
    census tract.

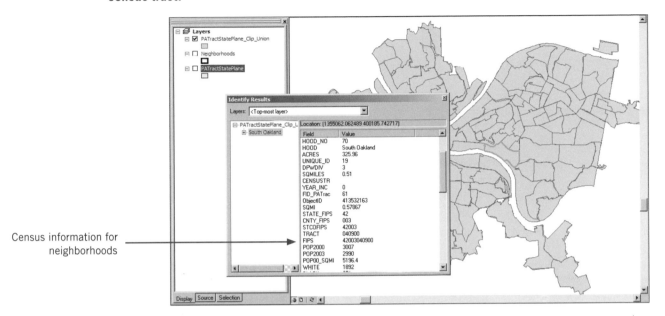

Census information for
neighborhoods

YOUR TURN

Open the Model window (in ArcToolbox, right-click your new model and choose Edit), add the
Dissolve tool to the model, and dissolve the tracts based on neighborhood names. Also, when setting
up the dissolve options, choose to summarize the population within each neighborhood.

Exercise Assignment 8-1

Build a study region for Colorado counties

GIS layers are typically available at a county or state level, but study areas sometimes need to be created for smaller areas such as neighborhoods or regions. A study area may also span across more than one county. GIS specialists can use the ArcView geoprocessing tools such as Clip, Union, and Dissolve to extract study area layers from a larger map collection or combine two or more areas together.

According to the U.S. Census, the western part of the United States is the fastest growing region. Colorado's population grew 30 percent from 1990 to 2000. Many Colorado residents are living in "exurbia"—the area beyond the suburbs and outside the limits of urban growth studies. This growth beyond the suburbs is becoming a problem because services such as police, fire, water, transportation, electricity, and so on, must be provided to residents and can be costly. In addition, many people living in exurbia still work in cities (rather than forming independent towns where they live), so transportation and pollution are an issue.

One solution to this problem is to define "smart growth"—boundaries which, according to the Urban Land Institute, call for compact suburban development integrated into existing commercial areas or new town centers, with proximity to transportation facilities. Smart growth policies that focus on land-use issues are defined as development that is environmentally sensitive, economically viable, community-oriented, and sustainable.

In this assignment, you will create a study area to study the population for two rapidly growing counties in Colorado, Denver, and Jefferson counties. You will create new shapefiles for an urban area study using polygon shapefiles downloaded from the U.S. Census Web site. Since we want to study two counties, some of the shapefiles need to be joined together, and some need to be clipped to a smaller study area. Additional studies would add other counties surrounding Denver and Jefferson counties.

Start with the following:

- **C:\Gistutorial\UnitedStates\Colorado\Counties.shp**—polygon shapefile of Colorado counties.
- **C:\Gistutorial\UnitedStates\Colorado\Streets.shp**—TIGER line shapefile of Jefferson County streets.
- **C:\Gistutorial\UnitedStates\Colorado\Streets2.shp**—TIGER line shapefile of Denver County streets.
- **C:\Gistutorial\UnitedStates\Colorado\MergedStreets.shp**—line shapefile temporarily used to append streets and streets2 using ModelBuilder.
- **C:\Gistutorial\UnitedStates\Cities_dtl**—point shapefile of detailed cities.
- **UA_08059.shp**—urban area polygons for Jefferson County, Colorado, downloaded from *www.esri.com* and saved to the Answers folder.
- **UA_08031.shp**—urban area polygons for Denver County, Colorado, downloaded from *www.esri.com* and saved to the Answers folder.

Create a study area map of Colorado urban areas

In ArcCatalog, create a new personal geodatabase called C:\Gistutorial\Answers\Assignment8\UrbanAreaStudy.mdb with the new study area shapefiles imported into it. Be sure to add all of the new study area layers from your personal geodatabase. See hints on what study areas to create.

In ArcMap, create a new map called C:\Gistutorial\Answers\Assignment8\Assignment8-1.mxd with a layout showing the urban area study area as one shapefile (downloaded study areas unioned together), one streets layer of streets in the urban area study only (streets appended and clipped using ModelBuilder), and a graduated point layer showing detailed city populations in the study area of Jefferson and Denver counties. Symbolize, rename, and label the layers to your liking. Consider showing the streets when zoomed to a detailed scale where you can see them.

Export the layout as C:\Gistutorial\Answers\Assignment8\Assignment8.pdf.

Creating study area hints
- Create a new feature class of just Jefferson and Denver counties called C:\Gistutorial\Answers\Assignment8\ UrbanAreaStudy.mdb\StudyAreaCounties.shp.
- Union UA_08059.shp and UA_08031.shp to create a feature class called C:\Gistutorial\Answers\ Assignment8\UrbanAreaStudy.mdb\StudyUrbanArea.shp.
- Create a new feature class for detailed cities that are within Denver and Jefferson counties called C:\Gistutorial\Answers\Assignment8\UrbanAreaStudy.mdb\StudyAreaCities.shp.

ModelBuilder hints to create study area merged streets
In ArcToolbox, create a new toolbox called StudyAreaStreets with the following model functions:
- Append streets.shp and streets2.shp, using them as the input layers and mergedstreets.shp as the output layer.
- Clip the appended streets to the Study Urban Area polygon.
Save the final merged and clipped streets as a feature class called C:\Gistutorial\Answers\Assignment8\ UrbanAreaStudy.mdb\StudyAreaStreets.

Questions
Perform the necessary queries and spatial analysis to answer the following questions. Save your answer in a document called C:\Gistutorial\Answers\Assignment8\Assignment8.doc.

1   List the names of all the detailed cities within the Urban Area.
2   What Denver and Jefferson county cities are within ten miles of Denver?
3   What is the total population of these cities?
4   What cities are within one mile of streets called Wadsworth?
    (Hint: FE_NAME=Wadsworth)

Exercise Assignment 8-2

Dissolve property parcels to create a zoning map

Many city planning departments use GIS to create property parcel and zoning maps. In this exercise, you will help a neighborhood community group create a zoning map for a citizen's meeting. The city planner provides a parcel map that has details about the type of zoning for each parcel; however, the citizen's group wants to see a general zoning map. You will create the zoning map by dissolving the parcel features based on a common value (zoning code).

Visit the city of Pittsburgh's Web site to learn more about zoning codes *(www.city.pittsburgh.pa.us/cp/html/land_use_control_and_zoning.html).*

Start with the following:

- **C:\Gistutorial\PAGIS\EastLiberty\Parcels**—parcel map for the East Liberty neighborhood of Pittsburgh, Pennsylvania, with zoning data.
- **C:\Gistutorial\PAGIS\EastLiberty\EastLib**—polygon outline for the East Liberty neighborhood of Pittsburgh, Pennsylvania.

Create zoning map

In ArcGIS, create a new personal geodatabase called C:\Gistutorial\Answers\Assignment8\ZoningMap.mdb and import the parcels into it.

In ArcMap, create a new map called C:\Gistutorial\Answers\Assignment8\Assignment8-2.mxd with a layout that includes the East Liberty parcels dissolved and shown as unique values for each zoning code. Consider grouping zoning codes together with similar color schemes to make them easier to read. Rename and label all layers appropriately.

Export the layout in a file called C:\Gistutorial\Answers\Assignment8-2.pdf.

Importing hints
- Before importing EastLib and Parcels into the ZoningMap.mdb, convert them to layer files by right-clicking them in ArcCatalog and choosing Create Layer. Once this is done, you can import the two new layer files into the geodatabase.

Dissolving hints
- Use the Dissolve dialog box from ArcToolbox instead of dissolve at the command prompt.
- Dissolve the parcels on the 'ZON_CODE' field. Call the new file C:\Gistutorial\Answers\Assignment8\ZoningMap.mdb\Zoning.
- In the Dissolve dialog box, add a summary of tax information for fields TAX_AREA, TAX_BLDG_A, and TAX_LAND_A. This will add these fields to the dissolved parcels, summarizing the tax values for each zoning type.

Questions

Add the following questions to C:\Gistutorial\Answers\Assignment8\Assignment8.doc.

There are two zoning codes whose land tax numbers are over two million.

5   What are those zoning codes?
6   What is the zoning code with the lowest land tax value?
7   What is its value?

What to turn in

If you are working in a classroom setting with an instructor, you may be required to submit the exercises you created in tutorial 8. Below are the files you are required to turn in. Be sure to use a compression program such as PKZIP or WinZip to include all three files as one .zip document for review and grading. Include your name and assignment number in the .zip document (YourNameAssn8.zip). *Do not* turn in interim files that are not in your final map (e.g., HHW participants geocoded point shapefile).

Note: *Do not* submit any of the original files that queries were performed from or .zip files that were downloaded for assignment 8-1. Only submit final shapefiles, projects, and Word documents.

ArcMap projects

C:\Gistutorial\Answers\Assignment8\Assignment8-1.mxd
C:\Gistutorial\Answers\Assignment8\Assignment8-2.mxd

Exported maps

C:\Gistutorial\Answers\Assignment8\Assignment8-1.pdf
C:\Gistutorial\Answers\Assignment8\Assignment8-2.pdf

Personal geodatabase

Important note: It is especially important to compact the personal geodatabases in this exercise. Compact them in ArcCatalog by right-clicking and choosing "Compact Database."
C:\Gistutorial\Answers\Assignment8\UrbanAreaStudy.mdb (includes shapefiles for Urban Areas, Study Area Counties, Study Area Cities, and Study Area Streets)
C:\Gistutorial\Answers\Assignment8\ZoningMap.mdb (includes Parcels shapefile)

Word document

C:\Gistutorial\Answers\Assignment8\Assignment8.doc

Create buffer points for proximity analysis
Conduct a site suitability analysis
Apportion data for noncoterminous polygons

GIS Tutorial 9

Spatial Analysis

The coordinates information associated with spatial data permits the use of special algorithms designed especially for GIS applications. For instance, it is possible to place buffers around features or retrieve features nearby other features for proximity analysis (for example, find crime locations near properties with crime-prone land uses such as bars). It is also possible to use spatial joins to carry out complex spatial processing, such as apportioning census tract data to police administrative areas. In this case, census tracts may be subdivided into two or more police administrative areas, so an approximation is needed to divvy up or apportion tract data to the police administrative areas. GIS is also useful for site selection analysis, especially when it involves several selection criteria, such as being in a business area, on a major street, and centrally located.

Buffer points for proximity analysis

Some land uses, like bars, attract crime. It is a good idea for police to keep track of crimes in the vicinity of bars, and it is possible to do this with GIS using circular buffers. Note: There are no *Your Turn* exercises in this chapter because there is sufficient replication of steps within the exercises.

Open map

1   **From the Windows taskbar, click Start, All Programs, ArcGIS, ArcMap.**

2   **Click the An existing map radio button in the ArcMap dialog box and click OK.**

3   **Browse to the drive on which the Gistutorial folder has been installed (e.g., C:\Gistutorial), select Tutorial9-1.mxd, and click Open.**

Tutorial9-1.mxd contains a map of the Lake precinct of the Rochester, New York, Police Department. Shown are assault crime offense points, bars, police car beats (with one patrol car assigned to each beat), and street centerlines.

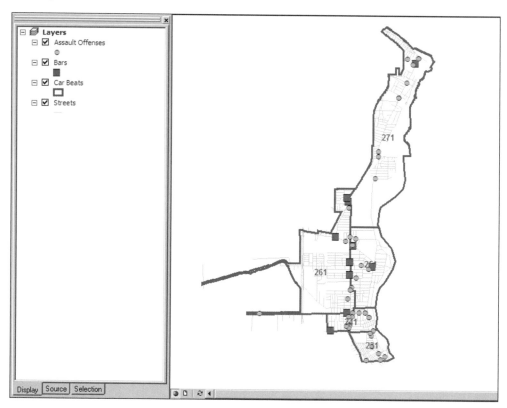

Buffer bars

1   Click the Show/Hide ArcToolbox Window button to open ArcToolbox.

2   In ArcToolbox, click the plus (+) sign beside the Analysis Tools toolbox to expand it, then expand the Proximity toolset.

3   Double-click the Buffer tool.

4   From the Input Features drop-down list, choose Bars.

5   Save the Output Feature Class as **\Gistutorial\LakePrecinct\Lake.mdb\Buffer_of_Bars**.

6   Click the Linear Unit radio button and type 0.25 in the field below it, then select Miles from the Units drop-down list to the right.

7   From the Dissolve Type drop-down list, choose ALL. (You may need to scroll down the dialog box to see this setting.)

8   Click OK, then click Close when the process is complete.

9   Change the symbology of the Buffer_of_Bars layer to a hollow fill.

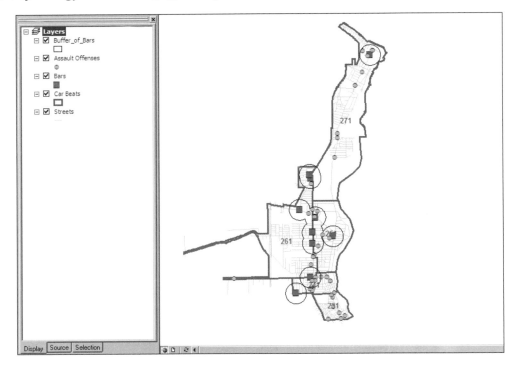

Extract assault offenses in bar buffers

1 In ArcMap, click Selection, Select by Location.

2 In the Select By Location dialog box, set the
options to select features from the Assault
Offenses layer that intersect the features in the
Buffer_of_Bars layer. Verify that your settings
match those in the graphic shown (at right),
then click Apply and Close.

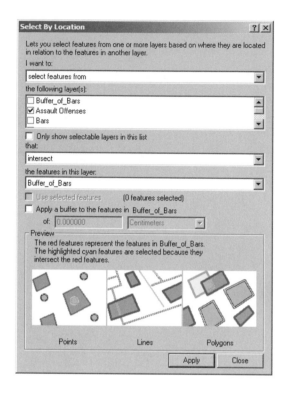

After running the Select By Location command, all the assault points within bar buffer zones
are selected.

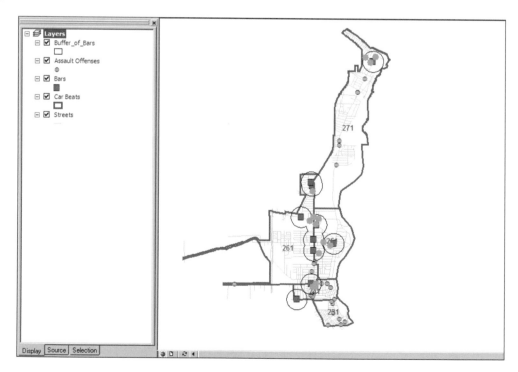

3   In the table of contents, right-click the Assault Offenses layer and click Data and Export Data.

4   In the Export Data dialog box, make sure that Selected features is chosen from the Export drop-down list and that Use the same Coordinate System as this layer's source data is selected. Name the output shapefile **AssaultsInBarsBuffers.shp** and save it in the **\Gistutorial\LakePrecinct** folder. Check your settings against the following graphic, click OK, then click Yes to add the layer to your map.

5   Turn off the Assault Offenses layer.

This is the kind of map that a task force working on problem bars would want for making its case to enforce laws at bars or close bars down. Another good example like this is drug dealing within 1,000 feet of a school, which can result in doubled sentences for arrested drug dealers.

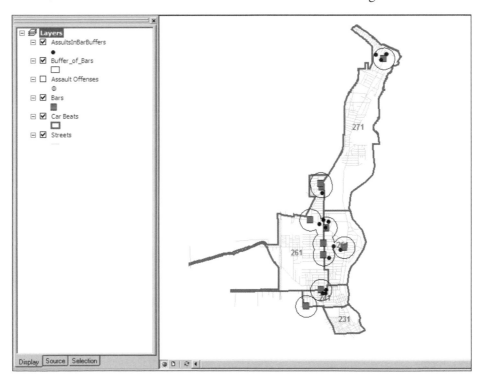

6   From the File menu, click Save to save your map.

Conduct a site suitability analysis

Suitability analysis is a common and classic type of GIS application. Typically, this type of analysis consists of several steps that include attribute- and location-based queries, buffers, spatial joins, and overlays. In this exercise, you will perform suitability analysis with the purpose of locating potential areas for new police satellite stations in each car beat of the Lake precinct of Rochester, New York. Criteria for locating these stations are that the site must be centrally located in each car beat (within a 0.33-mile radius buffer of car beat centroids), and that the site must be in retail/commercial areas (within 0.10 mile of at least one retail business and within 0.10 mile of major streets).

Open a map

1   If necessary, start ArcMap.

2   In ArcMap, open the **Tutorial9-2.mxd** from the **\Gistutorial** folder.

Tutorial9-2.mxd contains a car beat map of the Lake precinct of the Rochester, New York, Police Department. Also shown in the map are retail business points and street centerlines.

Add X and Y columns to car beats

1   In the table of contents, right-click the Car Beats layer and click Open Attribute Table.

2   In the Attributes of Car Beats table, click Options, Add Field.

3   In the Add Field dialog box, name the new field **X**, choose Double from the Type drop-down list, then click OK.

4   Click Options, Add Field.

5   Name the new field **Y**, set its Type to Double, then click OK.

Compute car beat centroids

The following steps use some Visual Basic code for creating car beat centroids. You do not have to understand the code, just type it in exactly as shown in the steps.

1   In the Attributes of Car Beats table, right-click the X column heading and click Calculate Values. Click Yes to calculate outside of an edit session.

2   In the Field Calculator, check the Advanced box.

This allows you to type in a Pre-Logic VBA (Visual Basic) Script Code.

3 In the Pre-Logic VBA Script Code field type:

```
Dim dblX As Double
Dim pArea As IArea
Set pArea = [Shape]
dblX = pArea.Centroid.X
```

4 In the X = field type **dblX**. Verify that your dialog box matches the following graphic, then click OK.

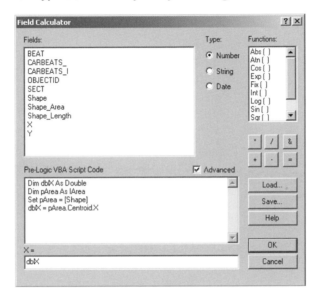

5 Open the Field Calculator for the Y field and click Yes to calculate values outside an edit session.

6 In the Field Calculator dialog box, check the Advanced box.

7 In the Pre-Logic VBA Script field type:

```
Dim dblY As Double
Dim pArea As IArea
Set pArea = [Shape]
dblY = pArea.Centroid.Y
```

8 In the Y = field, type **dblY**, then click OK.

Each record in the Attributes of Car Beats table now contains an X and Y coordinate value. Each X,Y pair represents the centroid of a police car beat. To learn more about using VB Script within the Field Calculator, and to see common scripting examples, search for *Making Field Calculations* in the ArcGIS Desktop Help.

X	Y
1397139.549464	1165093.524371
1404519.587559	1179549.785764
1402264.268132	1165279.502132
1400522.350349	1158989.873773
1402631.818900	1156203.703772

Map car beat centroids

You can directly map x,y coordinates as points.

1   In the Attributes of Car Beats table, click Options, Export.

2   In Export Data dialog box, name the output table **CarBeatCentroids** and save it in **\Gistutorial\ LakePrecinct\Lake.mdb**, then click OK. Click Yes to add the new table to your current map.

Make sure you save the file to Lake.mdb.

3   Close the Attributes of Car Beats table.

4   Click Tools, Add XY Data.

5   In the Add XY Data dialog box, choose CarBeatCentroids from the Choose a table drop-down list.

6   In the lower-right corner of the Add XY data dialog box, click Edit.

7   In the Spatial Reference Properties window, click Import.

8   In the Browse for Dataset window, navigate to **\Gistutorial\LakePrecinct\Lake.mdb**, click **lakecarbeats**, then click Add.

9   Click OK twice.

CarBeatCentroids Events is added as a layer to your map. The word "Events" is used because x,y data is often collected and used to represent events which occurred at a specific time and location.

10 Symbolize the CarBeatCentroids Events layer with a red color and a size value of 12.

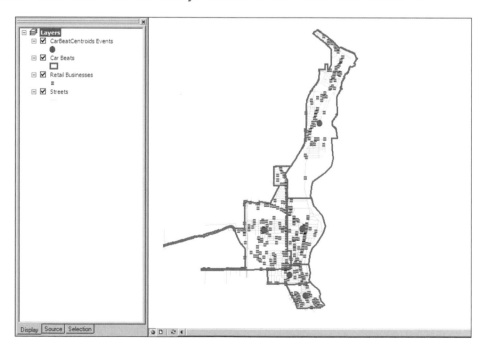

Buffer car beat centroids

1   If necessary, open ArcToolbox.

2   In ArcToolbox, expand the Analysis Tools toolbox, then expand the Proximity toolset.

3   Double-click the Buffer tool.

4   In the Buffer dialog box, click the Input Features drop-down list and choose CarBeatCentroids Events.

5   Save the Output Feature Class as **\Gistutorial\LakePrecinct\Lake.mdb\Buffer_of_Car_Beat_Centroids_Events**.

6   Make sure the Linear Unit option is chosen, then click in the distance field directly below it and type **0.33**. From the units drop-down list, choose Miles.

7   From the Dissolve Type drop-down list, choose ALL.

8   Click OK, then click Close when the process completes.

The Buffer_of_Car_BeatCentroids_Events layer is added to the map. Now you need to find areas within the car beat buffers that meet the remaining criteria.

9   Symbolize the buffers polygons with a hollow fill, set the Outline Color to Mars Red, then set the Outline Width to 1.

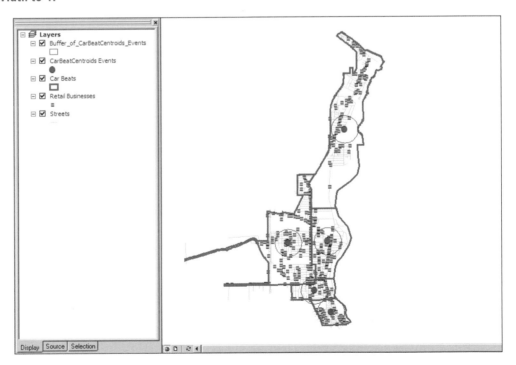

Buffer retail businesses

1 If necessary, open ArcToolbox.

2 Expand the Analysis Tools toolbox, then expand the Proximity toolset.

3 Double-click the Buffer tool.

4 Select Retail Businesses from the Input Features drop-down list.

5 Save the Output features as **\Gistutorial\LakePrecinct\Lake.mdb\Buffer_of_Retail_Businesses**.

6 Click the Linear Unit radio button, type **0.10** for the distance, and change the distance units to Miles.

7 From the Dissolve Type drop-down, choose ALL.

8 Click OK, then click Close when the process is complete.

The Buffer_of_Retail_Businesses layer is automatically added to the map.

9 Symbolize the new buffer layer with a hollow fill, set the Outline Color to Ultra Blue, and the Outline Width to 1.

10 In the table of contents, turn off the CarBeatCentroid Events and the Retail Businesses layers.

The intersection of the Buffer_of_Retail_Businesses and Buffer_of_CarBeatCentroids_Events nearly satisfies the suitability criteria, but you still need to buffer the streets.

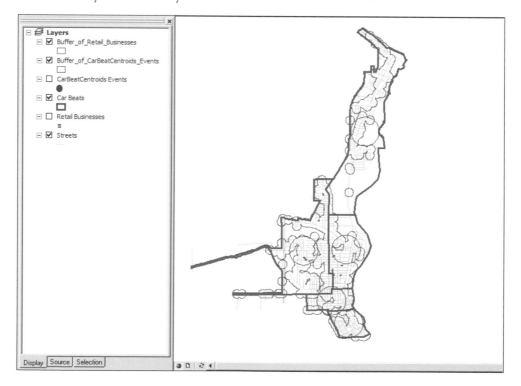

Select major streets

Major and commercial streets have FCC code values of A40 and A41 in the streets layer. You will select only those streets and then buffer them.

1   In ArcMap, click Selection, Select By Attributes.

2   In the Select By Attributes window, select Streets for the Layer and Create a new selection as the Method. Scroll down in the Fields box and double-click [FCC]. Click the = button, then click the Get Unique Values button. Double-click 'A40' in the Unique Values box, then click the Or button. Double-click [FCC], click the = button, then double-click 'A41'. Verify that your settings match those in the graphic shown at right, then click Apply and Close.

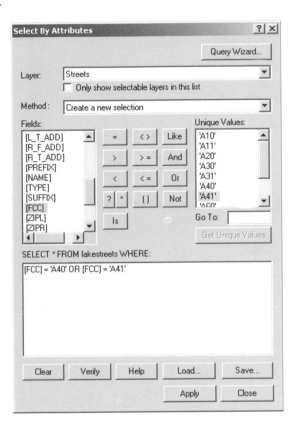

Major and commercial streets turn the selection color.

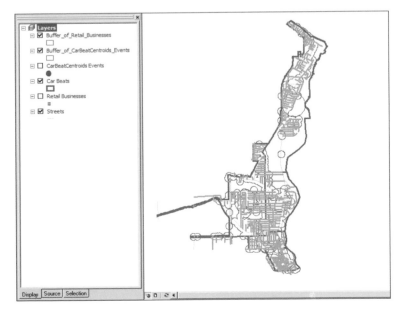

Buffer major streets

1   If necessary, open ArcToolbox.

2   In ArcToolbox, navigate to, then open the Buffer tool.

3   In the Buffer dialog box, set the Input Features to Streets.

4   Save the Output features as **C:\Gistutorial\LakePrecinct\Lake.mdb\Buffer_of_Streets**.

5   Choose the Linear Unit option, then set the distance to 0.10 Miles.

6   From the Dissolve Type drop-down list, choose ALL.

7   Click OK, then click Close when the process is complete.

The Buffer_of_Streets polygon layer is automatically added to the map.

8   Symbolize the new buffer layer with a hollow fill, set the Outline Color to Gray 60%, then set the Outline Width to 1.

9   In the table of contents, turn off the Streets layer.

The intersection of all three sets of buffers satisfies the suitability criteria. The latest buffer is mostly redundant, but it does rule out a few retail business buffers.

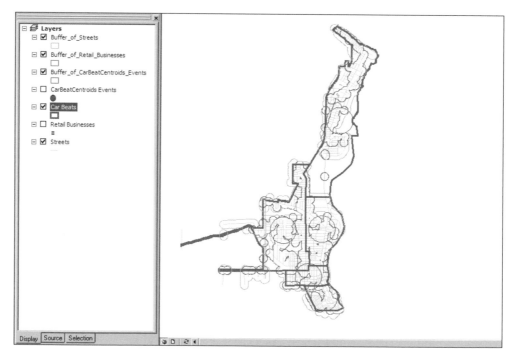

Intersect buffers

1 In ArcToolbox, expand the Analysis Tools toolbox, then expand the Overlay toolset. Double-click the Intersect tool.

2 From the Input Features drop-down list, choose Buffer_of_Streets, then choose Buffer_of_Retail_ Businesses from the list.

3 Save the Output Feature Class as **\Gistutorial\LakePrecinct\Lake.mdb\Streets_Retail_Intersect**.

4 Click OK, then click Close when the process completes.

The resulting intersection layer contains only the areas that overlap in the two input layers.

5 From ArcToolbox, open the Intersect dialog box again.

6 In the Intersect dialog box, set the Input Features to Streets_Retail_Intersect and Buffer_of_ CarBeatCentroids_Events.

7 Save the Output Feature Class as **C:\Gistutorial\LakePrecinct\Lake.mdb\SuitableSites**.

8 Click OK, then click Close when the process is complete.

9 Symbolize SuitableSites with a hollow fill, change the Outline Color to Leaf Green, then set the Outline Width to 1.

10 Click Selection, Clear Selected Features to clear the selected streets.

11 Turn off all layers except SuitableSites, Car Beats, and Streets.

12 Save the map.

That completes the task. The green areas are suitable for satellite police stations. Next, a staff person could work with realty companies to locate specific sites within the suitable areas.

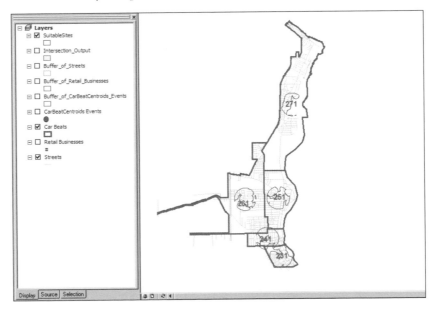

Apportion data for noncoterminous polygons

Often you will not have raw point data, but only aggregate data consisting of polygons. A good example is census data, which is totaled for polygon layers from counties down to blocks. Nevertheless, your need may be for much different types of polygon boundaries, namely, administrative areas such as police car beats (areas served by patrol cars). For example, the Rochester, New York, Police Department designed their administrative areas to meet police needs and, consequently, car beat boundaries do not always follow census tract boundaries. If you need census data by car beats, you will have to apportion (make approximate splits of) each tract's data to two or more car beats.

1 If necessary, start ArcMap.

2 In ArcMap, open the **Tutorial9-3.mxd** from the **\Gistutorial** folder.

Tutorial9-3 contains a map of car beats and census tracts in the Lake precinct of the Rochester Police Department. You will find several cases where car beats contain only portions of tracts.

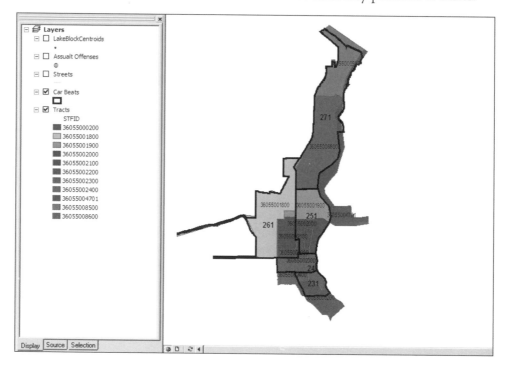

Approach to apportionment

Apportioning data from one set of polygons to another is a complex task, so much so that we thought it best to give you some background and a preview of steps. Census data from the census long form, such as data on educational attainment for the population aged 25 or older, is available at the census tract level but not at the block level. In contrast, short form census data is available down to the city block level.

<table>
<tr>
<td>

1 In ArcMap's table of contents, turn off Tracts layer and turn on the LakeBlockCentroids and Streets layers.

</td>
<td>

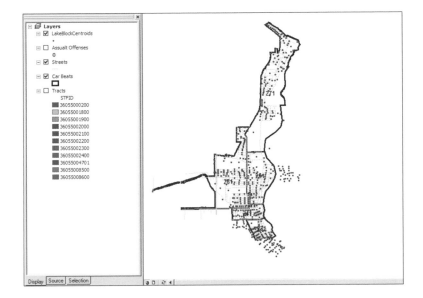

</td>
</tr>
</table>

The centroids have short form data allowing us to tabulate population for those 22 or older. The provided break points for general population do not allow us to tabulate 25 or older, but 22 or older is close enough in this case.

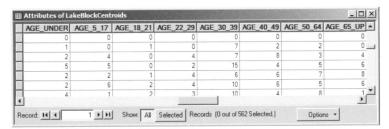

There are several alternatives for apportioning data for example, by area, length of street network, or the block centroids population. We chose the last method, because it is one of the most accurate. We *assume* that the variable being apportioned, in our case the number of people 25 or older who have less than a high school education, is spatially distributed within the census tract proportionally to general population aged 22 or older at the block level. We use block centroids instead of block polygons because the blocks are relatively small and can be safely represented by points to make the spatial data processing easier.

Note: If you merely need short-form census data, available for the block centroids, a simple spatial overlay of a polygon layer like car beats on block centroids (see tutorial 4) and the aggregation of resultant data is all that is needed instead of apportionment.

The math of apportionment

Let's take a look at one example. Below is a close-up of tract 360550002100, which is split between car beats 261 and 251.

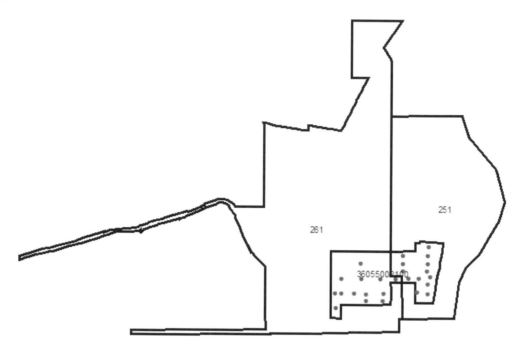

Tract 360550002100 has 205 people aged 25 or older with less than a high school education. For short, let's call this the under-educated population. How can we divide those 205 undereducated people between car beats 261 and 251?

Of the 26 blocks making up the tract, the 13 that lie in car beat 261 have 1,177 people aged 22 or older. The other 13 blocks, in car beat 251, have 1,089 such people for a total of 2,266 for the tract.

Apportionment assumes that the fraction of undereducated people aged 25 or older is the same as that for the general population aged 22 or older: 1,177 ÷ 2,266 = 0.519. For the other car beat, it is 1,089 ÷ 2,266 = 0.481.

Thus, we estimate the contribution of tract 36055002100 to car beat 261's undereducated population to be (1,177 ÷ 2,266)×205 = 106. For car beat 251, it is (1,089 ÷ 2,266)×205 = 99.

Eventually, by apportioning all tracts, we can sum up the total undereducated population for car beats 261 and 251.

Preview of apportionment steps

The following is a summary of the steps that you will complete in the following pages.

1   In the attribute table for block centroids, create two new fields: the census tract ID for each block and the sum across age groups for the general population aged 22 or older in each block.

2   In the attribute table for block centroids, sum the field for persons aged 22 or older by tract ID to create a new table.

3   Spatially join the tract and car beats layers to create new polygons that each have a tract ID and car beat number.

4   Spatially overlay the joined layer of tracts and car beats onto the block centroids to assign all the tract attributes (including the attribute of interest, undereducated population) and car beat attributes to blocks.

5   Join the table from step 2 to block centroids in order to make the apportionment weight denominator, total population aged 22 or older by tract, available to each block centroid.

6   For each block centroid, create new fields to store apportionment weight and apportioned under-educated population values, then calculate these values for the new fields.

7   Sum the apportionment weights by tract as a check for accuracy (they should sum to 1.0 for each tract), then sum the undereducated population per car beat, storing the results in new tables.

8   Join the table containing undereducated population by car beat to the car beats layer, then symbolize the data for map display.

Completing all of these steps and understanding the concepts and GIS implementation will be your crowning achievement in this tutorial textbook!

Create Tract ID and AGE22Plus fields in the attributes of block centroids

1 In ArcMap's table of contents, right-click the LakeBlockCentroids layer and click Open Attribute Table.

2 In the Attributes of LakeBlockCentroids table, click Options, Add Field.

3 In the Add Field window, type **TractID** in the Name box, change the Type to Text, change the Length to 11, and click OK.

4 In the Attributes of LakeBlockCentroids table, click Options, Add Field.

5 Name the new field **Age22Plus**, set its Type to Short Integer, then click OK.

6 In the Attributes of LakeBlockCentroids table, scroll to the right end of the table, right-click the column heading for TractID, click Calculate Values, and click Yes.

7 In the Field Calculator, set the Type option to String. In the Fields box, click FIPSSTCO, click the & button, then, in the Fields box, click Tract2000. Verify that your settings match those shown below, then click OK.

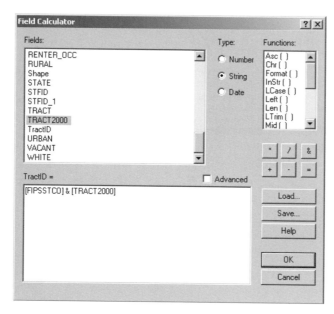

Values from the FIPSSTCO and Tract2000 field are concatenated and placed in the TractID field.

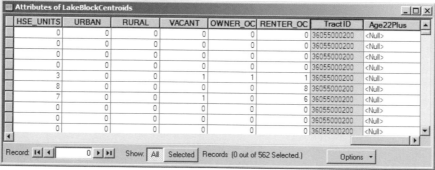

HSE_UNITS	URBAN	RURAL	VACANT	OWNER_OC	RENTER_OC	TractID	Age22Plus
0	0	0	0	0	0	36055000200	<Null>
0	0	0	0	0	0	36055000200	<Null>
0	0	0	0	0	0	36055000200	<Null>
0	0	0	0	0	0	36055000200	<Null>
3	0	0	1	1	1	36055000200	<Null>
8	0	0	0	0	8	36055000200	<Null>
7	0	0	1	0	6	36055000200	<Null>
0	0	0	0	0	0	36055000200	<Null>
0	0	0	0	0	0	36055000200	<Null>
0	0	0	0	0	0	36055000200	<Null>

Record: |◄ ◄ | 0 | ► ►| Show: All | Selected | Records (0 out of 562 Selected.) | Options ▼

8   In the Attributes of LakeBlockCentroids table, scroll all the way to the right, right-click the column heading for Age22Plus, click Calculate Values, and click Yes.

9   In the Field Calculator, clear your previous expression from the expression box. In the Fields box, click the AGE_22_29 field then click the + button; do the same for AGE_30_39, AGE_40_49, AGE_50_64, AGE_65_UP. Verify that your expression matches the one in the graphic below, then click OK.

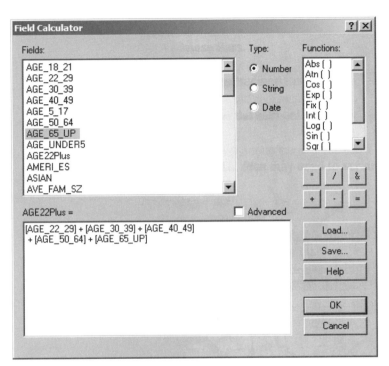

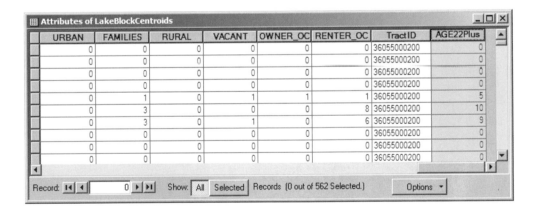

Sum Age22Plus by tracts

1   In the Attributes of LakeBlockCentroids table, right-click the TractID column heading and click Summarize.

2   For step 1 of the Summarize dialog box, choose TractID from the drop-down list.

3   For step 2, scroll down the list of fields, locate and expand the Age22Plus field, then check the Sum box.

4   For step 3, save the output table as **\Gistutorial\LakePrecinct\Lake.mdb\Sum_Age22Plus**.

5   Verify that your settings match those in the graphic shown at right, then click OK and Yes to add the new table to your map.

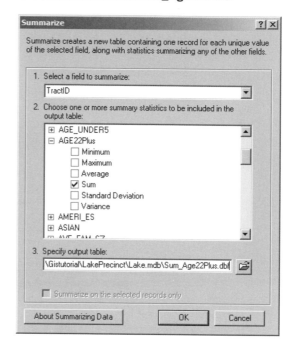

6   Close the Attributes of LakeBlockCentroids table.

7   In the table of contents, right-click the Sum_Age22Plus table and click Open.

This table contains tract-level data for the eleven tracts intersecting the Lake car beats.

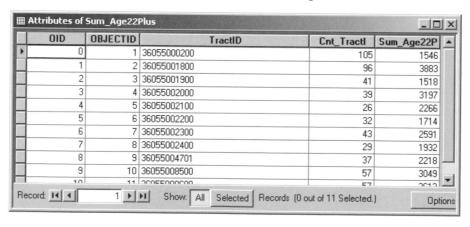

OID	OBJECTID	TractID	Cnt_TractI	Sum_Age22P
0	1	36055000200	105	1546
1	2	36055001800	96	3883
2	3	36055001900	41	1518
3	4	36055002000	39	3197
4	5	36055002100	26	2266
5	6	36055002200	32	1714
6	7	36055002300	43	2591
7	8	36055002400	29	1932
8	9	36055004701	37	2218
9	10	36055008500	57	3049

Intersect car beats and tracts

1 Close any open tables.

2 Open ArcToolbox.

3 In ArcToolbox, expand the Analysis Tools toolbox, then expand the Overlay toolset.

4 Double-click the Intersect tool.

5 From the Input Features drop-down list, choose Car Beats, then click the list again and choose Tracts.

6 Save the Output Feature Class as **\Gistutorial\LakePrecinct\Lake.mdb\Intersection_ CarBeatsAndTracts**.

7 Click OK, then click Close when the process completes.

The resulting layer contains polygons representing the areas where the car beats and census tract polygons overlapped.

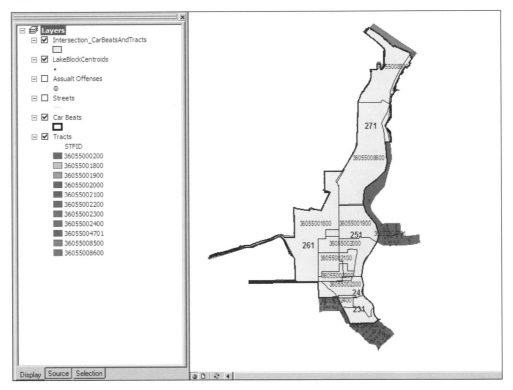

Overlay the intersection of car beats and tracts with block centroids

At this point, you will spatially overlay the joined layer of tracts and car beats with the block centroids to assign the tract and car beats attributes to the census blocks.

1 In the table of contents, right-click the LakeBlockCentroids layer, click Joins and Relates, Join.

2 In the Join Data dialog box, click the What do you want to join to this layer? drop-down list, and choose Join data from another layer based on spatial location.

3 For step 1, click the drop-down list and choose the Intersection_CarBeatsAndTracts layer.

4 For step 2, click the it falls inside option.

5 For step 3, save the output in **Lake.mdb** as **Join_Intersection_CarBeatsAndTracts_BlockCentroids**, then click OK.

The Join_Intersection_CarBeatsAndTracts_BlockCentroids is automatically added to your map.

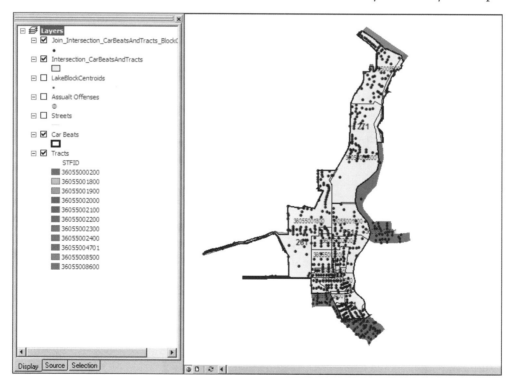

Join the summary attributes to the spatial join output

In this section, you will join the Sum_Age22Plus table to the block centroids in order to make the apportionment weight denominator—total population aged 22 or greater by tract—available to each block centroid.

1 Click the Display tab at the bottom of the table of contents.

2 In the table of contents, right-click the Join_Intersection_CarBeatsAndTracts_BlockCentroids layer, and click Joins and Relates, Join.

3 In the Join Data window, choose Join attributes from a table from the What do you want to join to this layer? drop-down list.

4 For step 1, select TractID from the drop-down list.

5 For step 2, select Sum_Age22Plus from the drop-down list.

6 For step 3, select TractID from the drop-down list.

7 Verify that your settings match those in the graphic shown at right, click OK, then click Yes to create an index for the field.

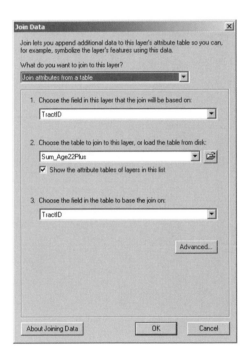

8 In the table of contents, right-click the Join_Intersection_CarBeatsAndTracts_BlockCentroids layer, then click Open Attribute Table. In the attribute table, scroll to the right and see that Sum_AGE22Plus and other tract data have been joined to the block centroids.

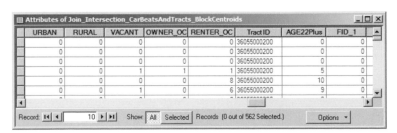

Compute apportionment weights

For each block centroid, you will now create and calculate new columns for the apportionment weight and apportioned undereducated population.

1   In the Attributes of Join_Intersection_CarBeatsAndTracts_BlockCentroids table, click Options, Add Field.

2   Name the new field **Weight**, set its Type to Float, then click OK.

3   In the Attributes of Join_Intersection_CarBeatsAndTracts_BlockCentroids table, click Options, Add Field.

4   Name the new field **UnderEducated**, set the Type to Float, then click OK.

5   In the Attributes of Join_Intersection_CarBeatsAndTracts_BlockCentroids table, locate then right-click the Join_Intersection_CarBeatsAndTracts_BlockCentroids.Weight column heading, click Calculate Values, and Yes.

In the Field Calculator, if you hover your cursor over a field in the Fields box (without clicking), a tool tip will appear displaying the entire field name.

6   In Fields box, click the Join_Intersection_CarBeatsAndTracts_BlockCentroids.AGE22Plus field, click the / button, scroll to the bottom of the Fields box, and click Sum_Age22Plus.Sum_AGE22P. Verify your settings match those in the following graphic, then click OK.

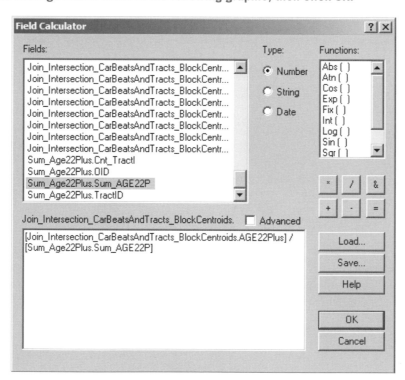

Compute apportionment values

1   In the Attributes of Join_Intersection_CarBeatsAndTracts_BlockCentroids table, locate and right-click the Join_Intersection_CarBeatsAndTracts_BlockCentroids.UnderEducated column heading. Click Calculate Values, then Yes.

2   Delete your previous expression, scroll to the bottom of the Fields list, click Join_Intersection_CarBeatsAndTracts_BlockCentroids.Weight field (the eighth row up from the bottom of the list), click the ✳ button, scroll about halfway up the Fields list, locate and click the Join_Intersection_CarBeatsAndTracts_BlockCentroids.NOHISCH field, click OK, and, if prompted with a warning message, click Yes.

The NOHISCH field is the number of persons with no high school education.

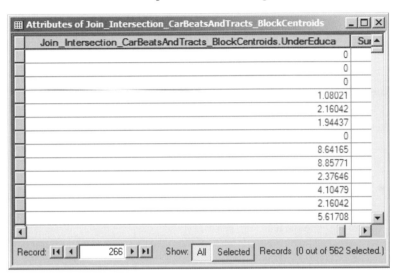

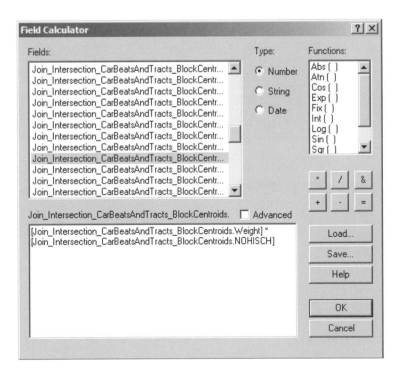

Sum weights by tract

Sum the apportionment weights by tract; they should add up to 1.0 for each tract.

1   Right-click the Join_Intersection_CarBeatsAndTracts_BlockCentroids layer in the table of
    contents, click Joins and Relates, Remove Join(s), Remove All Joins.

You will notice that the Weight and UnderEducated columns are the last columns in the table.

2   In the table, scroll to the left, locate and right-click the TractID column heading, and
    click Summarize.

3   For step 1, select TractID from the drop-down list.

4   For step 2, scroll down to and expand the Weight field, then check the Sum box.

5   For step 3, save the output table as \Gistutorial\LakePrecinct\Lake.mdb\Sum_WeightsByTract,
    click OK, then click Yes.

6   In the table of contents, right-click the Sum_WeightsByTract table, and click Open.

Note that the sum of weight for each tract is 1.0, which is a good check.

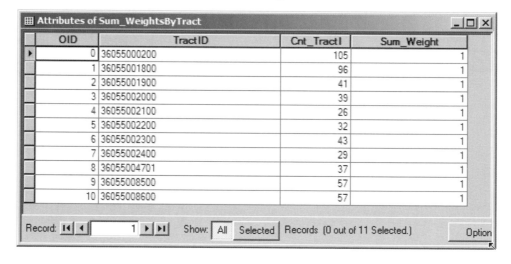

OID	Tract ID	Cnt_TractI	Sum_Weight
0	36055000200	105	1
1	36055001800	96	1
2	36055001900	41	1
3	36055002000	39	1
4	36055002100	26	1
5	36055002200	32	1
6	36055002300	43	1
7	36055002400	29	1
8	36055004701	37	1
9	36055008500	57	1
10	36055008600	57	1

Record: 1   Show: All   Selected   Records (0 out of 11 Selected.)   Option

7   Close the Attributes of Sum_WeightsByTract table.

Sum undereducated by car beats

Sum the undereducated population by car beat as a new table.

1   In the Attributes of Join_Intersection_CarBeatsAndTracts_BlockCentroids table, right-click the
    BEAT column heading and click Summarize.

2   For step 1, select BEAT.

3   For step 2, scroll down to and expand the UnderEducated field, then check the Sum box.

4   For step 3, save the output table as **\Gistutorial\LakePrecinct\Lake.mdb\Sum_UnderEducated**,
    then click OK and Yes.

5   Right-click the Sum_UnderEducated table in the table of contents and click Open.

The extra row with no beat value is okay for now, because it will not join to the car beats table.

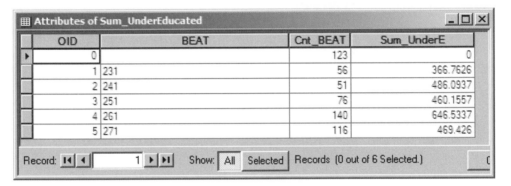

OID	BEAT	Cnt_BEAT	Sum_UnderE
0		123	0
1	231	56	366.7626
2	241	51	486.0937
3	251	76	460.1557
4	261	140	646.5337
5	271	116	469.426

Join Sum_UnderEducated to the car beat layer

In the following steps, you will join the table for undereducated population by car beat to the car beats layer and symbolize for display.

1 Click the Display tab at the bottom of the table of contents.

2 Right-click Car Beats in the table of contents and click Joins and Relates, Join.

3 In the Join Data dialog box, select Join attributes from a table from the What do you want to join to this layer? drop-down list.

4 For step 1, select the BEAT field from the drop-down list.

5 For step 2, select the Sum_UnderEducated table from the drop-down list.

6 For step 3, select the BEAT field from the drop-down list. Make sure your settings match those in the graphic below, then click OK and Yes.

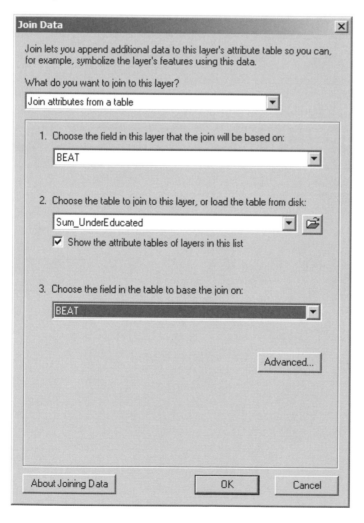

Map undereducated population by car beat

1   Close all open tables in the map.

2   In the table of contents, turn all layers off except Assault Offenses and Car Beats.

3   In the table of contents, right-click the Car Beats layer, then click Properties.

4   In the Layer Properties dialog box, click the Symbology tab. In the Show box, click Quantities, Graduated Colors.

5   From the Value drop-down list choose the Sum_UnderEducated, then click Classify.

6   In the Classification window, change the number of Classes to 3, then select Manual from the Method drop-down list.

7   In the Break Values box, type **450**, **550**, and **99999**, and click OK.

8   In the Layer Properties window, match the settings on the Symbology tab to those shown below, choose a monochromatic color ramp, and click OK.

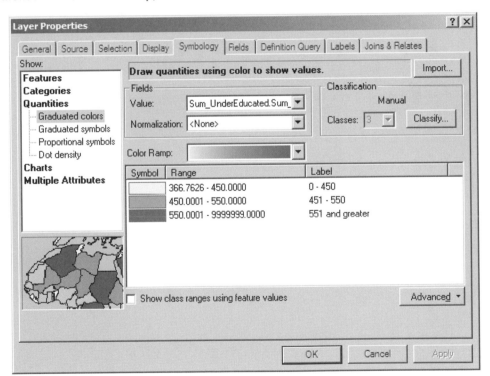

Wrap up

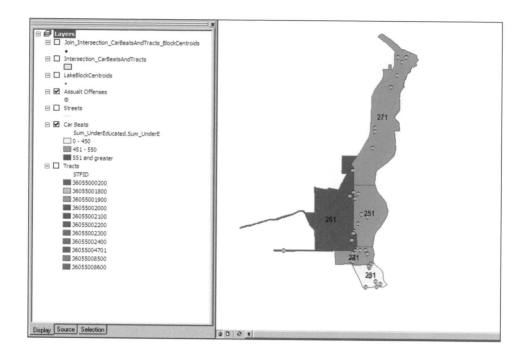

1   Save your map.

2   Close ArcMap.

Exercise Assignment 9-1

Analyze population in California cities at risk for earthquakes

Megacities are those defined as having a dense concentration of ten million or more people, many of whom have migrated from poor rural areas in search of work and live in slums. According to U.N. data, the five largest megacities are the greater Tokyo area with 35.3 million people, Mexico City with 19 million, New York–Newark with 18.5 million, Bombay with 18.3 million, and São Paulo with 18.3 million. Often, growth in megacities occurs so rapidly that authorities are overwhelmed.

When natural disasters occur in megacities, officials often need to move quickly to find resources to help people affected by the disaster. Knowing the population in areas where these disasters occur would greatly help in a recovery process, and GIS can help determine this information.

Earthquakes are one example of a natural disaster affecting millions of people. For example, Istanbul, which is highly vulnerable to earthquakes, grew from 1 million people in the 1950s to about 10 million today, a 10-fold increase in half a century. In the United States, California is a highly populated state that is vulnerable to various dangers, including earthquakes, tropical storms, and floods. In this exercise, you will use the spatial capabilities of GIS to create buffers around major earthquakes that have already occurred and analyze how many people live within 20 miles of these events.

Start with the following:

- **C:\Gistutorial\UnitedStates\California\CACounties.shp**—polygon boundary of California counties.
- **C:\Gistutorial\UnitedStates\California\Earthquakes.dbf**—database of earthquake locations in California with latitude and longitude data.
- **C:\Gistutorial\UnitedStates\Cities.shp**—point locations for major cities in California.

Create a map showing California earthquakes and population

In ArcCatalog, create a new personal geodatabase called C:\Gistutorial\Answers\Assignment9\ CAEarthquakes.mdb and import any new and relevant files to the project.

Begin a new map called C:\Gistutorial\Answers\Assignment9\Assignment9-1.mxd with a layout showing a 20-mile buffer around earthquakes whose magnitude is greater than 7; include a label of the total population within that buffer. Include another point layer of all California cities whose population is greater than 350,000. See hints.

Export the map to C:\Gistutorial\Answers\Assignment9\Assignment9-1.jpg.

Hints

- Add the Earthquakes.dbf file as an x,y event file and export it as a feature class to C:\Gistutorial\Answers\ Assignment9\CAEarthquakes.mdb\Earthquakes, and add it to your map from here.
- Create a 20-mile buffer around the earthquakes whose magnitude is greater than 7, call it C:\Gistutorial\ Answers\Assignment9\CAEarthquakes.mdb\Earthquakes_Buffer, and add it to your map from here.
- Use Select by Location or Clip to create a new feature class of cities in California that are within the 20-mile buffer of earthquakes whose magnitude is greater than 7, call it C:\Gistutorial\Answers\Assignment9\ CAEarthquakes.mdb\CAEarthquakeCities, and add it to your map from here.
- Spatially join the CAEarthquakesCities feature class and Earthquakes_Buffer feature class to a new feature class called C:\Gistutorial\Answers\Assignment9\CAEarthquakes.mdb\CitiesBufferJoin and add it to your map from here. Be sure to choose SUM when spatially joining so the summary of population is included in the new feature class. This way you can label the total population within that buffer. You might notice that there are two earthquakes affecting the same city and you are summing up that city's population twice (one for each individual buffer). This will still give you a good idea about how many people would be affected by earthquakes in that area. Another study may be to create individual buffers for cities that are close together.
- Create a feature class of major cities whose population is greater than 350,000 called C:\Gistutorial\Answers\ Assignment9\CAEarthquakes.mdb\majorcities.

Questions

Save the answers to your questions in a Microsoft Word document called C:\Gistutorial\ Answers\Assignment9\Assignment9.doc.

1 Which major earthquake (magnitude greater than 7) has the most detailed cities within 20 miles?

2 According to the detailed cities table, how many people are within 20 miles of that earthquake?

3 What California cities with populations over 350,000 have not yet been hit by an earthquake whose magnitude is over 7?

Exercise Assignment 9-2

Neighborhood walking distances and urban grocery store site selection

Many cities are trying to bring economic development into their downtown regions. One way to promote downtown environments is to demonstrate walking distances. Walkable catchments, sometimes referred to as "ped sheds," can be mapped to show the actual area within a five-minute walking distance from a neighborhood or town center or within ten minutes from any major transportation stop such as a rail station. Measuring the walkable catchment is simply a technique for evaluating how easy it is to move through an urban area and access neighborhood centers or transit facilities. The resulting maps are visual, highly accurate estimates of an area's walkability. Walkable catchment calculations are mathematically expressed by the actual area within a five-minute walking distance as a percentage of the theoretical area within a five-minute walking distance. The theoretical five-minute walking distance is shown as a circle with a radius of a quarter mile (1,320 feet) drawn around any particular center. This is an area of 125 acres. Calculating a ten-minute walking distance, the radius used is half a mile or 2,640 feet, resulting in a circle with an area.

Source: *www.cnu.org/cnu_reports/CNU_Ped_Sheds.pdf*

Study area background

In this exercise, you will study the walkability of an urban area of Pittsburgh, Pennsylvania. In a recent issue of the *National Geographic Magazine,* the zip code (15222) located in the heart of Pittsburgh was featured as one of the most interesting areas in the United States. You can read more about this area online at *magma. nationalgeographic.com/ngm/0308/feature6.*

Two neighborhoods making up the 15222 zip code, the Strip District and Central Business District, are adding a number of urban living condominiums and lofts. You will create point centroids for Pittsburgh zip codes to make a one-quarter-mile (five-minute) and one-half-mile (ten-minute) walking radius for the 15222 area. You can then show features within that distance (buildings, streets, and so forth).

You will also study the existing population in the 15222 zip code to determine what area is most suitable for a food store. The store should be located within a five-minute walking distance of the two most heavily populated census blocks for the 15222 zip code. This will be based on the 2000 census data. Another study could be done to determine areas around the new condos and lofts in the area.

Start with the following:

- **C:\Gistutorial\PAGIS\PghZipCodes**—Pittsburgh zip codes.
- **C:\Gistutorial\ PAGIS\CensusBlocks**—2000 Census blocks for the city of Pittsburgh.
- **C:\Gistutorial\ PAGIS\15222\15222Bldgs**—building footprints near and within the 15222 zip code.
- **C:\Gistutorial\ PAGIS\15222\15222Streets**—street centerlines within the 15222 zip code used to label street names.
- **C:\Gistutorial\ PAGIS\15222\15222Curbs**—curb lines within the 15222 zip code.

Map showing walkable catchment areas for neighborhood and grocery store site

Create a new personal geodatabase called C:\Gistutorial\Answers\Assignment9\StudyArea15222.mdb and import into it PghZIPcodes and the new files created below. See hints for the files to create and import. Be sure to load all files from the personal geodatabase for your final map.

Create a new map called C:\Gistutorial\Answers\Assignment9\Assignment9-2.mxd that includes a layout with two data frames:

- "15222 Walkable Catchment Area" showing a five- and ten-minute walking radius from the center of the 15222 zip code and background layers for 15222 buildings, curbs, and streets. Label the streets with the street name.
- "Food Store Site Suitability Study" zoomed to an ideal location for a grocery store based on the current population in the downtown area.

Export the map to a JPEG file called C:\Gistutorial\Answers\Assignment9\Assignment9-2.jpg.

Point centroid hints
- In the "15222 Walkable Catchment Area" data frame, add the PghZipCodes feature class from your personal geodatabase and create new fields that calculate the area and x,y centroids of the zip code polygons (see the steps in tutorial 9 on how to do this).
- Export the attribute table that now includes the x,y for the point centroids, save it as C:\Gistutorial\Answers\Assignment9\StudyArea15222.mdb\ZipXYData, and add the new table as x,y data. Export the x,y event points as a feature class called C:\Gistutorial\Answers\Assignment9\StudyArea15222.mdb\ZipCentroids.

Walking distance buffer hint
- Create and label five- and ten-minute walking distance buffers around the centroid point for the 15222 zip code only, and save them as C:\Gistutorial\Answers\Assignment9\StudyArea15222.mdb\Buffer5Minute and C:\Gistutorial\Answers\Assignment9\StudyArea15222.mdb\Buffer10Minute.
  Hint: Use feet and 1,320 and 2,640 as the buffer linear units.

Food store site selection hints
- In the data frame called "Food Store Site Suitability Study," add the PghZipCodes and CensusBlocks from the input layers.
- Select census blocks that have their center in the 15222 zip code, export these to a new feature class called C:\Gistutorial\Answers\Assignment9\StudyArea15222.mdb\CensusBlocks15222, add the new feature class to the map, and remove the original.
- Create three new fields to calculate the area and x,y centroids of the census block polygons.
- Create a table for the centroids called C:\Gistutorial\Answers\Assignment9\StudyArea15222.mdb\CensusBlockCentroids, and add the new table as x,y data.
- Symbolize the census block centroids by population, showing different colors for four population classifications (0–100, 101–200, 201–300, 300 and greater).
- Select only the block centroids with more than 300 people, and create two separate five-minute walking buffers called C:\Gistutorial\Answers\Assignment9\Zip15222.mdb\GroceryBuffer1 and C:\Gistutorial\Answers\Assignment9\StudyArea15222.mdb\GroceryBuffer2.
- Create an intersecting feature class of the two buffers called C:\Gistutorial\Answers\Assignment9\StudyArea15222.mdb\GroceryStoreSite.
- Show both five-minute buffers as outlines and the intersection buffer shaded. The intersection buffer is the ideal area for a new food store.

- Add buildings, curbs, and streets as background layers, and label accordingly on the map.
- Draw a black dot on and label the building where you would recommend locating a grocery store.

Question
Answer the following question in C:\Gistutorial\Answers\Assignment9\Assignment9.doc.

4   Explain your choice for locating the grocery store where you did. What other layers would you include for this study?

What to turn in
If you are working in a classroom setting with an instructor, you may be required to submit the exercises you created in tutorial 9. Below are the files you are required to turn in. Be sure to use a compression program such as PKZIP or WinZip to include all three files as one .zip document for review and grading. Include your name and assignment number in the .zip document (YourNameAssn9.zip).

ArcMap projects
C:\Gistutorial\Answers\Assignment9\Assignment9-1.mxd
C:\Gistutorial\Answers\Assignment9\Assignment9-2.mxd

Exported maps
C:\Gistutorial\Answers\Assignment9\Assignment9-1.jpg
C:\Gistutorial\Answers\Assignment9\Assignment9-2.jpg

Personal geodatabases
C:\Gistutorial\Answers\Assignment9\CAEarthquakes.mdb (includes CAEathquakeCities, CitiesBufferJoin, Earthquakes, Earthquakes_Buffer, and MajorCACities)
C:\Gistutorial\Answers\Assignment9\Zip15222.mdb (includes Buffer10Minute, Buffer5Minute, CensusBlockCentroids, CensusBlocks15222, GroceryBuffer1, GroceryBuffer2, GroceryStoreSite, ZipCentroids, and ZIPXYData)

Word document
C:\Gistutorial\Answers\Assignment9\Assignment9.doc

Appendix A

Data License Agreement

Important:

Read carefully before opening the sealed media package

Environmental Systems Research Institute, Inc. (ESRI), is willing to license the enclosed data and related materials to you only upon the condition that you accept all of the terms and conditions contained in this license agreement. Please read the terms and conditions carefully before opening the sealed media package. By opening the sealed media package, you are indicating your acceptance of the ESRI License Agreement. If you do not agree to the terms and conditions as stated, then ESRI is unwilling to license the data and related materials to you. In such event, you should return the media package with the seal unbroken and all other components to ESRI.

ESRI License Agreement

This is a license agreement, and not an agreement for sale, between you (Licensee) and Environmental Systems Research Institute, Inc. (ESRI). This ESRI License Agreement (Agreement) gives Licensee certain limited rights to use the data and related materials (Data and Related Materials). All rights not specifically granted in this Agreement are reserved to ESRI and its Licensors.

Reservation of Ownership and Grant of License: ESRI and its Licensors retain exclusive rights, title, and ownership to the copy of the Data and Related Materials licensed under this Agreement and, hereby, grant to Licensee a personal, nonexclusive, nontransferable, royalty-free, worldwide license to use the Data and Related Materials based on the terms and conditions of this Agreement. Licensee agrees to use reasonable effort to protect the Data and Related Materials from unauthorized use, reproduction, distribution, or publication.

Proprietary Rights and Copyright: Licensee acknowledges that the Data and Related Materials are proprietary and confidential property of ESRI and its Licensors and are protected by United States copyright laws and applicable international copyright treaties and/or conventions.

Permitted Uses:

Licensee may install the Data and Related Materials onto permanent storage device(s) for Licensee's own internal use.

Licensee may make only one (1) copy of the original Data and Related Materials for archival purposes during the term of this Agreement unless the right to make additional copies is granted to Licensee in writing by ESRI.

Licensee may internally use the Data and Related Materials provided by ESRI for the stated purpose of GIS training and education.

Uses Not Permitted:

Licensee shall not sell, rent, lease, sublicense, lend, assign, time-share, or transfer, in whole or in part, or provide unlicensed Third Parties access to the Data and Related Materials or portions of the Data and Related Materials, any updates, or Licensee's rights under this Agreement.

Licensee shall not remove or obscure any copyright or trademark notices of ESRI or its Licensors.

Term and Termination: The license granted to Licensee by this Agreement shall commence upon the acceptance of this Agreement and shall continue until such time that Licensee elects in writing to discontinue use of the Data or Related Materials and terminates this Agreement. The Agreement shall automatically terminate without notice if Licensee fails to comply with any provision of this Agreement. Licensee shall then return to ESRI the Data and Related Materials. The parties hereby agree that all provisions that operate to protect the rights of ESRI and its Licensors shall remain in force should breach occur.

Disclaimer of Warranty: THE DATA AND RELATED MATERIALS CONTAINED HEREIN ARE PROVIDED "AS-IS," WITHOUT WARRANTY OF ANY KIND, EITHER EXPRESS OR IMPLIED, INCLUDING, BUT NOT LIMITED TO, THE IMPLIED WARRANTIES OF MERCHANTABILITY, FITNESS FOR A PARTICULAR PURPOSE, OR NONINFRINGEMENT. ESRI does not warrant that the Data and Related Materials will meet Licensee's needs or expectations, that the use of the Data and Related Materials will be uninterrupted, or that all nonconformities, defects, or errors can or will be corrected. ESRI is not inviting reliance on the Data or Related Materials for commercial planning or analysis purposes, and Licensee should always check actual data.

Data Disclaimer: The Data used herein has been derived from actual spatial or tabular information. In some cases, ESRI has manipulated and applied certain assumptions, analyses, and opinions to the Data solely for educational training purposes. Assumptions, analyses, opinions applied, and actual outcomes may vary. Again, ESRI is not inviting reliance on this Data, and the Licensee should always verify actual Data and exercise their own professional judgment when interpreting any outcomes.

Limitation of Liability: ESRI shall not be liable for direct, indirect, special, incidental, or consequential damages related to Licensee's use of the Data and Related Materials, even if ESRI is advised of the possibility of such damage.

No Implied Waivers: No failure or delay by ESRI or its Licensors in enforcing any right or remedy under this Agreement shall be construed as a waiver of any future or other exercise of such right or remedy by ESRI or its Licensors.

Order for Precedence: Any conflict between the terms of this Agreement and any FAR, DFAR, purchase order, or other terms shall be resolved in favor of the terms expressed in this Agreement, subject to the government's minimum rights unless agreed otherwise.

Export Regulation: Licensee acknowledges that this Agreement and the performance thereof are subject to compliance with any and all applicable United States laws, regulations, or orders relating to the export of data thereto. Licensee agrees to comply with all laws, regulations, and orders of the United States in regard to any export of such technical data.

Severability: If any provision(s) of this Agreement shall be held to be invalid, illegal, or unenforceable by a court or other tribunal of competent jurisdiction, the validity, legality, and enforceability of the remaining provisions shall not in any way be affected or impaired thereby.

Governing Law: This Agreement, entered into in the County of San Bernardino, shall be construed and enforced in accordance with and be governed by the laws of the United States of America and the State of California without reference to conflict of laws principles. The parties hereby consent to the personal jurisdiction of the courts of this county and waive their rights to change venue.

Entire Agreement: The parties agree that this Agreement constitutes the sole and entire agreement of the parties as to the matter set forth herein and supersedes any previous agreements, understandings, and arrangements between the parties relating hereto.

Appendix B

Installing the Data and Software

GIS Tutorial includes two CDs—one with exercise data and one with ArcView 9 (Demo Edition) software. You will find both in the back of this book.

Installation of the exercise data CD takes about five minutes and requires 285 megabytes of hard disk space.

Installation of the ArcView 9 software CD takes approximately 35 minutes and requires at least 700 megabytes of hard disk space (more if you choose to load the optional extension products and the ArcGIS tutorial data). Installation times will vary with your computer's speed and available memory.

If you already have a licensed copy of ArcView 9, ArcEditor 9, or ArcInfo 9 installed on your computer (or accessible through a network), do not install the software CD. Use your licensed software to do the exercises in this book. If you have a licensed copy of ArcView 8.x, ArcEditor 8.x, or ArcInfo 8.x installed on your computer, you must uninstall it before you can install the software CD that comes with this book.

Installing the exercise data

Follow the steps below to install the exercise data. Do not copy the files directly from the CD to your hard drive. A direct file copy does not remove write-protection from the files, and as a result data editing exercises will not work. In addition, a direct file copy will not enable the automatic uninstall feature.

1   **Put the data CD in your computer's CD drive. In your file browser, click the icon for your CD drive to see its contents. Double-click the Setup.exe file to begin.**

2   **Read the Welcome.**

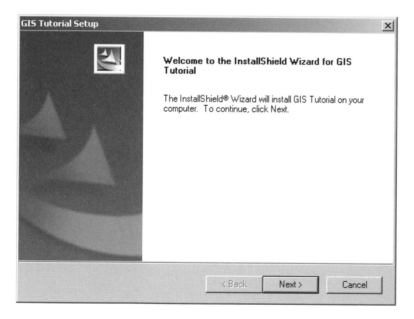

3   Click Next. Accept the default installation folder or click Browse and navigate to the drive or folder location where you want to install the data. If you choose an alternate location, please make note of it as the book's exercises direct you to C:\Gistutorial.

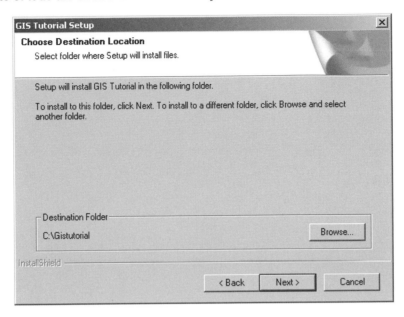

4   Click Next. The exercise data is installed on your computer in a folder called **Gistutorial**. When the installation is finished, you see the following message:

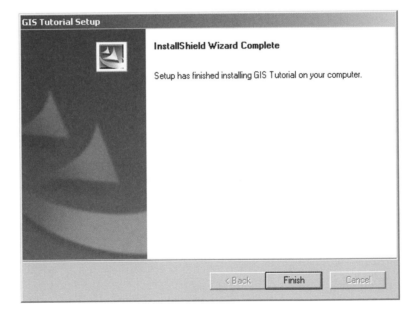

5   Click Finish.

If you have a licensed copy of ArcView 9, ArcEditor 9, or ArcInfo 9 installed on your computer, you are ready to start GIS Tutorial. Otherwise, follow the Installing the software instructions below to install and register the software.

Uninstalling the exercise data

To uninstall the exercise data from your computer, open your operating system's control panel and double-click the Add/Remove Programs icon. In the Add/Remove Programs dialog box, select the following entry and follow the prompts to remove it:

GIS Tutorial

Installing the software

The ArcView software included on this CD-ROM is intended for educational purposes only. Once installed and registered, the software will run for 180 days. The software cannot be reinstalled nor can the time limit be extended. It is recommended that you uninstall this software when it expires.

Follow the steps below to install the software.

1   Put the software CD in your computer's CD drive. In your file browser, click the icon for your CD drive to see the CD contents. Double-click the **Setup.exe** file to begin.

2   Read the Welcome.

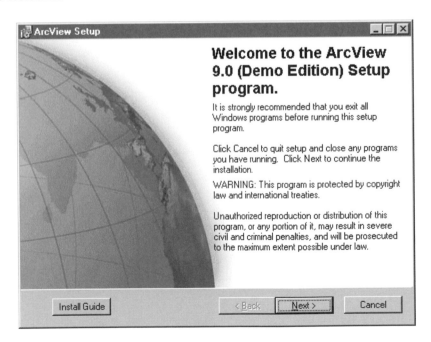

3   Click Next. Read the license agreement.

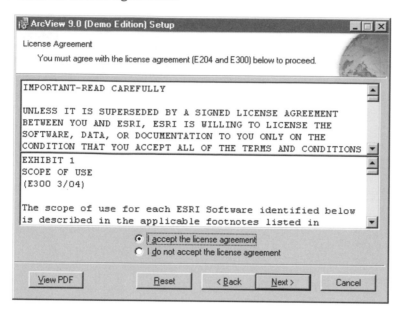

4   Click "I accept the license agreement" and click Next. The default installation type is Typical. A Typical install includes all functionality needed for this book. A Complete install adds extension products that are not used in the book but which you may want to explore on your own (subject to the 180-day time limit). A Complete install with all the extensions adds about 220 megabytes to the installation.

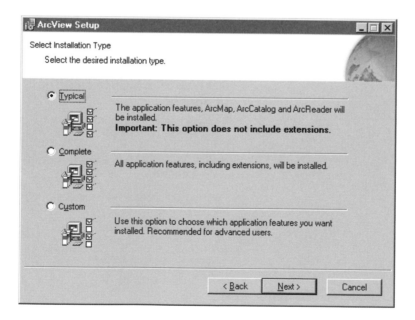

5   Click Next. Accept the default installation folder or click Browse and navigate to the drive or folder location where you want to install the ArcView software.

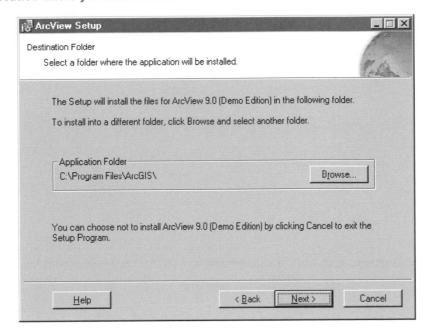

6   Click Next. Accept the default installation folder or navigate to the drive or folder where you want to install Python, a scripting language used by some ArcGIS geoprocessing functions. (You won't see this panel if you already have Python installed.)

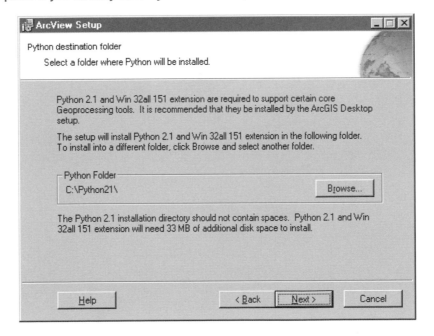

7   Click Next. The installation paths for ArcView and Python are confirmed.

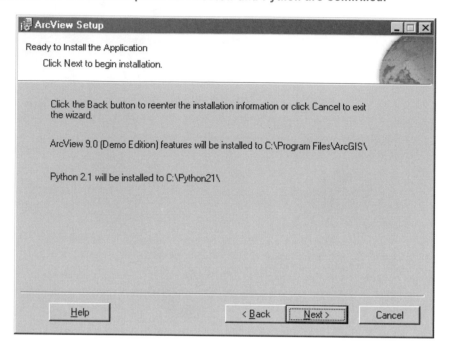

8   Click Next. The software will take some minutes to install on your computer. When the installation is finished, you see the following message:

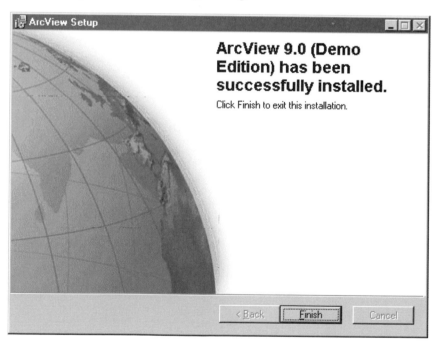

9   Click Finish. You are prompted to load the ArcGIS Tutorial Data, which adds about 375 megabytes
    to the installation. The book's exercises do not use this data; however, it is useful if you are
    evaluating one of the extension products.

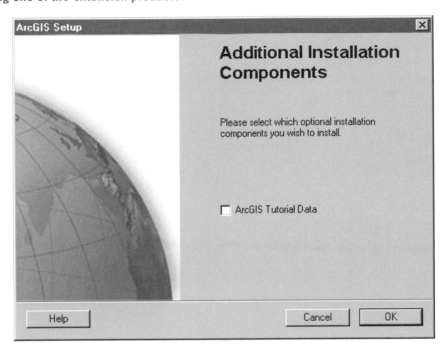

10   Uncheck the ArcGIS Tutorial Data box, and click OK. ArcView is now installed.

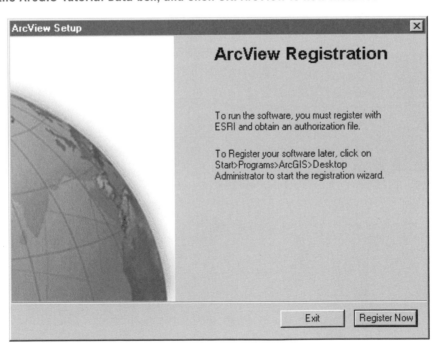

11   You can now either exit or register ArcView. If you have your registration code, click Register
     Now and follow the registration process; otherwise, click Exit. The registration code is located at
     the bottom of the software CD jacket in the back of the book.

If you have questions or encounter problems during the installation process or while using this book, please use the resources listed below. (The ESRI Technical Support Department does not answer questions regarding the ArcView 9 Demo Editing CD, the GIS Tutorial exercise data CD, or the contents of the book itself.)

- To resolve problems with the trial software or exercise data, or to report mistakes in the book, send an email to ESRI workbook support at *workbook-support@esri.com.*
- To stay informed about exercise updates, FAQs, and errata, visit the book's Web page at *www.esri.com/esripress/gistutorial.*

Uninstalling the software

To uninstall the software from your computer, open your operating system's control panel and double-click the Add/Remove Programs icon. In the Add/Remove Programs dialog box, select the following entry and follow the prompts to remove it:

ArcView 9.0 (Demo Edition)

Books from

ESRI
Press

Advanced Spatial Analysis: The CASA Book of GIS *1-58948-073-2*

ArcGIS and the Digital City: A Hands-on Approach for Local Government *1-58948-074-0*

ArcView GIS Means Business *1-879102-51-X*

A System for Survival: GIS and Sustainable Development *1-58948-052-X*

Beyond Maps: GIS and Decision Making in Local Government *1-879102-79-X*

Cartographica Extraordinaire: The Historical Map Transformed *1-58948-044-9*

Cartographies of Disease: Maps, Mapping, and Medicine *1-58948-120-8*

Children Map the World: Selections from the Barbara Petchenik Children's World Map Competition *1-58948-125-9*

Community Geography: GIS in Action *1-58948-023-6*

Community Geography: GIS in Action Teacher's Guide *1-58948-051-1*

Confronting Catastrophe: A GIS Handbook *1-58948-040-6*

Connecting Our World: GIS Web Services *1-58948-075-9*

Conservation Geography: Case Studies in GIS, Computer Mapping, and Activism *1-58948-024-4*

Designing Better Maps: A Guide for GIS Users *1-58948-089-9*

Designing Geodatabases: Case Studies in GIS Data Modeling *1-58948-021-X*

Disaster Response: GIS for Public Safety *1-879102-88-9*

Enterprise GIS for Energy Companies *1-879102-48-X*

Extending ArcView GIS (version 3.x edition) *1-879102-05-6*

Fun with GPS *1-58948-087-2*

Getting to Know ArcGIS Desktop, Second Edition Updated for ArcGIS 9 *1-58948-083-X*

Getting to Know ArcObjects: Programming ArcGIS with VBA *1-58948-018-X*

Getting to Know ArcView GIS (version 3.x edition) *1-879102-46-3*

GIS and Land Records: The ArcGIS Parcel Data Model *1-58948-077-5*

GIS for Everyone, Third Edition *1-58948-056-2*

GIS for Health Organizations *1-879102-65-X*

GIS for Landscape Architects *1-879102-64-1*

GIS for the Urban Environment *1-58948-082-1*

GIS for Water Management in Europe *1-58948-076-7*

GIS in Public Policy: Using Geographic Information for More Effective Government *1-879102-66-8*

GIS in Schools *1-879102-85-4*

GIS in Telecommunications *1-879102-86-2*

GIS Means Business, Volume II *1-58948-033-3*

GIS Tutorial: Workbook for ArcView 9 *1-58948-127-5*

GIS, Spatial Analysis, and Modeling *1-58948-130-5*

GIS Worlds: Creating Spatial Data Infrastructures *1-58948-122-4*

Hydrologic and Hydraulic Modeling Support with Geographic Information Systems *1-879102-80-3*

Integrating GIS and the Global Positioning System *1-879102-81-1*

Making Community Connections: The Orton Family Foundation Community Mapping Program *1-58948-071-6*

Managing Natural Resources with GIS *1-879102-53-6*

Mapping Census 2000: The Geography of U.S. Diversity *1-58948-014-7*

Mapping Our World: GIS Lessons for Educators, ArcView GIS 3.x Edition *1-58948-022-8*

Mapping Our World: GIS Lessons for Educators, ArcGIS Desktop Edition *1-58948-121-6*

Mapping the Future of America's National Parks: Stewardship through Geographic Information Systems *1-58948-080-5*

Mapping the News: Case Studies in GIS and Journalism *1-58948-072-4*

Marine Geography: GIS for the Oceans and Seas *1-58948-045-7*

Measuring Up: The Business Case for GIS *1-58948-088-0*

Modeling Our World: The ESRI Guide to Geodatabase Design *1-879102-62-5*

Past Time, Past Place: GIS for History *1-58948-032-5*

Continued on next page

When ordering, please mention book title and ISBN (number that follows each title)

Books from ESRI Press (continued)

Planning Support Systems: Integrating Geographic Information Systems, Models, and Visualization Tools *1-58948-011-2*
Remote Sensing for GIS Managers *1-58948-081-3*
Salton Sea Atlas *1-58948-043-0*
Spatial Portals: Gateways to Geographic Information *1-58948-131-3*
The ESRI Guide to GIS Analysis, Volume 1: Geographic Patterns and Relationships *1-879102-06-4*
The ESRI Guide to GIS Analysis, Volume 2: Spatial Measurements and Statistics *1-58948-116-X*
Think Globally, Act Regionally: GIS and Data Visualization for Social Science and Public Policy Research *1-58948-124-0*
Thinking About GIS: Geographic Information System Planning for Managers (paperback edition) *1-58948-119-4*
Transportation GIS *1-879102-47-1*
Undersea with GIS *1-58948-016-3*
Unlocking the Census with GIS *1-58948-113-5*
Zeroing In: Geographic Information Systems at Work in the Community *1-879102-50-1*

Forthcoming titles from ESRI Press
A to Z GIS: An Illustrated Dictionary of Geographic Information Systems *1-58948-140-2*
Charting the Unknown: How Computer Mapping at Harvard Became GIS *1-58948-118-6*
GIS for Environmental Management *1-58948-142-9*
GIS for the Urban Environment *1-58948-082-1*
Mapping Global Cities: GIS Methods in Urban Analysis *1-58948-143-7*

Ask for ESRI Press titles at your local bookstore or order by calling 1-800-447-9778. You can also shop online at www.esri.com/esripress. Outside the United States, contact your local ESRI distributor.

ESRI Press titles are distributed to the trade by the following:

In North America, South America, Asia, and Australia:
Independent Publishers Group (IPG)
Telephone (United States): 1-800-888-4741 • Telephone (international): 312-337-0747
E-mail: frontdesk@ipgbook.com

In the United Kingdom, Europe, and the Middle East:
Transatlantic Publishers Group Ltd.
Telephone: 44 20 8849 8013 • Fax: 44 20 8849 5556 • E-mail: transatlantic.publishers@regusnet.com

ESRI Press • 380 New York Street • Redlands, California 92373-8100 • www.esri.com/esripress